NEW AND
COLLECTED POEMS

U. A. Fanthorpe

NEW AND COLLECTED POEMS

Preface by Carol Ann Duffy

ENITHARMON PRESS

First published in 2010
by Enitharmon Press
26B Caversham Road
London NW5 2DU

www.enitharmon.co.uk

Distributed in the UK by
Central Books
99 Wallis Road
London E9 5LN

Distributed in the USA and Canada
by Dufour Editions Inc.
PO Box 7, Chester Springs
PA 19425, USA

ISBN: 978-1-907587-00-9 (hardback)

Enitharmon Press gratefully acknowledges the financial support of
Arts Council England, London.

The unpublished poems in the final section have been selected by R. V. Bailey,
Carole Satyamurti and Stephen Stuart-Smith.

British Library Cataloguing-in-Publication Data.
A catalogue record for this book is available
from the British Library.

Designed in Albertina by Libanus Press
and printed in England by
Antony Rowe Ltd.

BIBLIOGRAPHY

POETRY VOLUMES

Side Effects (Peterloo Poets, 1978)

Standing To (Peterloo Poets, 1982)

Voices Off (Peterloo Poets, 1984)

Selected Poems (Peterloo Poets, 1986, hardback; King Penguin, 1986, paperback)

A Watching Brief (Peterloo Poets, 1987)

Neck-Verse (Peterloo Poets, 1992)

Safe as Houses (Peterloo Poets, 1995)

Consequences (Peterloo Poets, 2000)

Christmas Poems (Enitharmon Press & Peterloo Poets, 2002)

Queueing for the Sun (Peterloo Poets, 2003)

Collected Poems 1978–2003 (Peterloo Poets, 2005)

Homing In: Selected Local Poems (The Cyder Press, 2006)

From Me to You (with R. V. Bailey: Enitharmon Press & Peterloo Poets, 2007)

New and Collected Poems (Enitharmon Press, 2010)

POETRY AUDIO CASSETTES

Peterloo Poetry Cassette No. 1 (with Elma Mitchell: Peterloo Poets, 1983)

Awkward Subject (Peterloo Poets, 1995)

Double Act (with R. V. Bailey: Penguin audiobook, 1997)

UA Fanthorpe Reading from her Poems (with R. V. Bailey: Poetry Archive, 2009)

For Rosie as always

CONTENTS

SIDE EFFECTS (1978)

The List	27
The Watcher	28
Jobdescription: Medical Records	29
For Saint Peter	31
Casehistory: Julie (encephalitis)	31
Casehistory: Alison (head injury)	33
Patience Strong	34
From The Remand Centre	35
After Visiting Hours	36
Earthed	37
Stanton Drew	38
Owlpen Manor	39
Brympton d'Evercy	40
Coire Dubh	42
Campsite: Maentwrog	44
The West Front at Bath	45
The Quiet Grave	45
Not My Best Side	48
Palimpsest	50
Some Modernisation Needed	50
My Brother's House	51
Rite	53
Carol Concert	54
Poem for Oscar Wilde	56
Only a Small Death	56
Family Entertainment	58
Ridge House (Old People's Home)	59
Men on Allotments	60
Pat at Milking Time	61
Canal 1977	62
Horticultural Show	63
Staff Party	64
Song	66

STANDING TO (1982)

Stations Underground	71
1. Fanfare	72
2. Four Dogs	74
3. At the Ferry	75
4. Rising Damp	77
5. Sisyphus	78
6. The Guide	80
7. The Passing of Alfred	81
The Conductor	83
Inside	85
Prolepsis	86
A Gardener	87
Not Quite Right	88
Resuscitation Team	90
Lament for the Patients	91
Spring Afternoon	93
Reports	93
Half-term	95
You will be hearing from us shortly	96
Only Here for the Bier	98
1. Mother-in-law	99
2. King's daughter	100
3. Army wife	101
4. Waiting Gentlewoman	102
Angels' song	103
BC:AD	103
Robin's Round	104
Reindeer Report	104
The Contributors	105
On Buying OS sheet 163	106
Princetown	106
Hang-gliders in January	107
In The English Faculty Library, Oxford	108

Haunted House   109
Rural Guerrillas   110
Getting it across   111
Pomona and Vertumnus   113
Janus   114
Genesis   115
Chorus   117
Father in the Railway Buffet   118
Birthday Poem   118
The Colourblind Birdwatcher   120
95   120
Child in Marble   121
Portraits of Tudor Statesmen   123
The Constant Tin Soldier   123
Standing To   132

VOICES OFF (1984)
Tomorrow and   137
Robert Lindsay's Hamlet   138
Armin's Will   140
Instead of the Last Post   142
Visiting Mr Lewis in January   143
Tony/Fabian O.S.B   144
Grandfather's Footsteps   146
Patients   147
Man to Man   148
Tyneside in December   150
Northmen   151
Air for an Heir   154
Circus Tricks   155
Second Time Round   156
Women Laughing   157
Cluny: Five Senses, Two Beasts and a Lady   158
London Z to A   160

St James's, Charfield   161
'Soothing and Awful'   162
Purton Lower Bridge   164
Growing Up   164
The First Years Arrive   166
Being a Student   167
The Cleaner   169
Knowing about Sonnets   170
Seminar: Life; Early Poems 171
Seminar: Felicity and Mr Frost 172
High Table   174
Chaplaincy Fell Walk   175
The Sheepdog   176
Local Poet   177
The Person's Tale   179
From the Third Storey   180

THE CRYSTAL ZOO (1985)
THE NEW EXETER BOOK OF
RIDDLES (1999)
Transitional Object   185
I Do Know How Awful I Am 186
My Lion Is a Unicorn   187
The Horse Speaks   188
The Heir   189
Riddle 1   190
Riddle 2   190

A WATCHING BRIEF (1987)
The Doctor   193
Downstairs at the Orangerie 194
La Débâcle. Temps Gris   195

Three Women Wordsworths   196
   1. Deer in Gowbarrow Park   196
   2. Undercurrents at the Dove and   197
     Olive Bough
   3. The Last   198
At Cowan Bridge   201
'These things were here'   202
Dear Mr Lee   204
'Very quiet here'   205
At Averham   206
Sounds and Silences   209
A Wartime Education   210
Washing-up   211
Eating Out   213
7301   213
Old Man, Old Man   214
Queueing Outside the Jeu de Paume
   in Light Rain   216
Difficilior Lectio   216
Looking for Jorvik   217
Dear True Love   219
Confessio Amantis   220
Homing In   221
Teacher's Christmas   222
S. Martin's College, Lancaster   223
In Residence   224
Going Down   224
Off Sick   225
Resignation Letter   226
Travelling Man   227
Sunderland Point and Ribchester   228
First Flight   230
Carthage: an historical guide   231
Terminal Feelings   233
Rag Trade   234

Of Mutability	234
M.S.	235
Bronwen	236
Unauthorised Version	237
Gaudy Ladies	239
Nativities	239
Garden Planning	240
Unfinished Chronicle	241

NECK-VERSE (1992)

As well as the Bible and Shakespeare . . . ?	247
Brauneberg on the River Mosel	247
Back to the Front	248
Children Imagining a Hospital	250
Clerical Error	250
The Comforters	251
Costa Geriatrica	252
Dear Sir	254
Descent	255
Diglis Lock	256
Doubles	256
Elegy for a Cat	257
Escaping	259
Familiars	260
Going Under	260
Half-past Two	261
Idyll	263
King Edward's Flora	263
A Life	265
May 8th: how to recognise it	267
Neighbours	268
The Old Lady and the Weather	269
The Poet's Companion	270

The Receptionist to her Watch   271
Superannuated Psychiatrist   272
Friends' Meeting House, Frenchay, Bristol   272
The Middle Passage   273
Reception in Bristol   274
Titania to Bottom   275
A Toy   276
The Two   277
Waiting   277
Word Games   278
    1. Comfortable Words   278
    2. Neck-Verse   280
Awkward Subject   282
Programmed   283
Notes at a Photographic Exhibition   284

SAFE AS HOUSES (1995)
Haunting   289
The Silence   289
The Room Where Everyone Goes   291
Tyndale in Darkness   293
The Doll's Children   301
Reading Between   302
Sirensong   304
Dying Fall   305
Collateral Damage   306
Last House   307
Counting Song   308
Death Row Poets   310
The Unprofessionals   311
A Major Road for Romney Marsh   311
DNA   312
Grand Union   313

At Swarkestone   314
Lostwithiel in February   315
Greensted Church   315
Helpston   316
Under the Motorway   317
What, in our house?   318
An Easy Day for a Lady   319
    1. The Climber   319
    2. The Father   320
    3. The Heir   321
Odysseus' Cat   322
He refuses to read his public's
    favourite poem   323
Deus v. Adam and Another   324
Woman Ironing   326
Painter and Poet   327
Colophon   328
Queening It   329
Water everywhere   331
Damage Limitation   332
On Worms, and Being Lucky   332
Daffodil Ministry   334
Atlas   335
The Absent-Minded Lover's Apology   335
Sister   336
Christmas Presents   338
Cat in the Manger   338
Christmas Sounds   339
The Invitation   340
The Wicked Fairy at the Manger   341

CONSEQUENCES (2000)

Consequences   344
    1. Found on the Battlefield   345
    2. Lost and Lost   346
    3. The Master of the Cast Shadow   346
    4. The Young Person's Guide to Arms   347
    5. Homily of the Hassocks   348
    6. Hats Off, Gentlemen. A Genius!   349
    7. The Uses of Architecture   350
    8. Master Shakespeare: His Maggot   351
    9. Ask a Silly Question   352
    10. Hundreds and Thousands   354
    11. Fox Unearthed   354
    12. The Fortune-Teller's Funeral   356
    13. At Staunton Harold   358
    Notes   359
Née   360
Kinch & Lack   361
Mother Scrubbing the Floor   362
Against Speech   363
Words for Months   363
Strong Language in South Gloucestershire   365
Three Poems for Amy Cook (1909–1998)   366
    1. Amy Sits for Her Portrait   366
    2. Amy Tells Us   367
    3. A Touch of Éclair   368
For OS 759934: 14.2.96. A Love-poem   369
Conygre Wood and Hyakinthoides
    Non-Scriptus   370
The Offshore Trip   370
The Burren   372
Seven Types of Shadow   372
New Highgate Cemetery: 4th April 1996   376
Underground   377

Widening the Westway   379
Maud Speaking   380
Gospel Truth   382
Overheard at Lumb Bank   383
Petition of the Cats Concerning
        Mr Peter Porter   384
Postcards   385
Look, No Hands   387
The Witness   388
Popular Fallacies   389
Sightings   389
Afterwards   391
Another Swan Poem   391
Olive   393
Post-op   394
Autumn Offer   395
The Gardener at Christmas   396
Christmas Traffic   397
Bird Psalm   397
Christmas in Envelopes   398

CHRISTMAS POEMS (2002)
The Sun Capers   401
What the Donkey Saw   401
I am Joseph   402
Lullaby: Sanctus Deus   402
The Wise Man and the Star   403
The Tree   404
Now   404
Open House   405
Not the Millennium   406

QUEUEING FOR THE SUN (2003)

Queueing for the Sun in Walbrook   409
The Gaoler's Story   411
Morning After   417
At Gunthorpe   419
Sprung   420
The Obituarists   421
The Dagda   422
Autumn Double   423
Driving South   425
The Vulgar Tongue   426
Caedmon's Song   426
Jonson at Hawthornden   427
The Man who Loved Gardens   428
Hardy Country   429
Workshop's End   431
Secret Garden   432
Route des Grappes   433
Marriage Lines   433
Herons   434
Caravan   435
The Apple War   436
West Bay in Winter   437
Wotton Walks   438
Extras   439
A Minor Role   440
Waiting Room   442
A Brief Resumé at Fifty   442
In Memory   445
What about Jerusalem?   446
A Wish for William Morris   447
The Benefactors   449
Candidates should pay special attention   450
Degree Day   451

Now What?   452
Pottery Class   453
The Little Children and their Wise Parents   453
Grandfather's Watch   454
Road Rage on the M6   455
Party Night   455
Agnus Dei: 2001   456
Wintersports   457
For Leo on 14.2.2000   457
Arthur's War   458
On the North Face   459
Needle Work   461
Libraries at War   461

NEW POEMS
1 January   465
12 April 2004   465
A Garden of Bears   466
Always   467
Administrator   468
Aberaeron   469
All Change   469
An Old Story   470
Another 'Last Signal'   473
But, Doctor...   474
Crop   476
Dictator   476
Either/Or   477
Entertaining Poets   478
Friendship   479
Fringe Town   480
FWIW: The Language Speaks   481
Gabriel   482
Growing Out   483

Harried   485
Lumb Bank, Early   486
Number One and the Butterfly   486
On a Dead Social Worker   488
On the Wing   488
Phalaenopsis   490
Poet at the Festival   491
Probably Unique in this State   492
Someone   494
Stroud   495
Thames Talking   496
The Beasts   497
The C Word   498
This and That: Guido Morris at St Ives   499
Three Goddesses   501
Tuesday   504
Two Men and a Dog   504
Two Nursery Rhymes for Today   506
Villanelle to Order   507
Will there be trumpets?   508

FOREWORD

On 18 April 1974, I started writing poems. Previously, like most bookish children, I'd viewed poetry as the spontaneous overflow of powerful feelings and had let rip whenever I experienced beauty, love, anger, humiliation etc. For sixteen years after that I'd been a teacher, dedicated to the cause of the un-split infinitive and the judicious use of the semi-colon. Then, at the beginning of that particular April, I found myself working as a hospital receptionist in Bristol and fiercely devoted to the cause of the out-patients, who were my business, and against the doctors, who were of course trained to understand and invariably had the last word, usually a medical cliché. At once I'd found the subject that I'd been looking for all my life: the strangeness of other people, particularly neurological patients, and how it felt to be them, and to use their words. Inevitably I had to break the rules and stop thinking in terms of correct spelling and punctuation. That was how the first book, *Side Effects*, came about. Subsequent collections derived their various origins from the death of my mother, my being a writer-in-residence in Lancaster, the distress of returning to the Bristol job I hoped I'd escaped from, responding to the challenge of various commissions, what happens to children after the war is over, obsession with civil war in the Balkans and the past that is still the present. Behind all of them lie preoccupations with the way people speak, birds, the landscape, cats, England, power, powerlessness and words, words, words. I would like to think there is a consistency about the poems, as well as the changes inevitable in widening experience. But that's for you, dear Reader, to say.

I've left out the poems that have somehow crept into collections and embarrassed me by their presence, and tried to include here poems that may be worth a second look. A few others, on the contrary, have crept in because they were published by other houses: *The Crystal Zoo* (for children) edited by Michael Harrison, was published by OUP in 1985; *The New Exeter Book of Riddles*, edited by Kevin Crossley-Holland and Lawrence Sail, was published by Enitharmon Press in 1999. Some Christmas poems, written over the years for friends, are placed here in the collections where they first appeared. Those which were published for the first time in *Christmas Poems* (illustrated by Nick Wadley, published jointly by Peterloo and Enitharmon in 2002) are printed under the heading *Christmas Poems*.

U.A. FANTHORPE

PREFACE

I first met U. A. Fanthorpe and her partner Rosie Bailey around 1987 at a poetry reading we did together in London's Silver Moon bookshop. Their kindness and tolerance are legendary, but what astonished me that first time I heard U. A.'s poems was how truly subversive she was – and this was all the more potent when deployed through her gentle and scholarly personality.

Many of us thought for years that she would have been the perfect Poet Laureate or Professor of Poetry at Oxford. I'm positive that, with Rosie at her side, she could have been both at once. This subtly subversive poet also understood the re-imagining of our traditions; the importance of the energy between the past and the present, particularly in poetry.

U. A. possessed an endearing patriotism that was founded lastingly on love, not shakily on superiority. All her poems, in fact, were sourced in love. She could make the difficult accessible and the accessible complex. She had not a smidgeon of pomposity or ego or self-regard. Indeed, if she had a fault as a poet, that fault was a closet virtue – modesty. She would have demurred herself, but U. A. Fanthorpe exerted a great influence on contemporary poetry. She was a brilliant performer of her work – aided and abetted by Rosie – and many of us learned much from her charismatic, hilarious and moving stage presence. And we continue to pass her influence on to new poets.

U. A. Fanthorpe revived the monologue in poetry – she loved Browning – and brought many marginalised voices to the centre, not least the voices of girls and women. I am only one of many poets who owe her a great debt and who is glad, always, to have her wonderful, warm, wise poems close.

CAROL ANN DUFFY

2010

SIDE EFFECTS
1978

THE LIST

Flawlessly typed, and spaced
At the proper intervals,
Serene and lordly, they pace
Along tomorrow's list
Like giftbearers on a frieze.

In tranquil order, arrayed
With the basic human equipment –
A name, a time, a number –
They advance on the future.

Not more harmonious who pace
Holding a hawk, a fish, a jar
(The customary offerings)
Along the Valley of the Kings.

Tomorrow these names will turn nasty,
Senile, pregnant, late,
Handicapped, handcuffed, unhandy,
Muddled, moribund, mute,

Be stained by living. But here,
Orderly, equal, right,
On the edge of tomorrow, they pause
Like giftbearers on a frieze

With the proper offering,
A time, a number, a name.
I am the artist, the typist;
I did my best for them.

THE WATCHER

I am a watcher; and the things I watch
Are birds and love.

Not the more common sorts of either kind.
Not sparrows, nor

Young couples. Such successful breeds are blessed
By church and state,

Surviving in huge quantities. I like
The rare Welsh kite,

Clinging to life in the far Radnor hills;
The tiny wren,

Too small for winter; and the nightingale,
Chased from her home

By bulldozers and speculating men.
In human terms,

The love I watch is rare, its habitat
Concealed and strange.

The very old, the mad, the failures. These
Have secret shares

Of loving and of being loved. I can't
Lure them with food,

Stare at them through binoculars, or join
Societies

That will preserve them. Birds are easier
To do things for.

But love is so persistent, it survives
With no one's help.

Like starlings in Trafalgar Square, cut off
By many miles

From life-supporting trees, finding their homes
On dirty roofs,

So these quiet lovers, miles from wedding bells,
Cherish their odd

And beastly dears with furtive fondling hands
And shamefaced looks,

Finding their nesting-place in hospitals
And prison cells.

JOBDESCRIPTION: MEDICAL RECORDS

Innocence is important, and order.
You need have no truck with the
Seamy insides of notes, where blood
And malignant growths and indelicate

Photographs wait to alarm. We like
To preserve innocence. You will
Be safe here, under the permanent
Striplighting. (Twenty-four hours cover.

Someone is always here. Our notes
Require constant company.) No
Patients, of course. The porter comes
And goes, but doesn't belong. With

His hairless satyr's grin, he knows
More than is suitable. Your conversation
Should concern football and television.
You may laugh at his dirty jokes,

But not tell any. Operations
Are not discussed here. How, by
The way, is your imagination?
Poorly, I hope. We do not encourage

Speculation in clerks. We prefer you
To think of patients not as people, but
Digits. That makes it much easier. Our system
Is terminal digit filing. If you

Are the right type for us, you will be
Unconscious of overtones. The contrasting
Weights of histories (puffy
For the truly ill, thin and clean

For childhood's greenstick fractures)
Will not concern you. You will use
The Death Book as a matter of routine.
Our shelves are tall, our files heavy. Have you

A strong back and a good head for heights?

FOR SAINT PETER

I have a good deal of sympathy for you, mate,
Because I reckon that, like me, you deal with the outpatients.

Now the inpatients are easy, they're cowed by the nurses
(In your case, the angels) and they know what's what in the set-up.

They know about God (in my case Dr Snow) and all His little fads,
And if there's any trouble with them, you can easily scare them rigid

Just by mentioning His name. But outpatients are different.
They bring their kids with them, for one thing, and that creates a
        wrong atmosphere.

They have shopping baskets, and buses to catch. They cry, or knit,
Or fall on the floor in convulsions. In fact, Saint Peter,

If you know what I mean, they haven't yet learned
How to be reverent.

CASEHISTORY: JULIE (ENCEPHALITIS)

She stands between us. Her dress
Is zipped up back to front.
She has been crying her eyes
Dark. Her legs are thinner than legs.

She is importunate.

I'm not mental, am I?
Someone told me I was mental,
But I lost me memory

'Cos our dad died.
It don't make sense though, do it?
After I've been a nurse.

Her speech is nothing.

If I been rude, I apologise.
I lost me memory
'Cos I had the flu, didn't I?
I thought it was 'cos our dad died, see.
But it was 'cos I had the flu.

What imports this song?

Married? O god forgive me.
Who to? Let's be fair,
If you're getting married,
You ought to know the man.
O, not Roy!
I didn't marry him, did I?
I must be mental.
I'll do meself in.

There is a willow.

He was different to my brothers.
God forgive me for saying this,
He was like a woman.
Children? O god, please help me,
Please do, god.

O rose of May.

I'm getting better,
The doctor told me so,
As god's me witness, touch wood.
O, I am hungry.
I hope you don't mind me asking,
Where's the toilet to?

Do you see *this,* O *God?*

What about me dad?
Me dad's not gone, is he?

CASEHISTORY: ALISON (HEAD INJURY)

(She looks at her photograph)

I would like to have known
My husband's wife, my mother's only daughter.
A bright girl she was.

Enmeshed in comforting
Fat, I wonder at her delicate angles.
Her autocratic knee

Like a Degas dancer's
Adjusts to the observer with airy poise,
That now lugs me upstairs

Hardly. Her face, broken
By nothing sharper than smiles, holds in its smiles
What I have forgotten.

She knows my father's dead,
And grieves for it, and smiles. She has digested
Mourning. Her smile shows it.

I, who need reminding
Every morning, shall never get over what
I do not remember.

Consistency matters.
I should like to keep faith with her lack of faith,
But forget her reasons.

Proud of this younger self,
I assert her achievements, her A levels,
Her job with a future.

Poor clever girl! I know,
For all my damaged brain, something she doesn't:
I am her future.

A bright girl she was.

PATIENCE STRONG

Everyone knows her name. Trite calendars
Of rose-nooked cottages or winding ways
Display her sentiments in homespun verse
Disguised as prose. She has her tiny niche
In women's magazines, too, tucked away
Among the recipes or near the end
Of some perennial serial. Her theme
Always the same: rain falls in every life,
But rainbows, bluebirds, spring, babies or God
Lift up our hearts. No doubt such rubbish sells.
She must be feathering her inglenook.

Genuine poets seldom coin the stuff,
Nor do they flaunt such aptly bogus names.
Their message is oblique; it doesn't fit
A pocket diary's page; nor does it pay.

One day in epileptic out-patients,
A working-man, a fellow in his fifties,
Was feeling bad. I brought a cup of tea.
He talked about his family and job:
His dad was in the Ambulance Brigade;
He hoped to join, but being epileptic,
They wouldn't have him. *Naturally*, he said,
With my disease, I'd be a handicap.
But I'd have liked to help. He sucked his tea,
Then from some special inner pocket brought
A booklet muffled up in cellophane,
Unwrapped it gently, opened at a page –
Characteristic cottage garden, seen
Through chintzy casement windows. Underneath
Some cosy musing in the usual vein,
And *See*, he said, *this is what keeps me going.*

FROM THE REMAND CENTRE

Eleven stone and nineteen years of want
Flex inside Koreen. Voices speak to her
In dreams of love. She needs it like a fag,
Ever since Mum, who didn't think her daft,
Died suddenly in front of her. She holds
Her warder lovingly with powerful palms,
Slings head upon her shoulders, cries *Get lost*,
Meaning *I love you*, and her blows caress.

AFTER VISITING HOURS

Like gulls they are still calling –
I'll come again Tuesday. Our Dad
Sends his love. They diminish, are gone.
Their world has received them,

As our world confirms us. Their debris
Is tidied into vases, lockers, minds.
We become pulses; mouthpieces
Of thermometers and bowels.

The trolley's rattle dispatches
The last lover. Now we can relax
Into illness, and reliably abstracted
Nurses will straighten our sheets,

Reorganize our symptoms. Outside,
Darkness descends like an eyelid.
It rains on our nearest and dearest
In car-parks, at bus-stops.

Now the bed-bound rehearse
Their repertoire of movements,
The dressing-gowned shuffle, clutching
Their glass bodies.

Now siren voices whisper
From headphones, and vagrant
Doctors appear, wreathed in stethoscopes
Like South Sea dancers.

All's well, all's quiet as the great
Ark noses her way into night,
Caulked, battened, blessed for her trip,
And behind, the gulls crying.

EARTHED

Not precisely, like a pylon or
A pop-up toaster, but in a general
Way, stuck in the mud.

Not budding out of it like gipsies,
Laundry lashed to a signpost, dieting on
Nettles and hedgehogs,

Not lodged in its layers like badgers,
Tuned to the runes of its home-made walls, wearing
Its shape like a skin,

Not even securely rooted, like
Tribesmen tied to the same allotment, sure of
The local buses,

But earthed for all that, in the chalky
Kent mud, thin sharp ridges between wheel-tracks, in
Surrey's wild gravel,

In serious Cotswold uplands, where
Limestone confines the verges like yellow teeth,
And trees look sideways.

Everything from the clouds downwards holds
Me in its web, like the local newspapers,
Routinely special,

Or Somerset belfries, so highly
Parochial that Gloucestershire has none, or
Literate thrushes,

Conscientiously practising the
Phrases Browning liked, the attitude Hughes noticed,
Or supermarkets

Where the cashiers' rudeness is native
To the district, though the bread's not, or gardens,
Loved more than children,

Bright with resourcefulness and smelling
Of rain. This narrow island charged with echoes
And whispers snares me.

STANTON DREW

First you dismantle the landscape.
Take away everything you first
Thought of. Trees must go,
Roads, of course, the church,
Houses, hedges, livestock, a wire
Fence. The river can stay,
But loses its stubby fringe
Of willows. What do you
See now? Grass, the circling
Mendip rim, with its notches
Fresh, like carving. A sky
Like ours, but empty along
Its lower levels. And earth
Stripped of its future, tilted
Into meaning by these stones,
Pitted and unemphatic. Recreate them.
They are the most permanent
Presences here, but cattle, weather,
Archaeologists have rubbed against them.
Still in season they will

Hold the winter sun poised
Over Maes Knoll's white cheek,
Chain the moon's footsteps to
The pattern of their dance.
Stand inside the circle. Put
Your hand on stone. Listen
To the past's long pulse.

OWLPEN MANOR

I am folded among my terraces
Like an old dog half asleep.
The sunlight tickles my chimneys.

I have never cared for grandeur.
This narrow handcarved valley fits
My casual autocracy. But I hold

What's mine. The long, undistinguished
Dynasty of Cotswold gentlemen,
Who never married cleverly, and made

Only a modest fortune in Ireland,
Suited my fancy. Owlpens, Daunts
And Stoughtons, I charmed them to a happy

Apathy. Even Margaret, my ghost of Anjou,
Pacing my Great Chamber in her high-crowned hat,
Knowing that tomorrow is Tewkesbury,

Walks in benevolence. My floorboards creak
In their infinite adjustment to time.
I have outlasted my successor on the hill,

I am permanent as the muted roar
Of white pigeons in my barn, as the drift
Of dry leaves in my ancient garden.

BRYMPTON D'EVERCY

1. *The Priest's House*

You can see they have lived close
To humanity for a long time. That numbed look,
Those finger furrows, take time to grow.
Casualties of the annual offensive
Between the treacly clay of Somerset,
The obstinate earthy hands of labourers,
They recline here now, stiffly at ease.

We are what they achieved. The hay
Raked, hedges laid, milk scoured, rats
Trapped, eels skinned, clothes scrubbed, earth
Dug by these laborious tools, with their
Immense genealogies and no future,
Resulted in us. Now, mud scraped off,
They find themselves suddenly rare.

The blacksmith, dairymaid, wheelwright,
Ditcher, haytrusser and shepherd have all
Stepped into the dark, but these slow, brutal things,
These hammers, bits, castrators, pitchforks,
This table on which dynasties of pigs
Have bled into the grain, these tired hats
Lasted. Now they inspect us, their artifacts.

The rain knocks on the roof. We feel
Fragile, apologetic. This elaborate world,
Which ended so suddenly that the cider press
Smells still of apples, watches mutely,
Knowing more about local weather than
We do. Furtively we sprint ten wet yards
Of grass to the chapel.

2. *The Chapel*

Whose consecrated air smells different,
Warm and encouraging. This lace, perhaps,
Retains a tender feeling for mankind.
But no. We found it wasn't that at all:
Just central heating, on for Evensong.

Three people lay there, all too beautiful
To be disturbed. The whiskered knight, encased
In scales like a huge salmon, held a pose
Gymnastically graceful and absurd.
A nervous lion peered behind his feet.

The rains of time had run the lady's dogs
(One at each heel) into her marble skirt,
But still her thick stone lips were sensual,
The wimple horning on her rigid brows
Still made it clear her faded blood was blue.

The solemn forehead and devoted eyes
Of the long priest focussed their holy thought
Upon a mass of stone between his hands,
Substitute for the chalice time had drowned.
He was too much in love to notice us.

3. The Garden

There is no room for us
Here. The past is too solid,
Too finished. The dead

Do not want us, except
As admirers. There are no
Cracks in their surface

For us to set root in.
But outside shining young vines
Grow green in the wet.

COIRE DUBH

If I stand still, I can hear only
The river's hollow comment, the bright
Interjection of the stonechat.
Room for you here, in a land scoured
Fit for sheep, eagles, deer; among
These humps and cones, these acres
Of glowing uneloquent water.

You are what they are looking for,
These hills, heaving unendingly their brutal
Heads, poring over each other's purple
Shoulders and white heads, unendingly
Watching for something, though I
Am seen, too; and the jet's
Mechanical shadow.

You, who are looked for, are the ones
Who are not here. Only
A caretaker lot, offering bed
And breakfast: frying Scotsmen,
Foresters, roadmen and surly girls
Ambitious for jobs in Oban.
The only poets left are headmasters
And civil servants,

And the English, whose temperate
Home-made syntax can't accommodate
This empty disorderly landscape.
Poets were flushed out of Scotland,
And who else speaks mountains?
Who else knows the heather's logic,
The corrie's semantics?

Selfconsciously our alien tongues
Baptise Ben Sausage and Ben Goitre,
Formal peaks, whose many-vowelled names
Hang about them, beautiful and personal
As clouds, and like clouds
Are unspoken. We are not the ones.
We tramp where you should live

In your jolly, squalid hovels,
Children of Big Mary of the Songs
(Seventeen stone singing-weight)
And Alasdair son of the Minister
Of Islandfinnan in Moidart; children
Of hereditary bards who composed in the dark,
With boulders on their bellies.

Who are not here. Whose absence
Sings louder than the stonechat
And the crunch of climbing boots,

Louder than the clicks of your dumb
And glossy descendants, in computer
Rooms, by cash registers, consuming
The fattening cake of exile.

CAMPSITE: MAENTWROG

This field contains the modest apparatus
Of suburb life, incubating under
Separate bell-jars, hurricane lamp-lit.

We observe it. Domesticated mum
In the permanent apron, and dad, reverting
In the wild to a feral state,

Shirt-sleeved, morose. The quarrelling lovers
Rained on, in the car, by dashboard-light.
He pitched the tent alone; they left at dawn.

Children fetching milk and water, making
Work a ritual, like games, and playing
Only with children from respectable tents.

The flat-capped fisherman, working his punctual
Day-shift on the river, whose dog
Knew to expect him at tea-time. And you

And me, patrolling the domestic purlieus,
Getting on with knitting and letters,
All of us practising our characteristic selves,

Despite the grass, and the apologetically
Insistent rain. Abroad we should be
Other, conforming to the strangeness

Of bread and air. Here we are just
Ourselves forced under glass. You have to pay more
For expensive weather. This is a cheap country.

THE WEST FRONT AT BATH

The headscarfed tourists in the comfy shoes
Obediently make their scheduled pause
Among the pigeons. Sun and stone confuse
The rhythm of their uninformed applause.
Where are we now? Would it be Bath, perhaps?
Five o'clock deftly shoots its slanted gleam
Across their eyes. A thoughtless pigeon claps
His wings. This moment is as much a dream
As Jacob's nightmare on the Abbey wall,
Alive with straining angels, who with wing
Correctly folded, desperately crawl
Along their monstrous ladder. Evening
Distorts their poise. Above it all sits God,
Watching the dreams, and finding both kinds odd.

THE QUIET GRAVE

(*for Cecil Sharp*)

Underground Rome waited solidly
In stone patience. Orpheus might lose
A beast or two, cracked apart by roots
Of brambled centuries, but still
Foundations lasted, knowing, like the princess,
That one day a ferret and a boy
Exploring a rabbithole would find an empire.

But this was a kingdom that lived

Some kinds of earth are reliable. The black
Peat of Somerset, and Norfolk mud
That tenderly cradled the deathship's spectral
Longrotted timbers. Some kinds of dryasdust
Air, too, responsibly cherish papyrus.

But this was a kingdom that lived
In the living air

Who held the keys of the kingdom?
Unfriendly old men in workhouses;
Bedridden ninety-year-olds terrorized
By highhanded grandchildren; gipsy women
With the long memories of the illiterate;
Old sailors who could sing only
Within sound of the sea. These
Held the keys of the kingdom.

Where was the kingdom?
The kingdom was everywhere. Under the noses
Of clerics devoted to folklore it lived
Invisibly, in gardens, in fields and kitchens,
In the servants' quarters. No one could find it
But those who were in it already.

When was the kingdom?
The kingdom was while women washed
And men broke stones. It was
Intervals in birdscaring; between
A cup too low and a cup
Too high; when a great-grandfather
Sang like a lark. Then
Was the kingdom.

Who cared for the kingdom?
An old woman gathering stones,
Who seized Sharp by his gentle-
Manly lapels, blowing her song into his mind
Through wrinkled gums. A surly chap
In Bridgwater Union, holding
Sharp's hand between his own grim bones,
Tears falling on all three. These
Cared for the kingdom.

What were the treasures of the kingdom?
Scraps of other worlds, prized
For their strangeness. A derrydown and a heyho,
And a rue dum day and a fol the diddle dee.
These were the treasures of the kingdom.

Who were the heirs of the kingdom?
The kingdom had no heirs, only
A younger generation that winked
At senility's music, and switched on the gramophone.

What was the end of the kingdom?
Massed choirs of the Federation
Of Women's Institutes filling
The Albert Hall; laconic
Improper poetry improved
For the benefit of schools;
Expansion of the Folk Song Industry. These
Were the end of the kingdom.

For this was a kingdom that lived
In the dying air

NOT MY BEST SIDE

I

Not my best side, I'm afraid.
The artist didn't give me a chance to
Pose properly, and as you can see,
Poor chap, he had this obsession with
Triangles, so he left off two of my
Feet. I didn't comment at the time
(What, after all, are two feet
To a monster?) but afterwards
I was sorry for the bad publicity.
Why, I said to myself, should my conqueror
Be so ostentatiously beardless, and ride
A horse with a deformed neck and square hoofs?
Why should my victim be so
Unattractive as to be inedible,
And why should she have me literally
On a string? I don't mind dying
Ritually, since I always rise again,
But I should have liked a little more blood
To show they were taking me seriously.

II

It's hard for a girl to be sure if
She wants to be rescued. I mean, I quite
Took to the dragon. It's nice to be
Liked, if you know what I mean. He was
So nicely physical, with his claws
And lovely green skin, and that sexy tail,
And the way he looked at me,
He made me feel he was all ready to
Eat me. And any girl enjoys that.
So when this boy turned up, wearing machinery,
On a really *dangerous* horse, to be honest,

48

I didn't much fancy him. I mean,
What was he like underneath the hardware?
He might have acne, blackheads or even
Bad breath for all I could tell, but the dragon –
Well, you could see all his equipment
At a glance. Still, what could I do?
The dragon got himself beaten by the boy,
And a girl's got to think of her future.

III
I have diplomas in Dragon
Management and Virgin Reclamation.
My horse is the latest model, with
Automatic transmission and built-in
Obsolescence. My spear is custom-built,
And my prototype armour
Still on the secret list. You can't
Do better than me at the moment.
I'm qualified and equipped to the
Eyebrow. So why be difficult?
Don't you want to be killed and/or rescued
In the most contemporary way? Don't
You want to carry out the roles
That sociology and myth have designed for you?
Don't you realise that, by being choosy,
You are endangering job-prospects
In the spear- and horse-building industries?
What, in any case, does it matter what
You want? You're in my way.

PALIMPSEST

Once the surface of the ground has been
The sidelong eyes of dawn and twilight
disturbed, the effect is, for all practical
catch in the net of their long shadows
purposes, permanent: the perfect
what is no longer there: grass offers
vestigia of a temple, as
its mute sermon on earth's derangement,
easily discernible in the
invisible and indelible
corn as on paper.
as children's hatred.

SOME MODERNISATION NEEDED

It wasn't inhospitable, exactly.
Preoccupied, perhaps. We didn't fit.
Our voices sounded gross, uncertain footsteps
Disturbed its poise. Side-set above the road,
Its four mild windows (two upstairs, two down)
Gazed south along the garden. Odds and ends
Of someone's life still hung around: a tin
Of Ajax in the kitchen, a tall-stalked
Geranium with little thirsty leaves,
And torn net curtains in the living room.

Despite its apathy it parted us.
You saw its future, on some August night,
Extended, painted, lived in, flushed with food,
Voices and flowers. Convivially chairs
Had clustered on the terrace. Someone played
These Foolish Things. Coffee, cigars and stock
Infused the air. This was how it would be.

The present held me in its frosted fist.
The house stayed sad and small, and smelt of cold.
Someone was dying upstairs in a slow
Damp-sheeted bed. The garden had turned strange.
The smell of its depression filtered through
Cracks in the window frames. The dying nose
Knew the sour drift of couchgrass, sliding sly,
Plaiting itself across the garden paths,
The whiff of mouldy blackberries, the thick
Polleny stink of asters run to seed.

We stood locked in our independent dreams,
Wondering why they weren't the same. The house
Shuffled its temperament between us both,
Equivocally fair. We took the key
Back to the agent, never talked of it,
The only house of all the ones we saw
To survey us, and keep its findings dark.

MY BROTHER'S HOUSE

Stood, like a fairyale, at the start
Of a wood. Vague fogs of bluebells
Absentmindedly invested it in summer.

Curdled dollops of snow
Flopped slowly in winter from invisible
Outstretched branches of firtrees.

The wood was a real wood, and
You could get lost in it. The trees
Had no names or numbers.

Jays, foxes and squirrels
Lived there. Also an obelisk in an odd
Corner, where nobody went.

The road to my brother's house
Had an air of leading nowhere. Visitors
Retreated, thinking of their back axles.

Blackberries and fifty-seven varieties
Of weeds had their eye on the garden.
Every year they shrivelled in flame,

Every day they returned unemphatic,
Not bothering to flaunt so
Easy a triumph. There was no garage

To uphold suburban standards, only
A shed where bicycles cowered among drips.
Indoors, all doors were always open

Or else jammed. Having a bath
Invited crowds, not just of spiders. Cats
Landed on chests with a thump and a yowl

In mid-dream. Overhead the patter of tiny
Paws or dense whirring of wings.
There were more humans around, too,

Than you quite expected, living furtive
Separate lives in damp rooms. Meals, haphazard
And elaborate, happened when, abandoning hope,

You had surrendered to bread
And butter. Massed choirs sang solidly
Through the masses of Haydn. Shoppers

Returned from forays with fifteen
Kinds of liversausage and no sugar.
When the family left, rats, rain and nettles

Took over instantly. I regret the passing
Of my brother's house. It was like living in Rome
Before the barbarians.

RITE

Foreign ground. It dips
Polished in every direction.

I long for squatter's rights
In a hymn book and part of a pew.
Snug C of E, where our fathers
Dozed anticipating roast beef, while shepherds
Slept by dogs, and Squire snored
At his private fireside, rousing
To contradict Rector. What one expects.

Here derelicts fling themselves down,
Agilely abject, and kiss the dirty lips
Of a picture. Untidily genuflecting
They visit the talkative candles. Saints
With flexible necks and symbolic fingers
Amble through goldleaf on impractical feet.
Ikons are scarfed like football crowds.
I stand in an uncommitted way
By the bookstall. Half the texts are Greek.

No choir. No priest, bell, book.
For landmark, the more desperate psalms,
Chanted in an even tenor which

Draws death's sting. No hymns,
But an impromptu hilarious
Madrigal group (three beards and one
Long skirt) intone delicately,

Guessing the note, dropping the music
Between tunes, and giggling
In harmony. This could go on
For ever. The derelicts
With random passion abase themselves.
Candles ebb. There is no heating.
My feet hurt.

In this holy web, where one-
Dimensional saints and floundering
Souls are safe together, I
Can find no place to be.
The polished floor caves in,
The smoke comes through.

CAROL CONCERT

Before the ice has time to form
On the carparked windscreens, before
A single carol has announced itself,
The performance happens.
(sing lullaby virgin noel)

These sculptured hairdos, these fairy-
Tale dresses, gothic embraces –
Sophie, long time no see! – are they
The approved offering
(sing lullaby virgin noel)

To the dull obligatory
Young men, whose correct accent, tie
And sex are paraded like expensive
Perfume? Or is it friends
(sing lullaby virgin noel)

Who get this oblation? Known once
Sweaty, tearful, giggling, asleep,
In the undesigning equality
Of youth, now moving high
(sing lullaby virgin noel)

Into the difficult heavens
Of Hotel Management in Kent,
Of sitting Oxbridge, of getting married?
In the carpark ice forms,
(sing lullaby virgin noel)

In the hall inarticulate
Strange friendships falter. *The standard
Of singing* (they say) *has gone down. They must
Be missing us.* Prefects
(sing lullaby virgin noel)

Like angels watch with wondering eyes.
Next year perhaps they too will sport
Long curtain-fabric skirts and Afro hair,
But their present faces
(sing lullaby virgin noel)

Deny complicity. The young
Bored man says he's having a ball,
While the choir with the innocent mouths
Of singers cry
Lullaby, virgin, noel.

POEM FOR OSCAR WILDE

Lane is cutting cucumber
Sandwiches, and the dogcart
Is coming round at the same
Time next week. The weather
Continues charming.

Reading Gaol and seedy France
Lurk in Cecily's garden
Under the pink roses. As
A man sows, so let him reap.
This truth is rarely pure,
And never simple.

Babies, handbags and lives are
Abandoned (I use the word
In the sense of *lost* or *mislaid*).
Sin, a temperance beverage,
Has stained somebody's lining.

This exquisite egg, which hatched
Ruin for you, who made it,
Retains its delicate poise.
Grief turns hair gold, and teacake
Can be tragic. The weather
Continues charming.

ONLY A SMALL DEATH

Only a small death, of course,
Not the full ceremony with mourners, a hearse,
Residuary legatees and a beanfeast
After the crematorium. Just a small, fully-
Conscious end.

Never again will you sleep in
This room, see sun rise through glass at this
Familiar angle, never again
Adjust to the shape of this bath, the smell
Of this cupboard.

You have died suddenly. The arrival
Of undertakers informs you of your
Decease. Their muscular detachment dissolves
Bonds between chairs and rooms, shelves
And their books.

The house offers its own valuation
Of the late owner. Dirt appears
In embarrassing contexts. If you were still
Alive, you would feel the need
To apologise.

Casual adjuncts of ordinary
Living, dustbins and drains, the
Unremarkable milkman, haloed in
The otherworldly glare of the last rites,
Achieve reality

Just as you end with them for ever.
Neighbours, paying a deathbed visit,
Acquire the tender resonance of friends,
But die as you go, birth exists on the edge
Of extinction.

The heir, arriving tactlessly early,
Retires till you finish dying. With you go
Archaic patterns of a home you will never
Come home to. Like an amputation, it will
Haunt you in the grave.

FAMILY ENTERTAINMENT

A nice evening for it. The firemen
Look in their yellow helmets
Just like the seven dwarfs.

Blue sky, green trees, red fire.
The ladies in the crowd wear floral
Dresses and sandals, the children less.

The dogs are well-behaved, lying
On the grass and panting politely. We
Behave well, too, taking care

Not to block anyone's view. We don't
Intrude on the group by the ambulance,
We preserve a proper distance

From the hosepipes and sirens. Fresh
From kite-watching and ball-games,
With the same detached attention,

We eye ruin. The dwarfs with their axes
Hack at the stockbroker's gothic, hand
Smoking armchairs through crazed windows.

Ashy carpet flakes over sills,
Torches wink in bedrooms, the intercom
Mutters away to itself. A hose leaks.

A neighbour runs past with a basin
And towels. Some of us imagine
The losses and injuries, but no one

Cares to find out. We are simply
A crowd, whose part is to watch.
The house will be ready again

For tomorrow's performance, the wounds
Washed off. Only, as we wander away,
We sniff the scorching in our own kitchens.

RIDGE HOUSE (OLD PEOPLE'S HOME)

Something dramatic ought to happen here.
These pools and pergolas, these long dim fish
Anticipate an entrance, and offstage
Butler and parlourmaid are polishing
Silver and dialogue impartially.
Edwardian high comedy, of course.
Epigrams fidget in the atmosphere.

The trees are close, too. Something might draw near
Under the dead beech leaves. A cloven foot
Moves otherwise than ours, and makes less noise.
The shadowed lawn looks knowing. Grass, of course,
Has contacts with the supernatural.
At night, perhaps, when no one is about,
Oberon's cavalry manoeuvre here.

But all's quiet now. The August sky is clear,
Wisteria hangs its leaflets undisturbed.
The weather and the garden both deserve
A compliment, but no one's here of course,
Except a sexless, ageless, shapeless shape,
Hunched underneath the cedar, muffled, rugged,
Which cannot see or smell, touch, taste or hear.

Dramatist to this house is Death. Austere,
Withdrawn, the scripts he writes. A single bed
Is his theatre. There the actor lies
Alone, and in the long dim hours explores
Dissolving senses. No one cares, of course.
The garden and the weather stay remote;
No god leaps from the clouds to interfere.

MEN ON ALLOTMENTS

As mute as monks, tidy as bachelors,
They manicure their little plots of earth.
Pop music from the council house estate
Counterpoints with the Sunday-morning bells,
But neither siren voice has power for these
Drab solitary men who spend their time
Kneeling, or fetching water, soberly,
Or walking softly down a row of beans.

Like drill-sergeants, they measure their recruits.
The infant sprig receives the proper space
The manly fullgrown cauliflower will need.
And all must toe the line here; stem and leaf,
As well as root, obey the rule of string.
Domesticated tilth aligns itself
In sweet conformity; but head in air
Soars the unruly loveliness of beans.

They visit hidden places of the earth
When tenderly with fork and hand they grope
To lift potatoes, and the round, flushed globes
Tumble like pearls out of the moving soil.
They share strange intuitions, know how much

Patience and energy and sense of poise
It takes to be an onion; and they share
The subtle benediction of the beans.

They see the casual holiness that spreads
Along obedient furrows. Cabbages
Unfurl their veined and rounded fans in joy,
And buds of sprouts rejoice along their stalks.
The ferny tops of carrots, stout red stems
Of beetroot, zany sunflowers with blond hair
And bloodshot faces, shine like seraphim
Under the long flat fingers of the beans.

PAT AT MILKING TIME

This enterprise is sick. The placid rats
Know it, roundhaunched and glossy, taking
Turns in the straw, like country dancers.

The dairy smells of defeat and sour milk.
Bank manager on Wednesday. Herb cheese
Drains peacefully through muslin into the churn.

The kids don't understand, knowing
Nothing but now, and the imperatives
Of suck, sleep, wriggle. In their world

It's normal to be fed at three o'clock
In the morning. What a field contains –
Sun, daisies, wind – is not to be imagined.

Growing up keeps them busy. But the milkers
Know, and are sad. They come to her pail
One by one, independently, as she calls them,

Christabel, *Infanta*, *Treasure* and *Nickel*,
Mosquito and *Gnat*, stepping thoughtfully,
Nibbling her straggly hair, weaving

Their sympathetic magic behind her back,
Watching through square-lensed eyes. Every day
There is less milk in their taut pronged teats.

Love is no help. Like cats they rub against her.
The church clock echoes oddly. The strident
Mew of a peacock slices the neutral air.

CANAL 1977

I remember this place: the conspiratorial
Presence of trees, the leaves' design
On uncommitted water, the pocky stonework
Ruining mildly in mottled silence,
The gutted pub, the dropping sounds
Inside the tunnel, I remember this place.

And before. I remember the sly lurchers,
The rose-and-castled barges, serious horses,
Coal smell, the leggers' hollow whoops
Down water, the bankrupt contractors
Grizzling into their beer, the trees and grass
Waiting to take over. I remember before.

And I remember the not-yet after,
When the money's raised and the sparetime Sunday
Navvying's over, the last intrusive sapling
Is ashes, when the bunting has bobbed, the first
Distinguished head ducked under the keystone,
There will be an after to be remembered

As the pleasurecraft purr their idle way
Into sunshine, and the smooth pink families
With their superior dogs enjoy the water,
The weather, the picturesque antiquity
That savaged so many who made it.
I remember after. And after

And before, the mute persistence of water
And grass and trees. Humanity goes out
Like a light, like the Roman-candle miners,
Shafting their pits on a donkey-winch, astraddle
A powderkeg, light in their teeth, a fuse in each pocket,
Lying foreign and broken in Gloucestershire churchyards now.

HORTICULTURAL SHOW

These are Persephone's fruits
Of the underyear. These will guide us
Through the slow dream of winter.

Onions her paleskinned lamps.
Rub them for strange knowledge. They shine
With the light of the tomb.

Drawn in fine runes along
Hard green rinds, the incomprehensible
Initiation of the marrow.

All orange energy driven
Down to a final hair, these carrots
Have been at the heart of darkness.

And parti-coloured leeks,
Their green hair plaited, like Iroquois braves,
Leaning exhausted in corners.

Holystoned the presence
Of potatoes, pure white and stained pink.
Persephone's bread.

Sacrificed beetroots
Display their bleeding hearts. We read
The future in these entrails.

Out in the world excitable
Ponies caper, Punch batters Judy, a man
Creates a drystone wall in thirty minutes,

Arrows fly, coconuts fall, crocodiles
And Jubilee mugs, disguised as children,
Cope with candyfloss, the band
Adds its slow waltz heart beat.

Here in the tent, in the sepia hush,
Persephone's fruits utter where they have been,
Where we are going.

STAFF PARTY

Silky and bland, like Roman emperors,
With kiss-curls trained across their noble brows,
They sit, my colleagues, laughing in the right
Self-conscious way at all the proper points.

I've known them for so long, and yet I don't
Know them at all. I know their parlour tricks,
Their favourite cardigans and recipes,
Their hairdressers, their views about the split
Infinitive, the Principal and What
Is Wrong with Modern Parents, know the names
Of children, husbands, cats. I know that when
Some local battle clouds relationships
(Shoplifting, drugs, the press or pregnancy –
So many trivial things can go astray
Besides the bigger, permanent mishaps:
The timetable, or the supply of ink),
Some will orate, some help, and some betray.

We know what each will do. But some cold hand
Stops us from knowing more. That's dangerous,
Even disloyal. For already we
Know more than's proper about all of us.

We know our reputations and nicknames,
Enthusiast, digressor, confidante,
The one who just can't concentrate on girls
Because she's getting married, and the one
Who never does her washing. Emperors
Preserved their Roman calm in public life,
Unless they liked it otherwise, but these
Statuesque Romans have Suetonius
Around them all the time, scribbling on desks,
Asking discursive questions, argus-eyed,
Flypaper-memoried historians,
Publishing every moment of the day
Sober surmises and fantastic truth.

Knowing all this, and knowing we are known,
We must respect the anonymity
We decent ladies all pretend to have,
Letting the Whore, the Genius, the Witch,
The Slut, the Miser and the Psychopath
Go down to history, if they really must,
While Caesar keeps his bright precarious gloss.

SONG

Don't eavesdrop on my heart,
    It's a sneak.
It will chat with any stranger,
Lifeguard, lover, doctor, tailor;
It just needs to feel an ear
    And it will speak.

Don't eavesdrop on my heart,
    It's illiterate.
The educated hand, eye, brain,
Turn words to shapes and back again;
My stupid heart could never learn
    The alphabet.

Don't eavesdrop on my heart,
    It's dumb.
In rainforests of tubes and pumps
It hangs, my heart, a third-world dunce;
Parrots can speak, but my heart just
    Communicates by drum.

Don't eavesdrop on my heart,
    It's clever.
And if your head should touch my breast
My heart would make its own arrest,
Develop hands, as trees grow leaves,
And hold you there forever.

STANDING TO
1982

STATIONS UNDERGROUND

Horace: Odes I, no. XXIV

durum: sed levius fit patientia
  Quidquid corrigere est nefas.

Loss hurts. Yet patience helps us to endure
The ills no human should presume to cure.

(tr. James Michie)

1. FANFARE

(for Winifrid Fanthorpe, born 5 February 1895, died 13th November 1978)

You, in the old photographs, are always
The one with the melancholy half-smile, the one
Who couldn't quite relax into the joke.

My extrovert dog of a father,
With his ragtime blazer and his swimming togs
Tucked like a swiss roll under his arm,
Strides in his youth towards us down some esplanade,

Happy as Larry. You, on his other arm,
Are anxious about the weather forecast,
His overdraft, or early closing day.

You were good at predicting failure: marriages
Turned out wrong because you said they would.
You knew the rotations of armistice and war,
Watched politicians' fates with gloomy approval.

All your life you lived in a minefield,
And were pleased, in a quiet way, when mines
Exploded. You never actually said
I told you so, but we could tell you meant it.

Crisis was your element. You kept your funny stories,
Your music-hall songs for doodlebug and blitz-nights.
In the next cubicle, after a car-crash, I heard you
Amusing the nurses with your trench wit through the blood.

Magic alerted you. Green, knives and ladders
Will always scare me through your tabus.
Your nightmare was Christmas; so much organised
Compulsory whoopee to be got through.

You always had some stratagem for making
Happiness keep its distance. Disaster
Was what you planned for. You always
Had hoarded loaves or candles up your sleeve.

Houses crumbled around your ears, taps leaked,
Electric light bulbs went out all over England,
Because for you homes were only provisional,
Bivouacs on the stony mountain of living.

You were best at friendship with chars, gipsies,
Or very far-off foreigners. Well-meaning neighbours
Were dangerous because they lived near.

Me too you managed best at a distance. On the landline
From your dugout to mine, your nightly
Pass, friend was really often quite jovial.

You were the lonely figure in the doorway
Waving goodbye in the cold, going back to a sink-full
Of crockery dirtied by those you loved. We
Left you behind to deal with our crusts and gristle.

I know why you chose now to die. You foresaw
Us approaching the Delectable Mountains,
And didn't feel up to all the cheers and mafficking.

But how, dearest, will even you retain your
Special brand of hard-bitten stoicism
Among the halleluyas of the triumphant dead?

2. FOUR DOGS

1. *Cerberus*

The first was known simply
As *the dog*. Later writers gave him a name,
Three heads, a collar of serpents,
And a weakness for cake.
They also claimed he could be
Calmed by magic, charmed by music,
And even, on one occasion, thrashed.

Later writers can seldom be trusted.
Primary sources are more reliable:
This dog guarded his master's gate,
Wagged his ears and tail at visitors,
Admitted them all, and saw to it
That nobody ever got out.

2. *Anubis*

The civil Egyptians made
Their dog half man. The dog end
Had the usual doggy tastes
For digging, and bones. But the human half
Was drawn to conservation and chemistry,
Liked pickling, preserving, dissecting,
Distillation; added artistry
To the dog's enthusiasm. Undertaking
Became Egyptian art.

3. *El Perro (Goya)*

There was a man who never blinked.
Helmeted in deafness, he set down
What he saw: the unembarrassed beastliness
Of humanity, country picnics, rape,

Blank-faced politicians, idiot obstinate kings,
Famine, firing-squads, milkmaids.
He charted nightmare's dominion
On his house's walls. To him appeared
The thing itself, snouting its way
Up from underground. He drew it
As it was: darkness, a dog's head,
Mild, mongrel, appalling.

4. *Shandy*

The fourth dog lives in my house with me
Like a sister, loves me doggedly,
Guiltily, abstractedly; disobeys me
When I am not looking. I love her
Abstractedly, guiltily; feed her; try
Not to let her know she reminds me
Of the other dogs.

3. AT THE FERRY

Laconic as anglers and, like them, submissive,
The grey-faced loiterers on the bank,
Charon, of your river.

They are waiting their turn. Nothing we do
Distracts them much. It was you, Charon, I saw,
Refracted in a woman's eyes.

Patient, she sat in a wheelchair,
In an X-ray department, waiting for someone
To do something to her,

Given a magazine, folded back
At the problem page: *What should I do*
About my husband's impotence?

Is a registry office marriage
Second-best? I suffer from a worrying
Discharge from my vagina.

In her hands she held the thing obediently;
Obediently moved her eyes in the direction
Of the problems of the restless living.

But her mind deferred to another dimension.
Outward bound, tenderly inattentive, she was waiting,
Charon, for you.

And the nineteen-stone strong man, felled
By his spawning brain, lying still to the sound
Of the DJ's brisk chirrup;

He wasn't listening, either. He was on the lookout
For the flurry of water as your craft
Comes about in the current.

I saw you once, boatman, lean by your punt-pole
On an Oxford river, in the dubious light
Between willow and water,

Where I had been young and lonely, being
Now loved, and older; saw you in the tender, reflective
Gaze of the living

Looking down at me, deliberate,
And strange in the half-light, saying nothing,
Claiming me, Charon, for life.

4. RISING DAMP

(for C.A.K. and R.K.M.)

'A river can sometimes be diverted, but it is a very hard thing to lose it altogether.' (J.G.Head: *paper read to the Auctioneers' Institute in 1907*)

At our feet they lie low,
The little fervent underground
Rivers of London

Effra, Graveney, Falcon, Quaggy,
Wandle, Walbrook, Tyburn, Fleet

Whose names are disfigured,
Frayed, effaced.

These are the Magogs that chewed the clay
To the basin that London nestles in.
These are the currents that chiselled the city,
That washed the clothes and turned the mills,
Where children drank and salmon swam
And wells were holy.

They have gone under.
Boxed, like the magician's assistant.
Buried alive in earth.
Forgotten, like the dead.

They return spectrally after heavy rain,
Confounding suburban gardens. They infiltrate
Chronic bronchitis statistics. A silken
Slur haunts dwellings by shrouded
Watercourses, and is taken
For the footing of the dead.

Being of our world, they will return
(Westbourne, caged at Sloane Square,
Will jack from his box),
Will deluge cellars, detonate manholes,
Plant effluent on our faces,
Sink the city.

Effra, Graveney, Falcon, Quaggy,
Wandle, Walbrook, Tyburn, Fleet

It is the other rivers that lie
Lower, that touch us only in dreams
That never surface. We feel their tug
As a dowser's rod bends to the source below

Phlegethon, Acheron, Lethe, Styx.

5. SISYPHUS

'The struggle itself towards the heights is enough to fill a man's heart.
One must imagine Sisyphus happy.'
(Camus: *The Myth of Sisyphus*)

Apparently I rank as one
Of the more noteworthy sights down here.
As to that, I can't judge, having
No time to spare for tourists.

My preoccupations are this stone
And this hill. I have to push
The one up the other.

A trivial task for a team, an engine,
A pair of horses. The interest lies
Not in the difficulty of the doing,

But the difficulty for the doer. I accept this
As my vocation: to do what I cannot do.
The stone and I are

Close. I know its every wart, its ribby ridges,
Its snags, its lips. And the stone knows me,
Cheek, chin and shoulders, elbow, groin, shin, toe,
Muscle, bone, cartilage and muddied skinprint,
My surfaces, my angles and my levers.

The hill I know by heart too,
Have studied incline, foothold, grain,
With watchmaker's patience.

Concentration is mutual. The hill
Is hostile to the stone and me.
The stone resents me and the hill.

But I am the mover. I cannot afford
To spend energy on emotion. I push
The stone up the hill. At the top

It falls, and I pursue it,
To heave it up again. Time not spent
On doing this is squandered time.

The gods must have had a reason
For setting me this task. I have forgotten it,
And I do not care.

6. THE GUIDE

The level-headed Greeks grasped
Their underworld, and charted it. Rivers,
Hills and dry land behaved
Geographically, appropriately. Sentence
Was passed by a panel
Of High Court Judges, with an assessor
To help with hard cases,
And the terrain, being logical,
Enforced the law.

Dante the bureaucrat invented
A new filing system for
The irregular dead, pigeon-holing them
As pertinently as the Mikado.
They fluttered and squeaked,
But he netted and mounted them,
Steady as Aristotle, knowing
The unutterable articulations of peace,
From purgatory to paradise, were based
On the accurate taxonomy of sin.

Dispossession, and the secrets
Of his beemaster father,
Taught Vergil more than men know.
He trudged further into suffering
And pity than other people,
Led to accept his vocation
By the annals of the hive. He knew
How drones die nobly
In midsummer air after mating,
Or sombrely, autumnal offerings;
How the workforce fly their wings
To rags, to death; how virgin knights

Are stabbed in their royal cradles;
How tired and failing monarchs
Undertake forced marches upcountry

To found new colonies. He knew
That the bees' god is the Future,
Which consumes first the loving,
The wise, the beautiful, the brave,
Because they are special, and favours
The ordinary bee, the bee-in-the-air,
Aeneas, the survivor.
So Orpheus has to die. So Rome
Goes on, as Vergil knew it would,
Monumentally second-rate city.

About Hell, too, he knew more
Than the others. Through blunt-edged Latin,
Its meanings scuffed by ages of misuse,
He found ways of wording the unsayable,
Fathomed echo-chambers behind the dulled
And vague, and told us:
Hell is a sort of underground bog.
There are no landmarks. In it
Those we have loved and failed
Turn their backs for ever.

7. THE PASSING OF ALFRED

'He (Tennyson) died with his hand on his Shakespeare, and the
moon shining full into the window over him . . . A worthy end.'
(Queen Victoria: Journal)

Our fathers were good at dying.
They did it lingeringly,
As if they liked it; correctly,

With earnest attention to detail,
Codicils brought up to date,
Forgiveness, confession, last-gasp
Penitence properly witnessed
By responsible persons. Attorneys,
Clerics, physicians, all knew their place
In the civil pavane of dying.

Households discharged
Their methodical duties: said farewell
In order of precedence, outdoor staff first,
Faithful hounds respectfully mourning,
Lastly the widow-to-be, already
Pondering a transformed wardrobe.

They died in the houses,
The beds they were born in,
They died where they lived, between
Known sheets, to the obbligato
Of familiar creaks and ticks.

We who differ, whose dears are absorbed
Into breezy wards for routine terminations,
Envy our fathers their decorous endings
In error. Nothing makes extinction easy.
They also died appallingly, over

The family breakfast-cups; bloodily
In childbed; graveyard coughed themselves
Into coffins; declined from heart-break
And hunger. And however resigned,
Orderly, chaste, aesthetic the passing of Alfred,
Remorse, regret still shadowed the living after.

Like us they ran from habit to tell good news
To dead ears; like us they dreamed
Of childhood, and being forgiven;
And the dead followed them, as they do us,
Tenderly through darkness,
But fade when we turn to look in the upper air.

THE CONDUCTOR

I am the conductor. I preside
Over the players, clothed in the swagger
Of my office. My imperative hands
Ordain volume and tempo. I am
The music's master.

This is the music, propped open before me:
Immense Unfinished Symphony of life,
Its intervals, blunt naturals and fugues,
Its resolutions, syncopations, shakes,
Scored for my players.

These are the players. (Stand up, friends,
And make your bows.) A random lot,
Amateurs all, for nothing at all disbars,
And finally all find parts that fit them
For my orchestra.

Listen! an excerpt: today's programme.
First subject, in flute's paediatric whine,
Transposed now to the key of senility,
Dribbling urine and spittle, difficult heartbeats
Plucking like harpstrings.

Each virtuoso has his own variation:
Depression's largo, schizophrenia's scherzo,
Mute music of the withdrawn, epileptic cadenzas,
The plagal cadence of the stretcher-borne dying,
Drum taps of the blind.

Listen again. The second subject
Is harder to hear, is sensed at last
In pauses, breves, a *did-not-come*, a rest,
A silence. For this symphony's name
Is also Farewell,

And as each player reaches his part's end
He tucks his instrument decently under his arm,
Snuffs out his candle, tiptoes demurely away
Into the dark and the stillness. For him
The concert's over.

I, the receptionist, must also play
My part, and go. I shoot my cuffs,
And watch my hectoring fingers, like the rest,
Sprout into rattlebones. And see
A new conductor,

Young, fetching, shifty, immortal,
Hermes bringer of dreams, the light-fingered,
Hermes who leads men's souls in another direction
From our world of unholy living
And wholly dying.

INSIDE

Inside our coloured, brisk world,
Like a bone inside a leg, lies
The world of the negative.

It is the same world, only somehow
Conviction has dribbled out of it,
Like stuffing from a toy.

A world of hypnotic clocks and unfinished
Goblin gestures. Nothing moves in a landscape
Fixed in hysteria's stasis.

This is the hushed network of nightmare.
You have lost touch with the sustaining
Ordinariness of things.

Suddenly the immense and venerable
Fallacies that prop the universe
Fail, the colossal flickering fabric
Which we must believe in so that it can be
Goes out.

Here malevolence is routine, the shadow
Is real and the world is shadow.
Here the happy-ever-after crumples
Into a rheumatoid hic-iacet.

Here the appalling and unexpected
Disaster is expected. Here the blood
Screams whispers to the flesh.

And here the alien wanders
Endless benighted streets where innocent households
Laugh behind blinds and believe in tomorrow
Like the milkbottles at the door.

PROLEPSIS

You look too young for the part,
Said the producer. *This is how we show*
Age on the stage.

She traced the firm ground round the eye,
Touching bone under. Make-up's black finger
Rehearsed what would come:

Mouth's drag, the florid swag
Of flesh round socket, cheekbone, chin.
The writing on the skin.

You wore age like a mask,
Young, bright, erect. Who could detect
Decomposition's mark?

Your new producer has a different touch
Who, like a headsman, can evoke
Death at a stroke.

You look too young for your age,
He said. *So let's pretend you're dead.*
He showed his hand

And touched your head.
One hemisphere's sure pilot faltered,
Brain's tempo altered,

One eye, arm, hand, side, leg and foot
Fell mute. We read you, dulled and stiff,
Half of Death's hieroglyph.

You will recover,
Claim you're mis-cast, demand a different role,
But we decipher
The writing on the soul.

A GARDENER

Ours are a job lot
From the Funny Farm: shambling gangs
Of overgrown dwarfs, waiting
To be told what to do,

Or austere, executive Scotsmen,
Who issue crisp, instantly misunderstood orders,
Decamping before incomprehension
Becomes too obvious.

This one materialised
Pruning an abandoned rambler
With placid accuracy.

We spoke. I asked, he taught me
To know growths of different years,
How each year sets its signature on roses
Like hallmarked silver.

I asked what course he'd done.
He explained the high-flying
Resolution of rootstock, the frailty
Of patrician grafts.

Next day he described
The enormous thirst of trees,
The flow of sap that makes each sprig

Stretch itself into leaves,
And how in winter, each
Of these great drinkers shrinks
Inside its bark, thinks slow
Thoughts as the sun runs low.

Sandwich course? I suggested,
Job in municipal gardens?
A televisual career?
Why waste such talent here?

I haven't seen him since,
But I know where he's been;
Hollyhocks thoughtfully barbered
Before frost blacks their tops.

I know he's still around,
One day with kindest cuts
Dressing our shaggy borders;
Another, transplanted hydrangeas

Suddenly look at home.
Our scrubby grounds grow spruce.
Not much more left to do.
Will he start on the dwarfs next?

But he keeps clear of me.

NOT QUITE RIGHT

Excuse me, staff-lady, but I feel rotten hungry and
thirsty, honest, I feel really ill. I'm very sincerely
grateful for having my life saved. I'm not a fool.

I died once. My wife saved my life with the kiss of life.
I feel rotten hungry and thirsty. Would you have such a
thing on you as a piece of chewing-gum or a sweet?
Any chance of your lovely company for a game of crib?

Not the blunt planes of the dull-minded,
The junket façade of the deranged;
Sanity's fine dry-point composed this profile.
Above it, hemispheres in disorder.

O the higher up the mulberry tree
The sweeter grows the berry.

Not the doll's strut of the retarded,
The see-saw footing of the insane;
He runs our corridors lightly, like a boy,
Left arm bent, hand signalling a corner.
He is a motorbike. OOOO oooo

O the higher up the mulberry tree
The sweeter grows the cherry.

Not the candid eyeballs of imbeciles,
Lunacy's limp and slippery pupils;
Regal the gaze of his eye from its socket
As he angles his head to chat.

O the higher up the mulberry tree
The sweeter grows the parsley.

We swap jargon. I call him lad,
Naming him too often, like a dog.
He looks with his sane eyes. He speaks.
He says nothing.

O the higher up the mulberry tree
The sweeter grows the herring.

He shuffles his thoughts' thumbed pack.
No joker ever trumps the brain's dead cells.
Yet once when, bothered by his gibberish,
I said to him: *Say something cheerful, lad,*
For goodness' sake, he looked me in the eye
Wisely, and spoke: *I've got my life, I'm alive.*
I'm not a fool.

O the higher up the mulberry tree
The sweeter grows the berry.

RESUSCITATION TEAM

Arrives like a jinn, instantly,
Equipped with beards, white coats, its own smell,
And armfuls of metal and rubber.

Deploys promptly round the quiet bed
With horseplay and howls of laughter.
We, who are used to life, are surprised

At this larky resurrection. Runs
Through its box of tricks, prick, poke and biff,
While we watch, amazed. The indifferent patient

Is not amused, but carries little weight,
Being stripped and fumbled
By so many rugger-players. My first corpse,

If she is a corpse, lies there showing
Too much breast and leg. The team
Rowdily throws up the sponge, demands soap and water,

Leaves at the double. One of us,
Uncertainly, rearranges the night-dress.
Is it professional to observe the proprieties

Now of her who leaves privately
Wheeled past closed doors, her face
Still in the rictus of victory?

LAMENT FOR THE PATIENTS

These were far from lovely in their lives,
And when they died, they were instantly forgotten.

These were the permanent patients, the ones
Whose disease was living. Their trophy, death,
Being to no one's advantage, was kept dark.

These had quiet funerals (*no flowers,
Please*), silent incinerations, hushed-up autopsies;
Their dying figured in obituary columns
Of local papers only.

On these specialists had practised specialities;
Had weighed and measured; had taken samples
Of blood and urine; had tested IQs,
Reflexes, patience; had applied
Shock treatment, drugs and nice hot cups of tea.
Of these specialists had washed their hands,
Having failed to arrive at a satisfactory
Diagnosis (anglicè: having failed to infect them
With a reason for living). Therefore they died.

To me came the news of their dying:
From the police (*Was this individual*

A *patient of yours?*); from ambulance
Control (*Our team report this patient
You sent us to fetch is deceased already*);
From tight-lipped telephoning widowers
(*My wife died in her sleep last night*);
From carboned discharge letters (*I note
That you have preserved the brain. We would certainly
Be very interested in this specimen*);
From curt press cuttings (*Man found dead.
Foul play not suspected*). I annotated their notes
With their final symptom: *died.*
Therefore I remember them.

These I remember:
Sonia, David, Penny, who chose death.
Lynn and Gillian, who died undiagnosed.
Peter, whose death was enigmatic.
Simple Betty, who suddenly stopped living.
Lionhearted Gertrude, who persevered to the end.
Patricia, so sorry for herself,
For whom I was not sufficiently sorry.
Julian, the interesting case. Alan,
Broken by a lorry, resurrected by surgeons,
Who nevertheless contrived at length to die.

Not for these the proper ceremonies, the solemn crowds,
The stripped gun-carriage, the slow march from *Saul,*
The tumulus, the friendly possessions
At hand in the dark. Not even
The pauper's deal coffin, brief office
Of the uncared-for. Only the recital
Of disembodied voices in a clerk's ear,
A final emendation of the text.

SPRING AFTERNOON

The doves purr in the trees. The wild inmates
Of Stoke Park Mental Hospital next door
Shout their improper comments from barred windows.

Forsythia burns. Homely wallflowers breathe out
The smell of heaven. The nurses and the patients
Are taking tea in deckchairs in the garden,

Under the trees. Depressives and obsessives
Call gaily to us as they play at croquet.
The epileptics doze off in the grass.

Caged in normality, we dumbly watch
From our dark office windows, feel that something –
Spring? or our sanity? – has let us down.

REPORTS

Has made a sound beginning
Strikes the right note:
Encouraging, but dull.
Don't give them anything
To take hold of. Even
Pronouns are dangerous.

The good have no history,
So don't bother. *Satisfactory*
Should satisfy them.

Fair and *Quite good,*
Multi-purpose terms,
By meaning nothing,
Apply to all.
Feel free to deploy them.

Be on your guard;
Unmanageable oaf cuts both ways.
Finds the subject difficult,
Acquitting you, converts
Oaf into idiot, usher to master.

Parent, child, head,
Unholy trinity, will read
Your scripture backwards.
Set them no riddles, just
Echo the common-room cliché:
Must make more effort.

Remember your high calling:
School is the world.
Born at *Sound beginning,*
We move from *Satisfactory*
To *Fair,* then *Find*
The subject difficult,

Learning at last we
Could have done better.

Stone only, final instructor,
Modulates from the indicative
With *Rest in peace.*

94

HALF-TERM

Always autumn, in my memory.
Butter ringing the drilled teashop crumpets;
Handmade chocolates, rich enough to choke you,
Brought in special smooth paper from Town.

(Back at school, the square tall piles
Of bread, featureless red jam in basins,
Grace, a shuffle of chairs, the separate table
For the visiting lacrosse team.)

Long awkward afternoons in hotel lounges,
Islanded in swollen armchairs, eyeing
Aristocratic horses in irrelevant magazines.
Should I be talking to Them?

(Back at school the raptly selfish
Snatch at self: the clashing
Determined duets in cold practising-
Rooms, the passionate solitary knitting.)

Inadequacies of presentation, perceived
By parents' temporary friends; hair, manners,
Clothes, have failed to adjust.
I don't know the rules of snooker.

(Back at school, the stiff reliable
Awkwardnesses of work. History test
On Monday morning. Deponent verbs.
I have never been good at maths.)

Saying goodbye. There are tears
And hugs, relief, regret. They,
Like me, return to a patterned life
Whose rules are easy. Unworthily

I shall miss chocolate, crumpets,
Comfort, but not the love I only
Sense as they go, waving to the end,
Vague in the streetlamps of November.

(Back at school the bullies,
Tyrants and lunatics are waiting,
I can deal with them.)

YOU WILL BE HEARING FROM US SHORTLY

You feel adequate to the demands of this position?
What qualities do you feel you
Personally have to offer?

                                              Ah

Let us consider your application form.
Your qualifications, though impressive, are
Not, we must admit, precisely what
We had in mind. Would you care
To defend their relevance?

                                              Indeed

Now your age. Perhaps you feel able
To make your own comment about that,
Too? We are conscious ourselves
Of the need for a candidate with precisely
The right degree of immaturity.

                                      So glad we agree

And now a delicate matter: your looks.
You do appreciate this work involves
Contact with the actual public? Might they,
Perhaps, find your appearance
Disturbing?

                                    Quite so

And your accent. That is the way
You have always spoken, is it? What
Of your education? Were
You educated? We mean, of course,
Where were you educated?
And how
Much of a handicap is that to you,
Would you say?
                          Married, children,
We see. The usual dubious
Desire to perpetuate what had better
Not have happened at all. We do not
Ask what domestic disasters shimmer
Behind that vaguely unsuitable address.

And you were born – ?

                                    Yes. Pity.

So glad we agree.

ONLY HERE FOR THE BIER

'I wrote these four poems because I was interested to see how the masculine world of Shakespeare's tragedies would look from the woman's angle. In fact, women exist in this world only to be killed, as sacrificial victims. So I imagined Gertrude (Mother-in-law), Regan (King's daughter), Emilia (Army wife) and the un-named waiting gentlewoman in *Macbeth* having a chat with some usual female confidante, like a hairdresser, or a telephone.' (U.A.F.)

Such a nice girl. Just what I wanted
For the boy. Not top drawer, you know,
But so often, in our position, that
Turns out to be a mistake. They get
The ideas of their station, and that upsets
So many applecarts. The lieges, of course,
Are particularly hidebound, and the boy,
For all his absentminded ways, is a great one
For convention. Court mourning, you know.
Things like that. We don't want a Brunhilde
Here. But she was so suitable. Devoted
To her father and brother, and,
Of course, to the boy. And a very
Respectable, loyal family. Well, loyal
To number two, at any rate. Number one,
I remember, never quite trusted . . . Yes,
And had just the right interests. Folk song, for instance,
(Such a sweet little voice), and amateur
Dramatics. Inherited *that* taste
From her father. Dear old fellow, he'd go on
For hours about his college drama group.
And the boy's so keen on the stage. It's nice
When husband and wife have a shared interest,
Don't you think? Then botany. Poor little soul,
She was really keen. We'd go for trips
With the vasculum, and have such fun
Asking the lieges their country names for flowers.
Some of them, my dear, were scarcely delicate
(The names, I mean), but the young nowadays
Don't seem to notice. Marriage
Would have made her more innocent, of course.
I can't think who will do for the boy now.
I seem to be the only woman left round here.

2. KING'S DAUGHTER

Being the middle sister is tiresome.
The rawboned heroics of the eldest
Are out of reach; so is the youngest's
Gamine appeal. It is impossible for the second child
To be special. One must just cultivate
One's own garden, neatly. For neatness and order
Matter in the world of the middle daughter,
The even number. Disorderly lives
Are distasteful. Adultery is untidy;
Servants should be accurate and invisible.
Individuals should have two eyes, or none;
One eye is unacceptable. I enjoy the beauty
Of formality, and have no objection
To offering father the elaborate rhetoric
He expects. There is a certain correctness
In the situation. One must object, however,
To the impropriety of those who propose
Different rules. One is no innovator:
Innovation is unfeminine. It is important
That ashtrays should be emptied, and always
In the same place, that meals be punctual.
One depends on one's servants to supply
Visual and temporal symmetry. Equally,
One relies on one's family to support
The proper structure of relationships. It is a pity
That one's father is so eccentric, that his friends
Are the sort of people one tries not to know,
That one's sisters are, in their different ways,
Both so unwomanly. One would never dream
Of asserting oneself in public, as they do.
One tries to cultivate the woman's touch.

3. ARMY WIFE

It's the place, I think. Everyone seems
To have gone to pieces here. Oh, not me,
My dear. I'm so used to the life. Just
Dump me down anywhere, and I'd make
A go of it – with reasonable living quarters,
Mind you, and good native servants,
Can't do without them! No, I don't count myself,
Nor Jim, of course. Jim keeps his cool
Whatever happens. We're old campaigners.
But take Mike. Such an awfully nice chap.
The new sort of officer, has a degree,
Staff College, all that sort of thing,
But absolutely no side. We think the world
Of Mike. So what does the silly ass do
But get himself mixed up with a native tart
(Very flashy girl – you've probably seen her around),
And a drunk-and-disorderly, and – oh, it's too shaming.
What the locals must be thinking! Mind you,
I blame the CO for all this. I know he's brilliant
In the field, but he *isn't* one of us, whatever
They may say. What's bred in the bone . . .
And somehow, here he's more noticeable.
There was that dreadful scene he made yesterday
About the laundry, and goodness knows
He ought to leave things like that
To his batman. Keeps a sword in his wardrobe,
They tell me. Yes, extraordinary, isn't it? A bit –
Well – *native*. And dear little Mrs CO –
Yes, isn't she a darling? Terribly good family,
But absolutely no side – she really has no idea
How to cope. I said to Jim, the trouble with you boys
Is, you need an enemy. Now the Wogs
Have packed up and gone home, you've simply

Nothing to do, so you get into trouble.
But Jim'll be all right. Jim keeps his cool
Whatever happens.

4. WAITING GENTLEWOMAN

If Daddy had known the setup,
I'm absolutely positive, he'd never
Have let me come. Honestly,
The whole thing's too gruesome
For words. There's nobody here to talk to
At all. Well, nobody under about ninety,
I mean. All the possible men have buggered
Off to the other side, and the rest,
Poor old dears, they'd have buggered off
Too, if their poor old legs would have
Carried them. HM's a super person, of course,
But she's a bit seedy just now,
Quite different from how marvellous she was
At the Coronation. And this doctor they've got in –
Well, he's only an ordinary little GP,
With a very odd accent, and even I
Can see that what HM needs is
A real psychiatrist. I mean, all this
About *blood*, and *washing*. Definitely Freudian.
As for Himself, well, definitely
Not my type. Daddy's got this thing
About selfmade men, of course, that's why
He was keen for me to come. But I think
He's gruesome. What HM sees in him
I cannot imagine. *And* he talks to himself.
That's so rude, I always think.
I hope Daddy comes for me soon.

ANGELS' SONG

Intimates of heaven,
This is strange to us,
The unangelic muddle,
The birth, the human fuss.

We sing a harder carol now;
Holy the donkey in the hay;
Holy the manger made of wood,
Holy the nails, the blood, the clay.

BC:AD

This was the moment when Before
Turned into After, and the future's
Uninvented timekeepers presented arms.

This was the moment when nothing
Happened. Only dull peace
Sprawled boringly over the earth.

This was the moment when even energetic Romans
Could find nothing better to do
Than counting heads in remote provinces.

And this was the moment
When a few farm workers and three
Members of an obscure Persian sect

Walked haphazard by starlight straight
Into the kingdom of heaven.

ROBIN'S ROUND

I am the proper
Bird for this season –
Not blessed St Turkey,
Born to be eaten.

I'm man's inedible
Permanent bird.
I dine in his garden,
My spoon is his spade.

I'm the true token
Of Christ the Child-King:
I nest in man's stable,
I eat at man's table,
Through all his dark winters
I sing.

REINDEER REPORT

Chimneys: colder.
Flightpaths: busier.
Driver: Christmas (F)
Still baffled by postcodes.

Children: more
And stay up later.
Presents: heavier.
Pay: frozen.

Mission in spite
Of all this
Accomplished:

MERRY CHRISTMAS

THE CONTRIBUTORS

Not your fault, gentlemen.
We acquit you of the calculatedly
Equivalent gift, the tinsel token.
Mary, maybe, fancied something more practical:
A layette, or at least a premium bond.
Firmly you gave the extravagantly
Useless, your present the unwrapped
Hard-edged stigma of vocation.

Not your fault, beasts,
Who donated your helpless animal
Rectitude to the occasion.
Not yours the message of the goblin
Robin, the red-nosed reindeer,
Nor had you in mind the yearly
Massacre of the poultry innocent,
Whom we judge correct for the feast.

Not your fault, Virgin,
Muddling along in the manger,
With your confused old man,
Your bastard baby, in conditions
No social worker could possibly approve.
How could your improvised, improvident
Holiness predict our unholy family Xmas,
Our lonely overdoses, deepfrozen bonhomie?

ON BUYING OS SHEET 163

I own all this. Not loutish acres
That tax the spirit, but the hawking
Eye's freehold, paper country.

Thirty-two inches of aqueduct,
Windmill (disused), club house, embankment,
Public conveniences

In rural areas. This is my
Landlocked landscape that lives in cipher,
And is truer than walking.

Red and imperial, the Romans
Stride eastward. Mysterious, yellow,
The Salt Way halts and is gone.

Here, bigger than the hamlets they are,
Wild wayside syllables stand blooming:
Filkins, Lechlade, Broughton Poggs.

Here only I discard the umber
Reticulations of sad cities,
The pull and drag of mud.

PRINCETOWN

In the town it seems just a local
Joke, like piskies or Uncle Tom Cobley,
Though in rather poor taste. Souvenir mugs
Insistent as fat-bottomed mums on seaside postcards,
And tiny priapic men: *Property*

Of HM Prison, Dartmoor.
Not to be taken away. But if you walk
The ripped-up railway, its stonework
The patient, perfect carving of cheap labour,
To the quarries, you begin to imagine
The bald, tanned pates, grotesque livery,
Automatic warders, routine hopelessness,
But far off, historic, like walking
The Roman Wall, reconstructing
A massive alert garrison from piles
Of rubbish. So here, until, nearing the town,
We saw the discreet bulk, shining in twilight,
Each window equally watted. And I remembered
The mother and daughter, arm in arm and crying,
Outside the cafe offering cream teas.

HANG-GLIDERS IN JANUARY

(*for C.K.*)

Like all miracles, it has a rational
Explanation; and like all miracles, insists
On being miraculous. We toiled
In the old car up from the lacklustre valley,
Taking the dogs because somebody had to,
At the heel of a winter Sunday afternoon

Into a sky of shapes flying:
Pot-bellied, shipless sails, dragonflies towering
Still with motion, daytime enormous bats,
Titanic tropical fish, and men,
When we looked, men strapped to wings,
Men wearing wings, men flying

Over a landscape too emphatic
To be understood: humdrum fields
With hedges and grass, the mythical river,
Beyond it the forest, the foreign high country.
The exact sun, navigating downwards
To end the revels, and you, and me,
The dogs, even, enjoying a scamper,
Avoiding scuffles.

It was all quite simple, really. We saw
The aground flyers, their casques and belts
And defenceless legs; we saw the earthed wings
Being folded like towels; we saw
The sheepskin-coated wives and mothers
Loyally watching; we saw a known,
Explored landscape by sunset-light,

We saw for ourselves how it was done,
From takeoff to landing. But nothing cancelled
The cipher of the soaring, crucified men,
Which we couldn't unravel; which gave us
Also, somehow, the freedom of air. Not
In vast caravels, triumphs of engineering,
But as men always wanted, simply,
Like a bird at home in the sky.

IN THE ENGLISH FACULTY LIBRARY, OXFORD

(*for R.K.M.*)

It is a house of stairs. Books strain
Alphabetically upwards. Critics sprang
To eminence on their pages, and these bowed
Figures muse of vaulting after,

Through duly attested up-gradings
To doctorates. Beneath the spires
The academics dream.

It is a house of light. Technology
Illumines the dark reading, the blurred word.
With perfect vision, the bright-haired
(At sea with their sex-lives, finances,
Their futures, their tutors, sentenced
To match next essay with surly text)
Pelt down the feint tracks of dead game.

It is a house of peace. Gentle-
footed librarians pace the precincts.
Owen's legacy lies quiet. Sotto voce
Students make assignations and jokes; softly
They sharpen their pencils; inaudibly biros
Utter the last judgment.

It is a charnelhouse. The untongued dead
Wince at the touch of the lucky living.

It is a charnelhouse. The quick and young
Choke on the breath of refractory clay.

Down in the cellars the dead men grumble
Resenting, resisting the patterns
We make of their bones.

HAUNTED HOUSE

At six the furniture begins to fade.
Slit trenches' mouths gleam stickily along
The Axminster. Fixed bayonets look out

From cupboards. Gas and cordite tinge the air.
Hats turn to helmets as they hang. Outside
Hillocks of quicklime wait to hold the dead.

Children don't find this house by chance. A brown
Obsequious mongrel bitch seduces them
Into the magic garden, where faint smoke
Curls round the lily leaves. The oriole,
Night heron, bustard, bee-eater, composed
And friendly, eye their visitors with grace
And never move away. Strange trees extend
Embroidered hands. The air purrs with desire.

This stair promises something. Painted heads
Smile in its angles. Glowing shoulders, lace,
Arms, ringlets, sapphires, eyes, attest some force.
Concealed among the bosoms, spiky heads
Of Samurai, speared, tiger-whiskered, peer
In search of enemies twin to themselves.

At last, the lady and her room. Tea waits;
Smart bread-and-butter; polished brandysnaps;
Hands patrol teacups; angel cake presides;
Gentleman's relish sounds a richer note.
The children eat and drink. The day grows dark.
At six the furniture begins to fade.

RURAL GUERRILLAS

The dead sticks of winter rise in their graves.
The future pokes through them, exploding
Like pointillist grapeshot.

Landroving weeds lay jagged boobytraps.
Young daffodils rear ponderous heads
The shape of torpedoes.

Along the hedgerows impatient snipers
Pepper the air with their random bright
Volleys, declaring green.

The shouts and stutters and shamefaced mumbles
Of garden birds: recruits rehearsing
The trenches' foul language.

In the air, incorrigible Cockney
Thumbs-up of chestnut buds, embarking
For the spring offensive.

Under the tarmac the depth charge daisies
Brace knees and shoulders for the moment
When they hijack the world.

GETTING IT ACROSS

(*for Caroline*)

'His disciples said unto him, Lo, now speakest thou plainly, and
speakest no proverb. Now are we sure that thou knowest all things.'
St John 16, vv. 29–30

This is the hard thing.
Not being God, the Son of Man,
– I was born for that part –
But patiently incising on these yokel faces,
Mystified, bored and mortal,
The vital mnemonics they never remember.

There is enough of Man in my God
For me to construe their frowns. I feel
The jaw-cracking yawns they try to hide
When out I come with one of my old
Chestnuts. *Christ! not that bloody*
Sower again, they are saying, or *God!*
Not the Prodigal bleeding Son.
Give us a new one, for Messiah's sake.

They know my unknowable parables as well
As each other's shaggy dog stories.
I say! I say! I say! There was this Samaritan,
This Philistine and this Roman . . . or
What did the high priest say
To the belly dancer? All they need
Is the cue for laughs. My sheep and goats,
Virgins, pigs, figtrees, loaves and lepers
Confuse them. Fishing, whether for fish or men,
Has unfitted them for analogy.

Yet these are my mouths. Through them only
Can I speak with Augustine, Aquinas, Martin, Paul,
Regius Professors of Divinity,
And you, and you.
How can I cram the sense of Heaven's kingdom
Into our pidgin-Aramaic quayside jargon?

I envy Moses, who could choose
The diuturnity of stone for waymarks
Between man and Me. He broke the tablets,
Of course. I too know the easy messages
Are the ones not worth transmitting;
But he could at least carve.
The prophets too, however luckless
Their lives and instructions, inscribed on wood,
Papyrus, walls, their jaundiced oracles.

I alone must write on flesh. Not even
The congenial face of my Baptist cousin,
My crooked affinity Judas, who understands,
Men who would give me accurately to the unborn
As if I were something simple, like bread.
But Pete, with his headband stuffed with fishhooks,
His gift for rushing in where angels wouldn't,
Tom, for whom metaphor is anathema,
And James and John, who want the room at the top –
These numskulls are my medium. I called them.

I am tattooing God on their makeshift lives.
My Keystone Cops of disciples, always
Running absurdly away, or lying ineptly,
Cutting off ears and falling into the water,
These Sancho Panzas must tread my Quixote life,
Dying ridiculous and undignified,
Flayed and stoned and crucified upside down.
They are the dear, the human, the dense, for whom
My message is. That might, had I not touched them,
Have died decent respectable upright deaths in bed.

POMONA AND VERTUMNUS

Lady of kitchen-gardens, learned
In the ways of the early thin-skinned rhubarb,
Whose fingers fondle each gooseberry bristle,
Stout currants sagging on their flimsy stalks,
And sprinting strawberries, that colonise
As quick as Rome.

Goddess of verges, whose methodical
Tenderness fosters the vagrant croppers,
Gawky raspberry refugees from gardens,

Hip, sloe, juniper, blackberry, crab,
Humble abundance of heath, hedge, copse,
The layabouts' harvest.

Patron of orchards, pedantic observer
Of rites, of prune, graft, spray and pick,
In whose honour the Bramley's branches
Bow with their burly cargo, from grass-deep
To beyond ladders; you who teach pears their proper shape,
And brush the ripe plum's tip with a touch of crystal.

I know your lovers, earth's grubby godlings:
Silvanus, whose province is muck-heaps
And electric fences; yaffle-headed Picus;
Faunus the goatman. All of them friends
Of the mud-caked cattle, courting you gruffly
With awkward, touching gifts.

But I am the irrepressible, irresponsible
Spirit of Now: no constant past,
No predictable future. All my genius
Goes into moments. I have nothing to give
But contradiction and alteration.

Me, therefore, the wise goddess picked
When I came to her, true to my bent,
In the form of an old woman.

JANUS

I am the two-headed anniversary god,
Lord of the Lupercal and the Letts diary.
I have a head for figures.

My clocks are the moon and sun,
My almanac the zodiac. The ticktock seasons,
The hushabye seas are under my thumb.

From All Saints to All Souls I celebrate
The da capo year. My emblems are albums,
The bride's mother's orchid corsage, the dark cortège.

Master of the silent passacaglia
Of the future, I observe the dancers,
But never teach them the step.

I am the birthday prescience
Who knows the obituary, the tombstone's arithmetic.
Not telling is my present.

I monitor love through its mutations
From paper to ruby. I am archivist
Of the last divorce and the first kiss.

I am director of the forgotten fiesta.
I know why men at Bacup black their faces;
Who horned at Abbots Bromley tread the mazes.

I am the future's overseer, the past's master.
See all, know all, speak not.
I am the two-faced god.

GENESIS

(*for J. R. R. Tolkien*)

In the beginning were the words,
Aristocratic, cryptic, chromatic.
Vowels as direct as mid-day,
Consonants lanky as long-swords.

Mouths materialised to speak the words:
Leafshaped lips for the high language,
Tranquil tongues for the tree-creatures,
Slits and slobbers for the lower orders.

Deeds came next, words' children.
Legs by walking evolved a landscape.
Continents and chronologies occurred,
Complex and casual as an implication.

Arched over all, alarming nimbus,
Magic's disorderly thunder and lightning.

The sage sat in his suburban fastness,
Garrisoned against progress. He grieved
At what the Duke's men did to our words
(Whose war memorial is every signpost).

The sage sat. And middle-earth
Rose around him like a rumour.
Grave grammarians, Grimm and Verner,
Gave it laws, granted it charters.

The sage sat. But the ghosts walked
Of the Birmingham schoolboy, the Somme soldier,
Whose bones lay under the hobbit burrows,
Who endured darkness, and friends dying,

Whom words waylaid in a Snow Hill siding,
Coal truck pit names, grimy, gracious,
Blaen-Rhondda, Nantyglo, Senghenydd.
In these deeps middle-earth was mined.

These were the words in the beginning.

CHORUS

We are here to bear witness.
We would much rather be somewhere else.
We are not necessary.

We stand on suburban carpets, we sit
On three-piece suites of uncut moquette,
Under the detached retina of television.
Summoned to bear witness, we attend.
We do not understand our part.

Inexorably on our thin inexperienced
Shoulders the stiff vestments descend.
Head and hand assume the dragging
Gestures of hierophants. Our bodies assent
To the ceremony. We have become The Chorus.

But this is absurd! We're not in a play.
In our world, this is the hour
For winding clocks, walking dogs, cleaning teeth.
We have embarrassing little needs. I should like
To go to the lavatory; to look at my watch; to yawn.

The protagonist has the gift of tongues,
The hurt heart will spurt words all night.
We know the future, but we must not say so.
Our part is to bear witness. This is not our play.
We are not expected to interfere.

We are not necessary, but we are needed.
We sit, stand, speak, are silent,
Responding to archaic, unexpected promptings
We are too polite to defy. In the satyr play
Tomorrow, how we shall burlesque all this!

FATHER IN THE RAILWAY BUFFET

What are you doing here, ghost, among these urns,
These film-wrapped sandwiches and help-yourself biscuits,
Upright and grand, with your stick, hat and gloves,
Your breath of eau-de-cologne?

What have you to say to these head-scarfed tea-ladies,
For whom your expensive vowels are exotic as Japan?
Stay, ghost, in your proper haunts, the clubland smokerooms,
Where you know the waiters by name.

You have no place among these damp and nameless.
Why do you walk here? *I came to say goodbye.*
You were ashamed of me for being different.
It didn't matter.

You who never even learned to queue?

BIRTHDAY POEM

'Here come two noble beasts in, a man and a lion.'

Conscientious; a quiet man,
Not helped by the naïve histrionics
Of Bottom, the adolescent tantrums
Of fluffy-chinned Flute.

A diffident reader; anxious
About his limitations; keen
To embark on the difficult labour
Of learning the cues for roaring.

Honest as sunlight
He stands before the giggling
Intelligentsia, disclaiming illusion.
They must not suppose he is
What he is not. He is just
A man as other men are.

His careful confession made,
Unlike poor knock-kneed Moonshine,
Capitulating to high-bred heckling,
He does his job properly,
Like the master-craftsman he is.

The lion performs his pantomime part:
He roars; he tears Thisbe's cloak.
Well roared, Lion! He thinks
His sedulous hours of rehearsing
Munificently tipped, being himself
Too candid to know irony.

This for you, Leo, whose lion likewise
Is *a very gentle beast*
And of a good conscience.

You share his carpenter's
Steadfast standards, intelligent fingers,
Joy in making. Even his name,
With all its subharmonics, defines
Precisely you: lion among ladies,
The joiner, Snug.

THE COLOURBLIND BIRDWATCHER

In sallow summer
The loud-mouthed birds
Peer through my hedges
As brown as swallows.

In acrid autumn
High-flying birds
Splay in formation
As brown as magpies.

In the wan winter
Audacious birds
Besiege my windows
As brown as robins.

In sepia spring
The punctual birds
Resume their habits
As brown as blossom.

95

Three storeys up, she lives under the eaves
In the sky's suburbs. From above
She knows the tabby shoulders of pigeons,
The painted hair of men.

Downstairs is another country, its frontier
A childgate. On slippered, uncertain feet,
Armed with a Zimmer, she mans
The landing, her treacherous border.

Goliath voices intone in her
Diminishing kingdom, declaiming the weather's
Intentions, the future's enormous transactions.
Her armchair's horizon is global.

In it she waits for her tiny Doomsday.
Her drawers are tidied for good, and then
Untidied again. Life keeps on being picked up,
Like a tedious piece of knitting.

So she idles out her epilogue
In her eyrie, looking down upon living
As a small, difficult theorem
She could solve once. And in her windows

Her small, difficult plants turning sunwards
Obstinately, perpetually flower.

CHILD IN MARBLE

Here lie I, 'little Julia',
Interred between inverted commas
Like a dead canary.

I alone know who I was, what
I would have done. For my parents
My lack of finish completes me.

I am their emblem of precocious
Mortality. They remember my passing,
My meningeal convulsions, my spasmodic screaming,

The trained nurse, the little frilly frocks
Quickly given away after, the unpredictable
Silences and weeping.

Under my green grave chippings
I repudiate my axiomatic pathos.
I am not just a dead baby,

Undistinguishable in albums from
My ringletted, be-smocked siblings,
Eponyms of childhood, so similar

That no one now knows who was which.
Under the secretive façade of childhood
I grasped the blueprint of my own definition.

They have sterilised me in the fires
Of my dying, and concluded me.
But I was the future I missed,

My revised version of childhood,
My histrionic adolescence, my flowering
Into brains and graces, my marriages,

My children, ungrown because of my going,
My implicit, uncompromised self, my dark corners.
I claim to have been me, not

What they remember, their child,
Formal and meaningless as a marble cherub,
Signalling mourning by an empty urn.

PORTRAITS OF TUDOR STATESMEN

Surviving is keeping your eyes open,
Controlling the twitchy apparatus
Of iris, white, cornea, lash and lid.

So the literal painter set it down –
The sharp raptorial look; strained eyeball;
And mail, ruff, bands, beard, anything, to hide
The violently vulnerable neck.

THE CONSTANT TIN SOLDIER

1. Breaking Day

Dying is easier.
Just a flick of somebody's finger,
Then the icy exactness of rigor mortis,
While posthumous flies and decorations settle,
A subaltern writes thirty-two letters
By torchlight to next of kin,
And the Germans advance in your boots,
Which are better than theirs.

It isn't always lucky to stay alive.
Some never recover from surviving.
The showy heraldry of scars excuses,
But not the chronic tic of terror,
Picked up on a foggy March morning
Between the Staffords and the Suffolks,
Between Bullecourt and Croisilles.
You will carry this day like a tumour
In your head for life, fusilier,
And no one will ever needle it out.

You remember the date:

21st March, 1918. Day
Of the Kaiserschlacht, day
Of the German Spring Offensive.
We, the beaten, have no name for that day
In our own language.

You remember your place:

Third Army, 34th Division,
102nd brigade. HQ Gomiecourt
(Which I never saw) under
Lt Col Charlton (whom I never
Saw again after. Only now, sixty years on,
A youngster tells me he was taken prisoner.
I thought him killed).
23rd Northumberland Fusiliers.

You remember the weather:

Sun on the 20th, following rain
And squally winds. Enemy weathermen
Prophesied continuing calm. It would be safe,
They said, to use gas against us. Then
An intense, still morning; no wind;
But ground mist ghosting
To dense, inimical fog.

You remember the timing:

0440 hours: artillery bombardment begins.
Five hours of General Surprise Fire.
The German brass, guns, mortars and howitzers,
Jarring in unison. It rained noise,
Mud, bone, hot lumps of jagged metal,

Gas, smoke, fear, darkness, dissolution
By the clock, if any clock ticked on.
0940 hours: infantry attack begins,
Across the broken earth, the broken men.
An orderly advance; they sauntered
Over the unstrung landscape.

You remember your state:

Fear, fog, solitude,
Between Bullecourt and Croisilles,
Between the Staffords and the Suffolks.
We had to man the Forward Zone,
But creeping with the creeping fog
Came in the enemy. We knew them
By the shape of their helmets. They were
Where we were. Nothing was where
It had been on the map, and no one
Was one of us. The counties melted,
And their quiet local voices. My friend
Died, I was on my own.

You remember your mood:

Orphaned. The formal beauty
Of rank, its cordial courteous bearing,
Had foundered. No one to give
Or receive orders. Our training
Was scrappy; we had never studied
The delicate art of retreat, and our trumpets
Had mud in their throats.

You remember your choice:

Flight. Through craters, corpses,
Stumps of horses, guns and trees,
Through fog and my everyman darkness.
What are the rules for the solitary
Soldier? Should he stand firm
To the last pointless volley,
Or lay down his arms at the feet
Of kind enemies, and be whisked
By their finished techniques
To a snug internment? No one
Had drilled enterprise into us.
Choice had been frightened to death.
I could do only what I did,
What the primitive man I muzzle
Inside me made me do: I ran.

You remember the sequel:

Rehabilitation. The comfort of being
Among confederates, men
Who had hobbled their way back, stubbornly,
Without heroism. Most of us still
Had our uses. Mine was liaison
With American troops. Gigantic,
Buoyant, ignorant, they trod
Our shellshocked fief, as once their ancestors
Trampled across the New World.
I guided them along the labyrinths,
Interpreted, explained, a ghost of war,
Leading the living down the dead men's trenches.

You remember your self:

I had archaic longings,
Yearned for the dead and the lost,
The officers, the other ranks, the men

I belonged with, who knew the same songs,
Shouted on United. Not even
Graves for most, just Memorials
To the Missing. I missed them,
All the canny Geordie lads
With their feet still through the night
And the days.

2. *Spoils of Peace*

Some of the dead were signallers:
Rupert the Fair and Wilfred the Wise,
Isaac the exile and innocent Ivor,
And Edward, who endured.

In various ways, these died,
And so, afterwards, in some ways,
Some of the living perhaps listened.

The dead can afford to be generous,
Having no superannuation rights.
These men squandered the spoils of war,
But I latched on to my red-edged learning,

Investing sensibly in job, house, car,
Wife and children, dog and skivvy.
Redoubts and outworks, manned by me,
To balk the enemy at my back.

I couldn't afford to be taken
The same way twice; kept short accounts,
Checked the wiring, planted sharp roses,
Trained the dog to the qui vive.

But upkeep has to be paid for. I traded
My craftsman's hands for a salesman's pay.
Built my house on my tongue. Charm
Was the mortar, the brickwork cheek.

In a world fit for heroes, heroism
Is de trop. You have to fight
With guile for your rights, against
The agenda-adept, the minutes-men.

I mastered the means that made men mine,
Not shadows, to fade in the gassed thicket,
But beefy reliable cheque-signing fingers,
Dewlaps to dance at my bagman's patter.

I held the line, from Wallsend to Workington,
Where the Romans were, I came.
Chatted up waitresses, chaffed the barmen,
Sold my soul to keep myself safe.

(Not between Croisilles and Bullecourt.)

Good morning!
              Good gracious!
                           Nice day.
                                   Delightful.
Any tonics, tinctures or pick-me-ups?
No.
Thank you. I'll call again.
                           Good morning.
                                   Nice day.

Where the wind whips over the fraying border,
Where homesick legions were whittled away,
On the frontier of failure I jobbed and prospered,
Natty, dapper, with my quickfire smile.

Not the dovetailed sockets, the tonguing and grooving,
The crisscross network I could have carved,
But a web of hardheaded sceptical buyers,
Whom I forced at jokepoint to be my friends.

Good morning!
          Good morning.
                    Nice day.
                            Yes.
Any false rumours, horrors or hangovers?
No thank you.
I'll call again.
          Do.
                    Good morning.
                            Good morning.
Shocking day.

Back at HQ the walls stood firm.
I saw to that. But the garrison
Could never be trusted. Maids
Came and went, children were born

And died. The dog too. I procured
Replacements, held weekly inspections,
Reviewed morale, kept up my payments,
Insured house, contents and livestock, checked

The defences. There was nothing amiss.
But somehow I had enlisted
A saboteur, not a friend (my friend
Died). She gave me nothing

To complain of; collaborated in all
Transactions, performed creditably
At trade functions, answered the telephone
Adequately. But I didn't like

The sort of book she read. Disaffection
Was plain in her children. The boy
A myopic coward, whose only solution
Was running away. Then the girl

Who died. I forget her name now,
But she cost me a mint of money
At the time, one way and the other.
As for the substitute, I recognized

A usurper in her. She'd have ousted
Me, taken my place if she could,
Mutinous, sulky, and damnably
Heir to my look and my hands.

I had carved out a kingdom
For my son to inherit. But he
Renegued, would have none of it,
Fancied his own improvident way,

Instead of cultivating my contacts.
Married a fatherless, unsuitable
Outspoken girl from down south somewhere,
Ran to the opposite end of the earth

And stayed there. Good riddance.
One less mouth to feed, one less craven
In the camp. The girl deserted too,
After a prolonged, costly education

Without a dividend. No hope there
Of a son-in-law, someone I could
Have trusted, canny chap, living close,
To keep an eye on the wiring, the blood-pressure,

Someone I could have taken to, without
That yellow streak in him. But I managed
Without. Anticipated the next assault
(Infirmity, loneliness, death) and took

Precautionary measures: transferred HQ
To a high-rise residence for the well-heeled,
Heated centrally, caretakered, with lift,
Where care would be taken.

Here we live now, annuitied. I ignore
The persistent trickle of offstage
Deaths, as my feebler contemporaries
Fall out. Life has taught me
To concentrate on living. This I do.

My primitive man is dead, crushed
By cordial years of cronies. I couldn't
Speak straight now if I tried.
I am the kerbside cheapjack's patter:

Ladies, watch what I do.
The genuine article. 20 pound in the catalogue,
18 in the shops, 15 in the sales. But from me –
Stand close, ladies – *a fiver!*
Ladies, watch what I do.

Watch, ladies, what I do.
Holidays abroad yearly, until age
Made us uninsurable. Now a five-star
Scottish hydro, where I am known

To the management. I am still standing to,
Between the Staffords and the Suffolks,
As I have been for most of my life.
I may be only a tin soldier,
But I have been constant.

STANDING TO

This is turning into a long war.
I must have been mobilised
In the womb. I know nothing
Of a pre-war world. I ponder
The finicky distinctions of peace.

Service is secretive,
Camouflage always
Congenial. Medals
Have not been worn for years.

Martial paraphernalia –
Barrage balloons, fly-by-night signposts,
Rationing, passwords, internment,
The planes marked *Us* and *Them* –

Are the apparatus
Of children's games.

The enemy is not
The one who declares war,
Who is as mortal as you.

The true enemy declares
Nothing, cannot be disposed of,
Is never indisposed.

I was set here
To watch. So I do,
And report, in cipher, to headquarters,
Which is an hypothesis.

Are there others recruited
Like me, encoding what they see,
Abandoned by Higher Command,
Unable to desert?

Is the war perhaps over,
Mine an irrelevant garrison?

I doubt my calling, but still hear
The thin paper voices
From south-coast resorts
Reporting flak, then falling
Suddenly silent.

VOICES OFF
1984

TOMORROW AND

(for J.R. who reads Cowper while dying of cancer)

Was and *will be* are both uneasy ground;
Now is the safest tense.

Terminal Care rests among recipes
On the kitchen table.

We choke the future back down our throats like
Incipient vomit,

With so much time ahead, for all we know,
For turning out cupboards,

Pottery courses, Greek holidays, Brahms,
Grandchildren, greenhouses,

Getting at last to the end of *Decline*
And Fall of the Roman

It's all indifferent to him. He won't
Be here. Our small concerns

Balk us with their familiarity.
His perspectives are strict.

Library fines and income tax returns
Have lost their sting. The huge

Ghouls that shadow old age have excused him.
His exacting lover

Arrogates all of him. He'll never grow
Senile, tiresome, lonely.

With stoic courtesy, unfortified
By rites of holy church,

He watches each tomorrow, appraises
Contour, climate, colour,

As if it were a new world, while his books
(Which he won't read again,

He says) rest idle on their shelves, and nights
Grow longer, and contain

More symptoms, and his friends come, go, come, go,
Swallowing hereafters,

And he transacts the same
Miniature feats of gallantry with which
Cowper restrained the dark

Once, as far as we know

ROBERT LINDSAY'S HAMLET

(*for Braham Murray*)

That's him, in the foetal position, among
The front row watchers,

Sweatshirt and jeans, nothing particular, you
Wouldn't look twice, till

He stands to pace that eccentric circuit, from
Clouds still hang on you

To *Cracks a noble heart*, with the special props
That signal the Prince:

Two swords, recorders, skulls, a cup and a book.
The junk has banked up

Along the years. He can't move a foot without
Dislodging clinker –

First Folio, the good Quarto, bright guesses
From dead editors,

A notion of Goethe's, a sad hometruth of
Seedy STC's,

Business inherited from great-grandfathers
Garrick, Kean, Irving –

Heir to all this, as his watchers are heirs
Of dead playgoers,

Coming to see what they already know, with
Astonish me! smiles.

Who could mine anything new from this heap of
Old British rubbish?

But this man, discarding limelight and ketchup,
Customary suits,

Delivered raw at each performance, elbows
Us along the trite

Life of the man who thought faster than any-
one ever, till we,

Losing our poise, are lost, like the ignorant
Playgoer, watching

The story, whispering at the wrong moment
Does he kill him now?

ARMIN'S WILL

Who's the fool?
Not him. He came late to folly,
Mastering it slowly, as a man
Climbs a ladder. I was born motley,
Cried quips to my cradle. He conned
The diehard jester's hornbook,
Huffed with Herod in the country dust,
Clowned with Kemp, whose wittiest
Joke was the rictus of jigged
Legs in his Norwich morris.
I dug that folly's grave. Alas,
Poor Yorick.

Who's the fool now?
He, she, they. We are all fools,
Save the master-fool, bright
In folly's livery. I taught him
My catechism, confirmed him
In foolosophy. He converted the globe.
Gone the simple servants, pissing dogs,
The wild men, the disintegrators.
Hic jacent. Here comes the new man,
Feste, Lear's fool, the touchstone,
With his scornful step, his sweet breast
And acid tongue. Here comes folly's falcon.
A fellow of infinite jest,
Horatio.

With a hey ho
I ruled my kingdom. A king
Was my fool. And fond, drunk, mad,
Silly, conceited, lear-witted, the clowns
My subjects acclaimed me. I stood apart,

Uttering judgments double-mouthed,
Their oracle and butt. He designed
My world for me, I lived
His image. But he'll not be true.
I see other worlds in his magic eye,
Deserts and islands show dim
In the blue of his iris. Rough colonies,
Fit only for Kemp's children.
Take away the fool, gentlemen.
Quite chap-fallen.

So I who ruled
The invisible kingdom
Devise and bequeath
My coxcomb to no man,
Having no heirs, only
Chance inheritors,
Who with a breath, an air,
Make my ghost walk –
Thief, savage, spirit,
A faded stripe of
Feste's omniscient motley.
But that's all one.

ARMIN, Robert (d. 1615). One of the 'Principall Actors' in
Shakespeare's plays . . . His fooling was more subtle than
Kempe's, and Shakespeare probably wrote the parts of
Touchstone, Feste and the Fool in *Lear* for him.
(F. E. Halliday: *A Shakespeare Companion*)

INSTEAD OF THE LAST POST

(*in memoriam Arthur Lowe*)

Great clowns are displaced tragedians,
We know
They laugh with tears in their eyes, but
On with the show
Until the last exit, on the way out
Down under,
Where jokes bounce raggedly, like boomerangs,
And stars surrender.

He was born middle-aged, bloodhound-eyed,
Balding, with a paunch, and never improved.

He was no one's idea of Hamlet,
Or Falstaff, either. He was High Street Man,

Ruling tiny pockets of empire
Grimly; the original *Disgusted*.

He shored up suburbia's dated
Embargos, the dismal symbiosis

Of flagging marriage, epitomised
The not-quite-gentlemen who thought they were,

His grammar-school h's faintly un-
reliable. He was never funny.

Had he told a joke he would have botched
The punch-line. He impeded laughter.

But somewhere on no man's land a smile
Detonates, like a masked battery.

VISITING MR LEWIS IN JANUARY

He bangs with a stick on the wall
To call his wife. She knows
He should have died last week

He leaves his teeth out now. Skin drags
Down to his mouth. His eyes swell
With life in the mortal face. He enjoys visitors.

His wife knows he should have died
He looks forward to spring. The garden
Is missing him. In spring he'll be out there,

Digging. It's getting lighter now
In the evenings. He notes the days,
The signs of spring. Someone

Has brought him purple crocuses,
Swollen, unhealthy. One has fallen over.
Two nurses call each day. He likes

Being teased about women. His wife
Knows he should   But really,
He ought to keep his teeth in. Can we

Make out what he says? I can't;
Easier to understand his paper headline:
SHOOTOUT ANGER HITS WHITEHALL

He told you what he'd do in April. I
Found her dull patience easier. The room
Smells unwell. The crocuses

Have an appointment with the doctor.
His wife knows   His teeth
Grin at us underwater.

TONY/FABIAN, O.S.B.

'The first degree of humility is obedience without delay.'
(*Sancti Benedicti Regula Monachorum*)

Requiems are for filmstars, kings,
Motorists, Irish, the old – the risk-takers.
You have caught us off guard, Tony,
Memories not yet primed for you to die.

The fathers will name another Fabian,
Frugally, like Victorian parents,
Tacking the dead child's name on
To the next baby. They are always ready.

We never imagined you an enigma,
Just a grace-note in our lives, who went and came,
Unpredictable and delightful as weather,
Whose laws we never trouble to learn.

Up before larklight with your breviary,
The washing machine running amok
Among the Hail Marys. Baffled
By violent domestic engines

Of Western culture, and
(*The Abbot said Go*)
By street curs, equivocal Spanish,
Faithless novices, suggestive motifs on Peruvian pots,

Treasuring your defeats for our enjoyment,
You with whom the overtures of friendship
Were needless, who received our female
Protestant otherness with love, no wonder

We never got round to keeping your letters.
And yet we should have known
You were not just Tony, were also Fabian,
Ordained, ordered, obedient,

Braced to endure exile from your calling
Of teaching gentle boys English, turning
Exile into vocation, your innocence
Surprised, but flowering in the slums of Lima.

And now Tony, secretly (internal bleeding),
Now Fabian, swiftly, with holy alacrity,
(*God said Come*) you have gone,
Unexpected, conclusive as a spent light bulb.

We failed to grasp your calling; you did not.

'These, therefore, immediately abandoning their own affairs and
forsaking their own will, dropping the work they were engaged on
and leaving it unfinished, with swift obedience follow up with their
deeds the voice of him who commands them.'
(*Sancti Benedicti Regula Monachorum*)

GRANDFATHER'S FOOTSTEPS

This garden's for the birds.
Offers rich turf where, heads akimbo,
Blackbird and thrush may angle after
The underground naked. Here are little
Castles for robin to be cock of,
Constant water, nest-box lodging,
Fat, grain, nuts, definitive diet
For all suburbia's birds.

These birds are for the man.
All day he watches and they work.
Architect, athlete, busker, butcher,
Musician, mimic, mobster, thief.
Birds fight to live; their clockwork fidgets
Amuse the impresario who made the set,
The watching man.

One blackbird is his pet.
A trail of crumbs will bring it to his feet,
And punctually each afternoon it comes,
Collects the farthest scrap, with untamed eye
Fixing him sideways, moving closer to,
Through second thoughts and doubts, till it's drawn in
Up to the last, best morsel, by his shoe,
Snatches, and whirring, scrams.

The game is not the man's
Alone. Something is watching him,
Silent and patient, coaxing him along
With little crying fits and wheezy spells,
A swimming head and spots before the eyes.
This tempered bait will fetch him by degrees,
As he the bird. His impresario
Will play the game.

PATIENTS

Not the official ones, who have been
Diagnosed and made tidy. They are
The better sort of patient.

They know the answers to the difficult
Questions on the admission sheet
About religion, next of kin, sex.

They know the rules. The printed ones
In the *Guide for Patients*, about why we prefer
No smoking, the correct postal address;

Also the real ones, like the precise quota
Of servility each doctor expects,
When to have fits, and where to die.

These are not true patients. They know
Their way around, they present the right
Symptoms. But what can be done for us,

The undiagnosed? What drugs
Will help our Matron, whose cats are
Her old black husband and her young black son?

Who will prescribe for our nurses, fatally
Addicted to idleness and tea? What therapy
Will relieve our Psychiatrist of his lust

For young slim girls, who prudently
Pretend to his excitement, though age
Has freckled his hands and his breath smells old?

How to comfort our Director through his
Terminal distress, as he babbles of
Football and virility, trembling in sunlight?

There is no cure for us. O, if only
We could cherish our bizarre behaviour
With accurate clinical pity. But there are no

Notes to chart our journey, no one
Has even stamped CONFIDENTIAL or *Not to be*
Taken out of the hospital on our lives.

MAN TO MAN

Your divers' bubbling summons has roused
Us at our mooring, where we lay
Waiting for Gabriel.

We are the men who foundered, who plunged
Smartly to our stations, under
The eyes of the bright king

In July weather, in a flat calm,
In home waters, among the fleet,
Without giving reasons.

The long wait spliced us. Artificers,
Officers, gunmen and bowmen,
Old salts, surgeons, sea-cooks,

Captain, Vice-Admiral, all of us
Lay together in our common
Catafalque like lovers.

Tides passed. The mild fish consumed our flesh,
Bones dropped neat and nice as rope coils,
Jaws fell, grinning welcome

To the certain resurrection, when
The lovely rigging of the bone
Leaps to the last whistle

Of Bo'sun Christ. But the next coming
Was yours, who harrowed our petty
Harvest of every day –

Boots, bricks, barrels, baskets, rigging-blocks,
Dice, daggers, dead-eyes, pipe-and-drum,
A bell, books, candlesticks,

Hairs of the ship's dog, bones of the rat
He might have caught, bones of the men
Embalmed in Solent mud.

What will you do with us, you to whom
The sea yields its secrets, who plumbed
Our permanent instant?

Museums will house our chattels. Even
Degraded wood has its uses.
Only our nameless bones

Remain dully unadaptable,
Impossible to show or sell,
Being the same as yours.

TYNESIDE IN DECEMBER

(for Bill Bailey)

Here wind and darkness rule;
Have rubbed out the intention
Of landscape, the intrusion of trees.

The race has adjusted, has grown
Four-square, double-glazed houses
For four-square practical people,
And small square gardens for long-
rooted indestructible rose-trees.

Here households practise existence by vivid
Electric embers, hymning home-baked
Hospitality and putting on weight.
Here law-fearing straight streets
Glow orange and violet by night
For ten o'clock's dauntless dog-walkers.

And the lighthouse is saying something
Comprehensible only to men at sea.

By a shivering tallow dip, here
In the old, unimaginable darkness and wind,
Bede soberly sifted miraculous evidence,
Divined the shape of the unmapped
Country's history, keeping the candle
From going out. And out
There, in the darkness, the wind and the rain,
Cuthbert practised the habit of being holy.

NORTHMEN

1.

Footloose seafarers, they pitched their lives
To the tune of the come-and-go sea,

With the breaker's thump sprang at new lands
To seize, singe, spoil, spill. With the long hiss

Of the waves' recession they withdrew,
Left coasts stamped with their passing's pattern,

Like sand marked with water-written runes
At low tide. Came back, at fuller flood,

To the same places, but more of them,
And scudding further inland, till the shires

Were awash with men tall as birch trees
And their snake-headed, monster-sailed ships,

Men who could not keep still, but scurried
Down Europe's scarred edge, steering by starlight,

The track of birds, old men's yarns of winds
And havens. Men on the move, to Man,

Ireland, Iceland, Sicily, Orkney,
Byzantium, Vladivostok, and

Lucky Leif Eiricksson's Vinland. Men
Uncompassed, men ready to travel

Wherever the sea would take them. At
Their coming the world fled, like holy

Cuddie's timid monks, sent scuttling
From safe place to safer, with the sea

Squalling behind, till they found dry land
For tired bones at Durham, and dug in.

2.
These are the things that chose to last: from
A hoard; a male grave; from a guard-house
Of the ring-fort; a boat-burial.

The records are riddles, chiselled in
Angular runes, hard letters for stone
Or bone, nothing so lax as parchment.

The messages are curt: *Ranvaig owns*
This casket. We went to meet the men
Of Frisia, and we it was who

Split the spoils of war. These died southward
In the Saracens' land. Ginne had
The stone laid, and Toke. . . . No more.

Their relics are savage, momentous:
A sword, ritually disfigured,
Then buried, like a man, at Gotland;

Eagle's wing bone drilled into a flute;
Antler, amber, tusk, oak, maple, jet,
Carnelian, all scored with water's

Perpetual scribblings. A smith lies
Buried at Bygland with his trophies
(Sword, spear, arrow, shield-boss, knife and axe,

Bridle, spur, stirrup). His tackle rests
Beside him, like a wife in his bed.
With these tools he made these grim children.

The sea chanted inside the gaunt swords,
Two-edged slashers of embedded waves
(Strips, heat-melted, forged to a polished

Patterned fierceness). And sea-fretted gold
On necks, arms, fingers, breasts of women,
Enlaced the living, attended the dead.

They fared like men far after gold, but
In the east they were food for eagles.
Like men therefore they died. Things have more choice.

3.
Adaptable as water, they swapped
Languages, garments, gods. Wherever
They settled, they conformed affably
To the prevailing rules. Their senses

Smoked by the sea's strict tempo, their wits
Edged by their bards' conundrums, were quick
To learn rhythms of lands and seasons,
Translating sea-lore to small-holdings.

So they vanished into the people
They became, leaving their Viking selves
Underground, buried with wild treasures
For ploughmen to stumble on after.

The terrible tide that soused Europe
Was soaked up by patient fields long since.
Only a few Norse names are standing
Still, like thistles, among the furrows.

AIR FOR AN HEIR

'Suddenly, you find that your child is not a malleable object, or an
offprint of yourself, but is the culmination of goodness knows how
many thousands of years and the genetic make-up of your ancestors.'
(H.R.H. Prince Charles, *Guardian*, 17.6.83)

This miniature vessel
    Contains the choice blood
Of William the Bastard
    And Albert the Good.

Charles in the oaktree
    And Charles in the dock
Contribute their mite
    To this chip off their block.

Hanoverian Georges,
    Though all of them odd,
Preserved the succession
    Ap Adam ap God.

These eyebrows, that temper . . .
    Oh, everyone knows
Through what wild centuries
    Roves back this nose.

Loaded with lineage
    From Odin to Guelph,
Good luck, midget Highness,
    Look out for yourself!

CIRCUS TRICKS

Clearly Eden. Figleaves are out,
But they wear their meticulous muscles
As casually as clothes. They can fly,
And do, briefly, to a thrumming rumble,
Silence, a major chord on brass.

They rule matter. Plates and skittles
Duck humbly to their palms, and bunting
Interminably issues from their elbows;
They gyrate on an ear, an unambitious bone.

Obliging creatures, rash with love,
Unselve themselves, and do the splits to please.
A seal flops after Eve; Adam lays
His head in the tiger's tolerant nutcracker chops;
Emeritus apes play silly monkey-tricks;
Elephants amble hand-in-hand; barbs bow
Their lovelocked heads; dogs bear the foolish ruff.

The whip is ornament. It merely points.
Nobody here gets hurt, except the child,
Artless in Eden, who assumes
All this is natural, the worried dullness
Of household pets, the sagging clothbound bodies
Of Mum and Dad just a mistake.

SECOND TIME ROUND

Is it the past or the future they endorse?

The past, where both chose someone
Other, since discreetly departed,
Leaving mementos like testy elderly terriers,
A stray grandchild or so,
And a nice little nest-egg, snugly invested?

Or the future, delicately indented
By his false-toothy smile and hearing aid,
Her look of mutton, expensively dressed
To look like mutton? How many years
Before the discreet departed get them down?

We know why wedding guests attend:
They come for the jamboree, to keep in touch,
From curiosity, perhaps, or perhaps
Because Mum brought them.

But the happy couple, so garlanded,
So old, with their safe deposits
And shaky health, their taut smiles aimed
Down the short barren aisle of the future –
Do they redress some colossal
Incarnate error, the second time round?

No. These lovers are victims
Of Hymen's awful idol,
That poses so sullenly, legged,
Tiered and anointed with ice,
By the bride and the groom and the knife
On the album's last page.

WOMEN LAUGHING

Gurgles, genderless,
Inside the incurious womb.

Random soliloquies of babies
Tickled by everything.

Undomesticated shrieks
Of small girls. Mother prophesies
You'll be crying in a minute.

Adolescents wearing giggles
Like chain-mail, against embarrassment,
Giggles formal in shape as
Butterpats, or dropped stitches.

Young women anxious to please,
Laughing eagerly before the punchline
(Being too naive to know which it is).

Wives gleaming sleekly in public at
Husbandly jokes, masking
All trace of old acquaintance.

Mums obliging with rhetorical
Guffaws at the children's riddles
That bored their parents.

Old women, unmanned, free
Of children, embarrassment, desire to please,
Hooting grossly, without explanation.

CLUNY: FIVE SENSES, TWO BEASTS AND A LADY

(*for Lindis Masterman*)

Unicorn eyes his head
In the lady's mirror. His tail has turned
Perpendicular with excitement as her hand lies
Human on his withers. Two cloven feet
Rest on her lap. This is for Lindis,
Who led me among the astute French faces,
Highbrow graffiti, imperial strut of trees,
Corks in the well-rinsed gutters, painted
Pools of Giverny. Lion looks out
Of his century at us. You can see his tongue.
He is trying not to snigger. *La Voie.*

With eight fingers and two thumbs the lady
Handles her portable organ. Her maid
Works the bellows gingerly,
Without conviction. Unicorn, who
Adores music, is capering mediaevally.
Language of elegant intercourse: *pardon, madame;*
Madame, je vous en prie. Merci, Lindis,
For the old man in the train admiring your accent,
Who gave us flowers, the girl dancing to
Tea for Two at night in a street café.
L'Ouïe. Lion's expression is equivocal.

Monkey has a sugarplum, so has Parrot.
Lapdog is willing the lady
To remember him too. Unicorn,
Having counted the calories,
Turns his head away. You can see
His double chin. Ah Lindis, the bread
And the ices and fruit, the impromptu
Memorable meals! The taste of lettuce!

Lion is frankly greedy. His toothy jaws
Are wide open. He might even
Be roaring. *Le Goût.*

Monkey, in a jacquerie haircut,
Snuffs a carnation. The lady
Creates something clever with flowers
And florist's wire. Her maid looks critical
(She has done the advanced course).
Inhaling the aromatic shopgirls
With Lindis, the aseptic Métro,
Probing noses bedded in Monet's chubby peonies.
Unicorn beams. He enjoys this
Petit Trianon lifestyle. *L'Odorat.*
Lion is trying to look naïve.

Unicorn is having his horn stroked
By the lady. He is thrilled to bits;
His ears are askew with
Respectful passion. Lindis explains
The art of making salad. Insular hands
Explore the sober shapely planes
Of everyday ware. Glancing encounters
With foreign skin, with paving stones that cry *Mort*
Héroïquement pour la France. Lion's face bulges
With suppressed giggles. He is trying
To catch our eye. *Le Toucher.*

The lady discards her jewels;
This signifies free will. Her maid
Is looking poised. Lion and Unicorn
Have reverted to heraldry, null
As supporters on a By Appointment shopfront.
The teacher rubs in the moral: *Vous pouvez devenir*
Esclaves de vos passions de bonbons.

Her manycoloured infants digest the formula.
They are learning the art of
Being French. *A mon seul désir*
Says the tent, unexpectedly.

Lindis has led me through the tapestry
Into France, among flowering
Sonorous abstractions, martial trees;
Into a promised home county, where Rabbit,
Fox, Lamb, Wolf, Goat, Panther and Duck
Amble among the mille-fleur marginalia,
While Danton and St Louis, masquerading
As Tenniel's familiars, frisk
For Marie-Antoinette, who is also Alice,
And they all speak a language
Which I cannot pronounce, but I know.

LONDON Z TO A

Her buildings come and go like leaves.
Ziggurats bud. New highways soar
Like suckers, ambitious into air.

Behind the boarded windows
Pruning happens.

In the marble city only the barbarous
Street names last.

And driving south
Down remembered gone roads the cheesy
Cockney faces blossom in witty
Brittle façades: *Stark Naked
Ltd.; A Touch of Glass; Den*

Of Antiquity; Just Looking; Just 4 U;
Hat Trick. The strictly dapper parks
Offer no comment. But the corner pubs
Honour forgotten generals, dispossessed peers,
A stag, a tree; and streaming rude
Over tarmac and paving, barks, bellows, halloos,
Men, dogs and cattle, Lewisham awash
With their steaming muddy passage,
The Kentish Drovers.

ST JAMES'S, CHARFIELD

(a redundant church)

Someone has left riddles here,
Relic of the interrogative mode
Licensed to be used in churches.

The seven signs of Charfield:

A *bier,* since all flesh is,
And churchyards are never redundant,
Dying remaining the most
Favoured single activity.

A *sparrow,* claws up, for the fallen,
And to remind us how many we are worth.

A *Bible,* revised but sinister:
He also suppressed the hill-shrines
And the sacred poles in Judah.
Jehoshaphat, professing urban religion.

An *organ,* midget, defunct,
Which roared *Aargh* like a maniac
Being touched.

Emptiness, left behind by pews,
Vestments, guidebooks, kneelers,
The gaudy clutter of mortality. What stays
Is anybody's guess. It flutters,
And is full of light.

Pinned to the door, a *list*
Of the churchyard's flora: *I do hope*
That you will be able to manage
This interesting site in the best way
For the wildlife. And names,
Instead of the flower-arrangers, the flowers:
Cow-parsley, columbine, cuckoo-pint, daisy.

Last, the *memorial,*
In discreet granite memory
Of *those who lost their lives*
In the railway accident at Charfield:
Persons from Belper, Milverton,
Gloucester, Sheffield; couples
From Leicester, Derby, Plymouth;
Two children, never identified,
The hairs of whose heads someone
Omitted to number.

                                                    Please,
No weedkiller to be used in the churchyard.

'SOOTHING AND AWFUL'

(Visitors' Book at Montacute church)

You are meant to exclaim. The church
Expects it of you. Bedding plants
And polished brass anticipate a word.

Visitors jot a name,
A nationality, briskly enough,
But find *Remarks* beyond them.

I love English churches!
Says Friedrichshafen expansively.
The English are more backward. They come,

Certainly, from Spalding, Westbury-on-Trym,
The Isle of Wight; but all the words
They know are: *Very Lovely; Very Peaceful; Nice.*

A giggling gaggle from Torquay Grammar,
All pretending they can't spell *beautiful*, concoct
A private joke about the invisible organ.

A civilized voice from Cambridge
Especially noticed the well-kept churchyard.
Someone from Dudley, whose writing suggests tight shoes,

Reported *Nice and Cool.* The young entry
Yelp their staccato approval:
Super! Fantastic! Jesus Lives! Ace!

But what they found,
Whatever it was, it wasn't what
They say. In the beginning,

We know, the word, but not here,
Land of the perpetually-flowering cliché,
The rigid lip. Our fathers who piled

Stone upon stone, our mothers
Who stitched the hassocks, our cousins
Whose bones lie smooth, harmonious around –

However majestic their gifts, comely their living,
Their words would be thin like ours; they would join
In our inarticulate anthem: *Very Cosy*.

PURTON LOWER BRIDGE

Affable water lips and chats
Along iron-bound banks. A cruiser's wake
Wags unendingly after it, floats flouncing
Like cross dowagers with long memories.
Not many boats in autumn. Boys
Lend a hand with ropes, show their catch
(A dead eel). The low swung bridge
Opens when needed, smoothly, like a sliced smile.

This is the human scale: nothing too much.
But half a mile downstream sprawls Glumdalclitch,
Naked, enormous, careless, bright with mud,
Red sun squat on her, pocked by birdfeet, cables,
Monstrously tidal, impossible, uncivil,
Desirable, the lethal river Severn.

GROWING UP

I wasn't good
At being a baby. Burrowed my way
Through the long yawn of infancy,
Masking by instinct how much I knew
Of the senior world, sabotaging
As far as I could, biding my time,
Biting my rattle, my brother (in private),

Shoplifting daintily into my pram.
Not a good baby,
No.

I wasn't good
At being a child. I missed
The innocent age. Children,
Being childish, were beneath me.
Adults I despised or distrusted. They
Would label my every disclosure
Precocious, naive, whatever it was.
I disdained definition, preferred to be surly.
Not a nice child,
No.

I wasn't good
At adolescence. There was a dance,
A catchy rhythm; I was out of step.
My body capered, nudging me
With hairy, fleshy growths and monthly outbursts,
To join the party. I tried to annul
The future, pretended I knew it already,
Was caught bloody-thighed, a criminal
Guilty of puberty.
Not a nice girl,
No.

(My hero, intransigent Emily,
Cauterised her own-dog-mauled
Arm with a poker,
Struggled to die on her feet,
Never told anyone anything.)

I wasn't good
At growing up. Never learned
The natives' art of life. Conversation
Disintegrated as I touched it,

So I played mute, wormed along years,
Reciting the hard-learned arcane litany
Of cliché, my company passport.
Not a nice person,
No.

The gift remains
Masonic, dark. But age affords
A vocation even for wallflowers.
Called to be connoisseur, I collect,
Admire, the effortless bravura
Of other people's lives, proper and comely,
Treading the measure, shopping, chaffing,
Quarrelling, drinking, not knowing
How right they are, or how, like well-oiled bolts,
Swiftly and sweet, they slot into the grooves
Their ancestors smoothed out along the grain.

THE FIRST YEARS ARRIVE

You could mistake it for a holiday.
Rucksacks around, and dormobiles,
And people running to and fro with bundles.
But no one eats. That comes later

And is significant. They will eat
When the crowd has gone, with the new
Uncertain friends. But still you could
Mistake it for a holiday. There are

Grans sitting on beds, and younger sisters
On windowsills; the dog walks up
And down outside on a lead.
And no one cries. That is significant

And came earlier. *We're past*
The worst moment says a mother wryly.
Hers will be later, when she moves
An un-needed chair away from the breakfast table.

Fathers dashingly shoulder trunks upstairs,
Feeling their age. But you could still mistake.
They aim at a bright surface. No one
Cuddles in public. That comes later

And is significant. The time to go.
Misery keeps to itself. In one room three
Keep the door closed, and mother
Has taken her shoes off. Grief

Is not taken on holiday, or qualms.
The new uncertain friends, the well-used walls,
Even the virginal files, may hold more learning
Of false notes than is practised at home.

But that comes later, a holiday away,
Beyond the sphere of grans and younger sisters,
When, families gone, they have eaten and drunk,
And each lamb's left alone in the well-used thicket.

BEING A STUDENT

(4th week, 1st Year)

Unless you become the eternal kind
It lasts three years; time
To get married, divorced,
Re-married, or for Christ's ministry.

Standing-water time. Time
So much wanted that
When it comes, you can't believe
That it's here. Am I truly

That godlike thing? Do junior
School kids, seeing me, think
Student, the way they recognise
A blackbird, the way I did?

The feeling hasn't arrived yet.
Inside I'm still last year's
Sixth-former, pretending. At home they'd see
Through my jeans and leg-warmers

To the uniform self, caged
Between O and A. Here I'm defined
By last year's crop. The cleaner
Thinks I'll turn out like the girl

Who had this room before. *Easy
Meat!* she says, and sucks
Her cheeks, investigating the wastepaper
Basket for signs of sin.

My spelling mistakes are old
Friends to my new tutor. He keeps
Calling me *Mandy,* too. He sees
Three or four of me, cloudily.

And all the time the great
Term revolves, like the gerbils'
Wheel at home, and light falls
In unique patterns each day

On the sea and the fell,
And none of it comes again ever,
So rich, so wild, so fast,
While inside me I haven't

Even arrived here yet.

THE CLEANER

I've seen it all, you know. Men.
Well, I've been married for thirty-two years,
I can do without them.
I know what they're after.

And these students. They're young, you know.
They don't know what it's all about,
The first years. And these post-grads;
I know what they're after.

They're older, you know. And by Christmas
They've finished here, they've gone. A girl
Can get hurt. I've been here eight years.
I've seen it happen.

Sometimes I say to her friend
You ought to talk to her. Does she know
What she's doing? And the friend'll say
Yes, she does know. Well, I hope I did right.

No need for any of 'em to have a baby,
But do they know? I feel a mother, like.
Once I did ask. I said *Do you know*
And she said O *yes we know how far we're going.*

But these post-grads are older,
They take advantage. These girls, mind,
They're not all as innocent as you'd think.
Twenty stubs in the ashtray.

I can tell a lot from that.

KNOWING ABOUT SONNETS

Lesson 1: 'The Soldier' (Brooke)

'[The task of criticism] is not to redouble the text's self-understanding,
to collude with its object in a conspiracy of silence. The task is to
show the text as it cannot know itself.'
(Terry Eagleton: *Criticism and Ideology*)

Recognising a sonnet is like attaching
A name to a face. *Mister Sonnet,* I presume?
    If I
And naming is power. It can hardly
Deny its name. You are well on the way
To mastery. The next step is telling the sonnet
What it is trying to say. This is called Interpretation.
    If I should die
What you mustn't do is collude with it. This
Is bad for the sonnet, and will only encourage it
To be eloquent. You must question it closely:
What has it left out? What made it decide
To be a sonnet? The author's testimony
(If any) is not evidence. He is the last person to know.
    If I should die, think this
Stand no nonsense with imagery. Remember, though shifty,
It is vulnerable to calculation. Apply the right tests.
Now you are able to Evaluate the sonnet.
    If I

That should do for today.
  If I should die

                              And over and over
The new white paper track innocent unlined hands.
Think this. Think this. Think this. Think only this.

SEMINAR: LIFE; EARLY POEMS

Young poet projects identical scowl from five new
Paperback jackets. Face of a man
With narrowed eyes, face of a man with a dream.

Red-hair opens brilliant new briefcase,
Inscribes the date, left-handed,
And heads her page: *H. B. Yeats.*

Trouble over by the window: *How d'you say it?*
I thought it was Yeets, like Keats.
A reading-list suppresses him, starred

For quality, like brandy. And dates
Silence frivolity: 1865–1939.
Bright sweater notes: *He saw alot of changes.*

'A foreigner writing in English.' They ponder
The foreign-ness of Ireland, poets, the past,
This man, who was *proud of his ancestry,*

Who hoped to bring books to the people's doors,
And music too, perhaps. Here he has brought
A load of trouble. *Grew up in Slygo*

(Red-hair again) *where still believed*
In lepry . . . (how d'you spell it?). *Married a median*
Who believed in automatic writing

(Whatever that is). Pause to consider
ANIMA MUNDI (caps. for awkward tongues),
Reality of the invisible. 'Does anyone here

Believe this?' *It's a Christian idea*
(Snaps SCM) *Th' real world is yet to coom.*
Cowed by infallibility, they license

H.B.'s outré creeds, noting merely
Believed in cycles. So now a poem –
Faeryland, talking worms. They resent it

Without knowing why. *He could*
Have made it easier, couldn't he?
The face dreams on. And music too, perhaps.

SEMINAR: FELICITY AND MR FROST

(for Helen and Felicity Clark)

Two truth-tellers are here;
Marigold-headed Felicity (three)
Has come because of a hole in the roof.
Mr Frost, who is dead, comes in black
On white. He has something to tell us.

Both try hard. Felicity
Has drawn a house, silent
As thinking. *Can we have a door?*
She whispers. Mr Frost has brought a wall

With holes in it. The holes grow
Larger and darker as the sun
Walks round the room. Felicity
Opens her mouth in a yawn like a hole.

I didn't understand the story
The man was telling us she says clearly
Underneath the table. Mr Frost
Sticks to his story, but his voice is opaque.

After a cuddle, a thumb-suck, Felicity
Touches the book with her hand,
Gravely. It is snowing now in Mr Frost.
He has written a very short poem

And Felicity has found a jimmy in it
(*Secret world,* her mother explains).
Mr Frost's world is secret too.
There are woods in it, and miles to go,

And snow. It has started to rain
Where we are. Felicity stands on a chair
To look out. *Don't ever have children,*
Her mother smiles at the students.

And miles to go. *You said*
Don't have children (Felicity cancels
Her secret world). The students are concerned.
It is still raining. Her mother translates:

I didn't mean it. And snowing.
Mr Frost is preoccupied. He
Has promises to keep. And miles to go.

HIGH TABLE

Their equable virginity has borne
No heirs. Their successors are
Fecundly and frequently married,
Or bisexual, or male. These
Are the daughters of a dynasty
Of perpetual and celibate curates,
Descended from the Venerable Bede.

For decades they manned
Their ivory turrets, named after
Three saints (one apocryphal),
A bluestocking, an English lady.
Mistresses of the negative, they elected
An apostolic succession of able girls,
High-flyers all, with plenty
Of moral bottom.

Chastely they cherished their élite,
Reserving the deepest passions
For Jane Austen, Dr Johnson, Sterne,
The safe and barren dead.
Now they endure the faltering,
Falling, failing of their favourites,
But grace their dubious unions, god-
mother their grubby offspring, read
Their liberated, unbalanced novels, still
Offer kindness and Fuller's walnut cake.

They are extinct. Their vowels,
Cool and accurate as lettuce,
Are tuned to a defunct mode.
Learning lingers purely, like the down,
Among their wrinkles, but their writ

No longer runs. These assassins,
Whose *No* slewed lives, watch learning
Leave their strict streets for new
Irresponsible freeways, their dicta
Relegated to dismissive foot-notes.

Venerable falcons, cataract-hooded,
Jessed by the tight arthritis-leash,
Caged still in your vocation, stooping
Still on the disorganised dead –
But no longer your lifelong quarry,
Only Kipling, Stevenson, Scott,
The ones your book-riddled childhood
Randomly caught by heart –

Tyrants; we who can see now
How flimsy your toy palaces,
How brief your majesty, pardon
Your stiff integrity, as it nibbles
At your own white bones.

CHAPLAINCY FELL WALK

There is always one out in front
With superior calves and experienced boots;

Always a final pair to be waited for,
Not saying much, pale, rather fat;

And the holy ones in the middle, making it
Their part to acclimatise the lonely and new,
Introducing cinquefoil, a heron, a view;

And a stout one who giggles, uniting us
In wonder at her unfaltering chokes;
But alarming too. For what is she laughing at?

And remote presence of hills;
And the absence of you.

THE SHEEPDOG

After the very bright light,
And the talking bird,
And the singing,
And the sky filled up wi' wings,
And then the silence,

Our lads sez
We'd better go, then.
Stay, Shep. Good dog, stay,
So I stayed wi' t' sheep.

After they cum back,
It sounded grand, what they'd seen:
Camels, and kings, and such,
Wi' presents – human sort,
Not the kind you eat –
And a baby. Presents wes for him.
Our lads took him a lamb.

I had to stay behind wi' t' sheep.
Pity they didn't tek me along too.
I'm good wi' lambs,
And the baby might have liked a dog
After all that myrrh and such.

LOCAL POET

Can't see so well now; his hearing
Isn't what it was. But he can still
Smell where a fox has been among the dahlias.

The birds have flown, the loft's empty,
But he still writes for *Pigeon Post*,
Plays cards with his ancient neighbour,

Works the garden. And suddenly,
A year ago, the Muse pounced:
He is her man in Gloucestershire.

The opposition doesn't worry him. *Betjeman, now –*
He rhymes too far apart. I have 'em close
Like church bells. I'm ready for publication.

Each poem's numbered like a show bird;
There's a prospectus: 'Purchasers will find them
Humorous, informative, historical.'

And so they will, they will. The W.I.
Like his stuff, and the Horticultural.
His voice helps. *Double Gloucester,*

Though it shouldn't be, he says. I had the best
Education available at that time.
But I liked to play with the wild boys,

And they spoke broad. Now he's the poet
For wild things, looks with a pigeon's eye
As far north as Evesham, tells how blackbirds

Lob home though ivy, where to find
The fishbone mixen of a kingfisher's nest,
Honours the useful stream by the elastic factory,

Explains how to direct hounds (*they know
Who Charlie* is), records shy Royalty's local earths,
The tragedy of the lame stray greyhound bitch

Whose litter the fox ate, gulls
Trailing wireworms down strict furrows,
Long dead shires with hooves

As big as buckets, and remembers
Ol' Tucker Workman trapping the badger
Using his legs like tongs. But most of all

I like his garden ones, about the flowers
He grows but cannot spell, bees feverish
For marrow pollen, the evening mating call

Of woodlice, his iambic prescription
For limp cauliflowers of calomel dust
(*Obtainable from Boots*). How can I tell him

The competition judge won't pick his poems?
The Horticultural, the W.I. –
They ask him back, they think he's good,

And they know what he's on about. *This judge –
Where's he from, anyway? He won't know here.*
We settle which to send. He's disappointed

By what I like. I know he has no chance
Of winning. Does he trust me? No, I think.
Can he suspect I'll write about our talk,

And steal all his best lines? I hope he can't.
I hope he won't read this.

THE PERSON'S TALE

'In consequence of a slight indisposition, an anodyne had been
prescribed, from the effects of which (the author) fell asleep . . . On
awaking . . . (he) eagerly wrote down the lines that are here preserved.
At this moment he was unfortunately called out by a person on
business from Porlock, and detained by him above an hour . . .' (S.T.C.)

That the Muses have no more fervent
Devotee than myself may not be generally
Known outside Porlock. As a man of the cloth
I am, I trust, superior to mere vulgar
Appetite for fame. 'Full many a gem
Of purest ray serene . . .' I am, I hope, resigned
To being such a gem; an unseen blush.
But to allow myself to be presented
By Mr C– to posterity as a *person*
Goes beyond the limits of even clerical
Diffidence. It was, I may say, in pursuit
Of my pastoral duties that I made
The not inconsiderable journey from my parsonage
To the farmhouse, at Mr C–'s own
Most vehement behest. Prepared for any
Extreme office, I presented myself
Before Mr C–. *Sir*, said I, *I am here.*
The very man, quoth he, clasping me in
A distasteful embrace. *Most reverend sir –*
Then for two hours detained me at his door
With chronicles of colic, stomach, bowels,
Of nightly sweats, the nightmare, cramps, diarrhoea
(Your pardon, Delicacy! Merely the word appals),
All the while straining me to his bosom, like
His own deplorable Mariner, neglected hygiene
Rendering contiguity less than welcome,
The more as I infallibly discerned
The less pleasing features of addiction
To the poppy, prescribed, he affirmed,
As anodyne against the dysentery.

And now, it seems, I am the guilty *person*
Who cut off inspiration in its prime.
Quite otherwise. Myself had on the way
Entertained the notion of an Acrostick, a form
Of harmless mirth whereby I have achieved
Some slender fame among the Porlock fair.
Alas! the frail thing could not survive
Two hours of Mr C–'s internal ills.
I am the loser, first of my Acrostick,
Then of my character, for surely *person*
Denotes nonentity, a man of straw –
And the proud name of Porlock sullied too!

FROM THE THIRD STOREY

(*for Hazel Medd*)

'"You have to be selfish to be a writer."
"Monstrously selfish?"
"Monstrously selfish," she said.'
(David Plante: Jean Rhys in *Difficult Women*)

Aunt Jane scribbles in the living-room.
When visitors come, she stuffs her work
Under the blotter, and joins in the chat.

(In the third storey, a curious
Laugh; distinct, formal, mirthless.)

Daughter Charlotte's first care is to discharge
Her household and filial duties. Only then
May she admit herself to her own bright sphere.

(There were days when she was quite silent;
Others when I could not account for
The sounds she made.)

Home duties are a small part of
The Reverend William's life. Reverently
Elizabeth, wife and mother, furnishes his study,
And writes in the dining-room,
Which has three doors.

(A vague murmur, peculiar
And lugubrious. Something
Gurgled and moaned.)

George is Agnes's husband. He and
Mistress Marian (*what do people call her?*)
Write in one room at their desks, drudging
To pay off his marriage's debts.

(A savage, a sharp, a shrilly sound.
The thing delivering such utterance must rest
Ere it repeat the effort. It came
Out of the third storey.)

Sister Virginia, childless wife,
Fathoms the metaphor of room.
But who is One? The upstairs lunatic –
Might she not be Oneself?

(A snarling, snatching sound,
Almost like a dog quarrelling.)

Between affairs, before marriages,
Jean (*I have called myself so many
Different names*) buys twelve technicoloured
Quill pens to cheer her bare table
In bedsit Fulham. And writes,

(She was standing, waving her arms,
Above the battlements, and shouting out
Till they could hear her a mile off.)

And sets the mad wife free to tell
Truth of mistress, divorcée, mother,
Aunt, daughter, sister, wife:

Now at last I know
Why I was brought here
*And what I have to do.**

Note: The last stanza consists of the last words of Antoinette
Cosway/Bertha Mason in Jean Rhys's *Wide Sargasso Sea*, when
she is just about to set fire to Thornfield Hall.

THE CRYSTAL ZOO

1985

THE NEW EXETER BOOK
OF RIDDLES

1999

TRANSITIONAL OBJECT

Sits, holding nurse's hard reassuring hand
In her own two small ones.

Is terrified. Mews in her supersonic
Panic voice: *Help. Help. Please.*

Cries for Mummy, Daddy, Philip, the bus. Tries
To get up, to escape.

Is restrained by adult, would-be comforting
Hands and arms. Fights them.

Is brought a sweet warm drink, and is too shaky
With fear to swallow it.

The nurse cuddles her, snuggles the young amber
Ringlets against the grey.

Is not to be consoled. Her only comfort
The white blanket she hugs.

Whispers, *Help. Help. Please.* Cries for Mummy, Daddy,
Philip. She is 83,

Resisting childhood as it closes in.

I DO KNOW HOW AWFUL I AM

I have two of me.
Constantly they betray me.

One, the old gipsy,
Brown, wrinkled, with white eyelids,

Who laughs her way out
Of tight corners, holds fortune

Between her fingers,
Spits luckily on highways,

Coerces hazels,
Has no birth certificate.

This old wretch cons me,
Promises her favours,

But sends her daughter,
Pale, suburban and speechless,

Limp autumn crocus,
Whose magic is exhausted.

Naturally, when
I need such mild company,

The deplorable
Witch, her mother, comes instead.

MY LION IS A UNICORN

My lion is a unicorn.
He, sunbrowed and splendid,
Distributes love with lavish
Paws and growls goldenly.
She, tenderhoofed and weighed
Down with incongruous
Ivory lumber, shivers
With nerves, and is
Scared of virgins.

My lion is as strong as a
Ten-ton-truck. He tosses
Pancakes and cabers with his
Debonair tail. But my
Unicorn suffers from
Cold sores, hay fever and
A weak back, not to mention
Chilblains on the sensitive
Tip of her horn.

My lion is as hot as a
Boiling kettle. He hugs
Me to his royal mane and
Comforts me. But my sad
Unicorn creeps into
My bed and whimpers, *Please
Make me happy make me
Happy.* Darling unicorn,
You need my lion
To comfort you.

THE HORSE SPEAKS

No, not a speaking part this time,
But those are my hoofs you can hear
Four-in-a-bar-ing away. They missed
A chance to cheer up the back rows,
Not giving me a cue for a whinny,
But composers are always stingy
Over cadenzas. To be perfectly frank,
This boot-saddle-to-horse stuff
Never appeals to me much. I prefer
The peaceful world of the slow movement,
With grass in it. But even there
Sensational elements will intrude – cuckoos,
Thunderstorms, larks ascending. They can't
Leave well alone. In the present case,
Imagine me at my most statuesque,
Quietly nodding over a moonlit nosebag,
Dreaming of non-achievement. In bursts the Hero,
Inflicts saddle, bridle, spurs and purpose,
Helter-skelters into a spiteful landscape
Of black wire and barbed hedges. The moon, of course,
Goes down at once. And Heroes
Always ride cross-country.
                              The end?
Oh, the Hero gets there, naturally.
So presumably the horse does too,
In an interestingly exhausted condition.
Where? Funny you should ask me that.
I forget where we were going;
I always did confuse Ghent with Aix.

THE HEIR

It was very quiet on the island after
They all went back to Milan. Sounds
And sweet airs dwindled and petered out
As the fleet dissolved on Ariel's calm sea.

Caliban missed the music, being
A susceptible monster. The whole island
Was his now, sun, moon and yellow sands,
Filberts and freshets, but somehow

Vacant, and not worth having. Twangling
Instruments and spiteful hedgehogs
In retrospect mingled. He didn't know
Exactly what he was missing,

But he missed it. Prospero, he thought,
Had shipped harmony with the baggage
Back to Milan. Poor mooncalf, he didn't realise
They had all gone back to invest

In Olivetti and Neapolitan
Ice cream, abandoning magic
And music together. Only Ariel
Went on playing for love, and he never

Touched down on the island again.
His memories were quite distinct, and all
Of tyranny. So the island was soundless, airless,
Dumb to name Caliban king.

RIDDLE 1

Awash in the watery airway, I drift
But never stray from my moorings.

Child of a year, I am born
In the spray, fade in the fall.

My submissive brethren wait man's time;
I create my own moment,

Leaning from my twiggy rigging
Into the wind's hand, finding

A mutineer's grave in my grassy landfall.
Wasps are my monument.

Answer: a windfall

RIDDLE 2

A door	but not a door
In homes	but not for humans
I have no hole	for a key, nor a handle
Those who flash through me	having no fingers.
I am way out	and way in
For the night-watchers	the long-whiskered.

Answer: a cat-flap

A WATCHING BRIEF
1987

THE DOCTOR

(Sir Luke Fildes: *The Doctor*, Tate Gallery)

'That Jackson, he's another one.
If he goes on opening windows we'll all
Die of pneumonia.'
                    The native obsessions:
Health and the weather. Attendants have
The dogged, grainy look of subjects. Someone,
Surely, is going to paint them?

'You don't have a bad heart yet, do you?'

'Not that I know of.'
                    'They can examine you.'

'But they don't really know.'

                    The painters knew.
Gainsborough eyed his lovely, delicate daughters
And rich fat brewers: Turner his hectic skies.
They brooded on death by drowning (Ophelia, in real water);
Cloud without end; storm; storm coming on;
Bright exophthalmic eyes, consumptive colours,
And gorgeous goitred throats; the deluge,
The end of the world, and Adam's
Appalling worm-wrapped birth.
                    Such patient watchers
Have eyes for those who watch. The child
Frets in its fever, the parents
Grieve in the background gloom. But the doctor,
Who has done all he can, and knows nothing
Will help or heal, sits raptly, raptly,
As if such absorbed attention were in itself
A virtue. As it is.

DOWNSTAIRS AT THE ORANGERIE

I mount guard all day,
Feet apart in my correct shoes, arms crossed,
My mouth tucked into the policeman's slot,
Watching through powerful spectacles, listening
Through short-cut hair. For here,
Between the Maître and the Lion of France,
Rules are appropriate. Upstairs is different. With
Their disgusting nudes, their crazy Picassos, it is hard
To expect decorum. I have seen
Kissing upstairs, and worse. But here,
In my underwater world, I insist on etiquette.
Water-lilies are modest and delicate plants;
They cannot turn their heads and look away.
I protect their perpetual innocence. The Japanese
Can be relied on; there is some affinity
Between them and my children. But the Germans!
The Dutch! the faithless English! the dam-Yankees!
They move incessantly, they point, they speak aloud,
They touch. Criminal language, criminal behaviour.
I bark at them incomprehensibly: *N'touch! C'est interdit!*
They flinch, but will not go. My waterlily world
Lives only in their absence. Then the still
And permanent things are eloquent
In their own way. I'm deaf to it,
But that is not important. I have my place.
I pace my precious, my mysterious world,
Master the frivolous mob, and bow my head
To Clemenceau and Monet as I pass
Their bearded busts. I keep the peace
Of this, their world and mine. I have
No oriflamme, no florid pose, no torch,
But I serve France.

LA DÉBÂCLE. TEMPS GRIS

Seine. Facing south. Mid-day.
No sun. Cloud heavy over Lavacourt,
No boat, no body. Water, ice, snow,
Houses, trees, hills, cloud, sky.

This picture means nothing
More than it shows. The tree standing alone
Is not me, though I understand
Why you might think so. Wrongly.

Not a thing here means
Anything but that it is here,
Now. I am the witness, bound to set down
What I see. This is what I see,

Watch. Begin with the water.
It is undisturbed. In it flower stilly
The crooked refractions of poplars.
The poplars grow up from underwater,

The poplars grow up from above water.
Ice and snow come between tree and reflection.
In this weather reflection does not grow into tree.
Ice bars it. Begin again with the water.

There is one ice-free patch. Here
The reflections are. Beyond, brash ice
That tomorrow will be free water.
I painted the water first, lying under.

Ice slabs jolt to edged poses:
Planks, tents, scrubbing brushes, gables,
Lobsters, slices of cake. Light on ice
Shines green, blue, yellow, red,

Rashers of colour run along
The slab-slides. Water and film and ice
Mirror the hummocky pink-grey cloud.
This is the moment. I have trapped it.

Moving did happen. Poplars
Were felled by snow; these can be seen.
An ice-clamped-solid reach can be deduced
From the gashed floes. People

Live in the houses, perhaps. I will not say.
I record what I see: the silent
Unclenching of the still-clenched river.
The Break-up of the Ice. The weather, grey.

THREE WOMEN WORDSWORTHS

1. DEER IN GOWBARROW PARK

(*for David Webb*)

Not a gallant old warhorse of a poem,
Scarred from the student wars, but an indomitable
Little hackney, docile with twelve-year-olds,
Who may not understand *inner eyes* and
Tranquil recollecting, but know a *King Alfred*
When they see one, and can imagine lots.

Years later William knocked it together;
Mary gave her two lines. But it was Dorothy
Did the fieldwork, across the daffodilled years,
On a threatening misty morning, April,
1802. A boat is floating in the middle
Of the bay. Cows cause a diversion.
They see that yellow flower that Mrs C.
Calls *pilewort*; wood-sorrell; daffodils, naturally.

Waves at different distances, and rain,
And a sour landlady (*it is her way*),
And excellent ham and potatoes. Warm rum
And water for two – seven shillings all told.
We enjoyed ourselves, she says, *and wished
For Mary.* You hand us that day,

Dorothy, sister, all the random details, the furze bush
Opposite Mr Clarkson's, dry clothes afterwards,
William reading Congreve by the fire, how it rained
When you went to bed, and *N.B. Deer
In Gowbarrow Park like skeletons,*
With, of course, daffodils, *about the breadth
Of a country turnpike road.*

From William and Mary the official version,
Framed, in focus, ready to be declaimed,
Public as tapestry, concluding with a Thought.

The National Trust can use a poem like this.
But your straggle of unplanned delights and scrambles,
Texture of wind and wetness, glancing
Touch of the day, like (N.B.) the Gowbarrow deer
Defy the taming mind, your presence just
An urgent breathless charge: N.B., N.B.

2. UNDERCURRENTS AT THE DOVE AND OLIVE BOUGH

Complaint of the Guide:
All those portraits of Him, she says, not one of Her,
'Exquisite sister' with the wild eyes, only
One prim silhouette, image of Jane Austen,
And painful studies of senility.

Record of the House:
Sitting-room where the women clerked for William;
Bedroom lined with *The Times* to keep out damp,
Where children, sister slept, but not the Poet; door
William had built, *being disturbed*
By matters of a domestic nature.

Testimony of the Rug:
My wool is Grasmere wool,
Spun, dyed and knitted for the Poet's knees.
Rhubarb, mulberry, blackberry, old man's beard,
Begonia, nettles, privet, parsley, broom
She picked and steeped, poor feckless Willy's wife.
I represent long and unvalued hours
Of trivial effort. *It look some little time,*
She said of me.

Sign of the Sheepfold:
Built nearly in the form of a heart
Unequally divided.

3. THE LAST

'I shall forever feel thankful for the Almighty's goodness for
having spared me to be the solitary lingerer.'
(Mary Wordsworth, 7th February, 1855)

She was a stayer-on, a knitter-up
Of others' untidy lives. Adept
At self-effacement, she shared honeymoon,
Husband, house, claimed nothing
For herself but to be of use.

Brother died, children died, adored adorable Dora
Died; Dorothy, incontinent and senile baby,
Farted and belched, shrieked, sang and swore and spat;

The most wonderful Friend in the world
Blurred and faded away.
At length even He died. And five years later
She died, *that poor Miss Wordsworth.*

Still she lived on, since somebody had to,
To name the Work and nurse it into print,
As he had known she would, dear Idiot Man,
With his bad nights, his love-child, his headaches,
Who never noticed things till Dorothy wrote them

Into his journal; was put right by eight-year-olds;
Couldn't take it in, the leech-gatherer's message; missed
The crowning moment when they crossed the Alps;
Whom she thanked tenderly after eight hard years of marriage
For *the first letter of love that has been*

Exclusively my own.

NOTES
These three poems are perhaps a gloss on Coleridge's remark
about Wordsworth: 'living wholly among *Devotees* – having every
the minutest Thing, almost his very Eating and Drinking, done for
him by his Sister, or Wife.' I wasn't thinking about this remark when
I wrote these poems but it struck me afterwards. The more
immediate cause was a visit to Dove Cottage at Grasmere. (U.A.F.)

1. *Deer in Gowbarrow Park*

The woman here is Dorothy, whose Journal entry for 15th April, 1802,
was used by William to write the poem *Daffodils* in 1804.

Mary gave her two lines: Mary's lines are:

> 'They flash upon that inward eye
> Which is the bliss of solitude'.

2. Undercurrents at the Dove and Olive Bough

The woman here is Fanny, née Graham, wife of William's younger son Willy. His was not a successful career. Dove Cottage was, before the Wordsworths came to it, a small pub called the Dove and Olive Bough. William refers to this in *The Waggoner* (1806):

> 'There, where the Dove and Olive Bough
> Once hung, a Poet harbours now,
> A simple water-drinking Bard . . .'

It was not generally regarded as a suitable house for a family, as it was so small.

painful studies of senility (line 5): by S. Crosthwaite (1833) and J. Harden (1842). Dorothy's Alzheimer's Disease seems to have become serious in 1829, when she was 58.

door (line 9): This was inserted while the Wordsworths lived here. It meant that William could walk straight from the garden to the sitting room without encountering the household working in the kitchen.

Built nearly in the form of a heart/Unequally divided (lines 22–23): Dorothy's description in her Journal (11th October, 1800) of the sheepfold which she and William went to look at that day. (The next day he began writing *Michael*.)

3. The Last

This woman is Mary Wordsworth (née Hutchinson). The epigraph is from a letter she wrote on 7th February, 1855, after Dorothy's death. William had died in 1850, Dorothy on 25th January, 1855.

The most wonderful Friend in the world (line 9): Coleridge (died 1834).

the Work (line 14): the 'poem on his own life', which he never gave a name to. Mary sent it to Moxon to be published under the title of *The Prelude*.

AT COWAN BRIDGE

(for Elsa Corbluth)

This place has elected to lie low.
Houses are called *Private Road*
And *Private Property.*

Everything is ostentatiously eating:
Free-ranging hens and geese, a fat horse,
A goat tethered to its larder.
Black-snouted lambs nuzzle and crop.
The local store sells local lemon curd.
Two miles away at the teashop they hope
To delight your palate, and restore
Those jaded tastebuds.

And dandelions do well. Their mop heads stare
Up at the sun. But the scrawny ash
Hugs back its green.

Discreet of you not to die here,
Maria, Elizabeth, elder daughters,
Who caught death here.
The river's a true witness. It sings
A bleak song: children were cold here,
And children were hungry. The lion-headed fell
Averts its gaze, but you can see where winter
Has rubbed it raw. Here children died,

But were buried elsewhere. Here discretion
Is expected of the dead. Outside the chapel
Jesus assures the lunging lorries, in a dying fall,
I am the resurrection and the life
At Easter, in late hot April.
It makes no difference. Not many birds are singing.

What resurrection for the chilled children,
Blighted and broken, bundled home to die,
Killed off between July and June,
Silent singers, aged ten, aged nine?

Flesh is finished with. Something persists
In a sister, unrelenting, stunted;
In a dead child's voice outside a midnight window
Crying *Let me in, let me in.*

Here daffodils came
And have lived to regret it. In dwarfish clumps
They glower along the verge.

'THESE THINGS WERE HERE'

(*for Gladys Mary Coles*)

And still are, Father. It is only
Your forging eye that's missing, water-watcher,
Weed-watcher, weather-watcher, Father head-in-air,

In this your cloud-capped county. (*My dear Baillie,
The clouds are more interesting than in any other
Place I have been.*) But for *us*, trailing you,

Summer sky was an unregenerate dull white over all.
(*Proper August weather,* snarled the natives.) No time
To visit your burly Ribble. But that grand barn

We did finally pitch on. Ill at ease
On holy ground, we trespassed into the wrong one,
Claimed to identify your great As in the beams,

Knew privately this wasn't what had fetched you,
Asked a farmworker, sloshing through mud, one of your
Simple people, for whom beauty of inscape

Was buried away. Yes, he said, he knew which barn
It was, opened gates, walked us gravely through
(*There's a few cattle in, but you won't mind that*)

And there they were, as you saw them, the massive baulks
In high dimness above the dozy bullocks, vaulting adze-edged alphas,
Signifers for you of Who begins and ends. Here, Father,

As in so many places, you endured exile. (*My dearest Mother,*
By daylight I feel the strangeness of the place.) Yet here
In this great strange barn, which was also *ours,*

You found a likeness for the harvest-home
Of Christ, his mother, and all his hallows;

And for those whom your church could not then contain,
Those much loved holy heretics, *my dear Baillie,*
Dead *so dear to me* Henry Purcell, *dearest Bridges,*
My dear Canon, my dearest Mother,

And for those *simple people* who have hands to build
And eyes to see, who open gates, there seems here now to be
All the room in the world.

'July 19, 1872. Stepped into a barn of ours, a great shadowy barn,
where the hay had been stacked on either side and looking at the
great rudely worked timberframes – principals(?) and tie-beams, which
make them look like big bold As with the cross-bar high up – I thought
how sadly beauty of inscape was unknown and buried away from
simple people and yet how near at hand it was if they had eyes to see
it and it could be called out everywhere again . . .'
(G. M. Hopkins's *Journal*)

DEAR MR LEE

Dear Mr Lee (Mr Smart says
it's rude to call you Laurie, but that's
how I think of you, having lived with you
really all year), Dear Mr Lee
(Laurie) I just want you to know
I used to hate English, and Mr Smart
is roughly my least favourite person,
and as for Shakespeare (we're doing him too)
I think he's a national disaster, with all those jokes
that Mr Smart has to explain why they're jokes,
and even then no one thinks they're funny,
And T. Hughes and P. Larkin and that lot
in our anthology, not exactly a laugh a minute,
pretty gloomy really, so that's why
I wanted to say Dear Laurie (sorry) your book's
the one that made up for the others, if you
could see my copy you'd know it's lived
with me, stained with Coke and Kitkat
and when I had a cold, and I often
take you to bed with me to cheer me up
so Dear Laurie, I want to say sorry,
I didn't want to write a character-sketch
of your mother under headings, it seemed
wrong somehow when you'd made her so lovely,
and I didn't much like those questions
about *social welfare in the rural community*
and *the seasons as perceived by an adolescent*,
I didn't think you'd want your book
read that way, but bits of it I know by heart,
and I wish I had your uncles and your half-sisters
and lived in Slad, though Mr Smart says your view
of the class struggle is naïve, and the examiners
won't be impressed by me knowing so much by heart,

they'll be looking for terse and cogent answers
to their questions, but I'm not much good at terse and cogent,
I'd just like to be like you, not mind about being poor,
see everything bright and strange, the way you do,
and I've got the next one out of the Public Library,
about Spain, and I asked Mum about learning
to play the fiddle, but Mr Smart says Spain isn't
like that any more, it's all Timeshare villas
and Torremolinos, and how old were you
when you became a poet? (Mr Smart says for anyone
with my punctuation to consider poetry as a career
is enough to make the angels weep.)

PS Dear Laurie, please don't feel guilty for
me failing the exam, it wasn't your fault,
it was mine, and Shakespeare's,
and maybe Mr Smart's, I still love *Cider*,
it hasn't made any difference.

'VERY QUIET HERE'

(picture postcard of Aldeburgh sent by Thomas Hardy to his sister,
Kate Hardy, on 11th May, 1912)

(*for Bill Greenslade*)

In Wessex no doubt the old habits resume:
Fair maidens seduced in their innocent bloom,
May-month for suicide, and other crimes
(Two Dorchester murders discussed in *The Times*),
Mutilation of corpses, infanticide, rape,
And so many reasons for purchasing crêpe.
All stirring at home. But here vacancy reigns;
I have nothing to watch but my varicose veins.

Very quiet here.
Not an apprentice has perished this year.

I envy Crabbe the matter that he saw:
Those wasting ills peculiar to the poor,
Decline and dissolution, debts and duns,
The dreary marshes and the pallid suns –
So much for him to write about. And I
In Wessex homely ironies can spy.

None of that here.
Even dear Emma a trifle less queer.

Deck-chaired and straw-hatted I sit at my ease,
With each blighted prospect determined to please.
Inside my old skin I feel hope running on –
Perhaps a changed life when poor Emma is gone?
Strange foreknowings fret me: guns, music and war,
A corpse with no heart, a young Briton ashore
Walks here where I sit with the atheist Clodd,
Discussing the quirks of that local cult, God.

I ponder how
Time Past and Time to Come pester me now.

AT AVERHAM

Here my four-year-old father opened a gate,
And cows meandered through into the wrong field.

I forget who told me this. Not, I think,
My sometimes reticent father. Not much I know

About the childhood of that only child. Just
How to pronounce the name, sweetly deceitful

In its blunt spelling, and how Trent
Was his first river. Still here, but the church

Closed now, graveyard long-grassed,
No one to ask in the village. Somewhere here,

I suppose, I have a great-grandfather buried,
Of whom nothing is known but that, dying, he called

My father's mother from Kent to be forgiven.
She came, and was. And came again

To her sister, my great-aunt, for
Her dying pardon too. So my chatty mother,

But couldn't tell what needed so much forgiving,
Or such conclusive journeys to this place.

Your father, pampered only brother
Of many elder sisters, four miles away,

Grew up to scull on this river. My father,
Transplanted, grew up near poets and palaces,

Changed Trent for Thames. Water was in his blood;
In a dry part of Kent his telephone exchange

Was a river's name; he went down to die
Where Arun and Adur run out to the sea.

Your father, going north, abandoned skiffs for cars,
And lived and died on the wind-blasted North Sea shore.

They might have met, two cherished children,
Among nurses and buttercups, by the still silver Trent,

But didn't. That other implacable river, war,
Trawled them both in its heady race

Into quick-march regiments. I don't suppose they met
On any front. They found our mothers instead.

So here I stand, where ignorance begins,
In the abandoned churchyard by the river,

And think of my father, his mother, her father,
Your father, and you. Two fathers who never met,

Two daughters who did. One boy went north, one south,
Like the start of an old tale. Confusions

Of memory rise: rowing, and rumours of war,
And war, and peace; the secret in-fighting

That is called marriage. And children, children,
Born by other rivers, streaming in other directions.

You like the sound of my father. He would
Have loved you plainly, for loving me.

Reconciliation is for the quick, quickly. There isn't enough
Love yet in the world for any to run to waste.

SOUNDS AND SILENCES

(for David)

Sound heard only in childhood:
Interminable mumbling like rock-doves

Over early-morning tea, after last night's differences,
Of parents in their bedroom, creating today.

Conversations we might have had,
But didn't; the smothered grievances:
She loves you better than me; You
With your nose in a book. The uncleared air.

Scraps of learning stage-managed
To impress outsiders: cycling through tolerant suburbs
Shrieking bad extrovert French, playing
At being other; postcards in cuneiform.

Unplanned confidings of drunkenness
Which, as sobriety settles, we conspire
To forget. The mazy toastings
Of deadest philosophers, most indifferent stars.

Stalking neglected churches on unpretending
Bedfordshire uplands, your moped illegal,
Exhaustless. Conversation was basic shouts,
Small talk about roodlofts.

Drowned utterance of your just-got-home self,
Shrugging off the commuter, communing with terrapins
And watersnails. Silence eddied round you.
I watched; tried not to see.

Distant arpeggios of our mother playing
Rustle of Spring downstairs, at night, after dinner.
We listened, scared. Did she mean
To charm our childhood, or retrace her own?

Was she playing perhaps because she was happy?
Why did the innocent tinkle alarm us?
Where were we going?

A WARTIME EDUCATION

Lessons with Mam'zelle were difficult.
Le général would crop up in the middle of
The most innocent Daudet. Tears for *la France,*
La belle France embarrassed our recitation
Of nouns with tricky plurals: hibou, chou, *hélas*, bijou.

A father in uniform conferred status. Mine,
Camping it up with the Home Guard in Kent
On summer nights, too human for heroics.

Bananas and oranges, fruit of triumphant
Decimated convoys, were amazements
Of colour and light, too beautiful to eat.
(In any case, eating three bananas
Straight off, one after the other,
Was certain death. We all knew that.)

Struggling through adolescence, trying
To accommodate Macbeth, parents, God,
Teachers of mathematics, it was hard
To sustain plain hatred for *the Hun,*

Known only as nightly whines, searchlights, thuds, bomb-sites.
Might he not, like Aeneas, have reasons
(Insufficient, but understandable) for what he did?
I found it hard to remember which side

I was on, argued endlessly at home,
Once, rashly, in a bus, and had to be defended
By mother from a war-widow. *Careless talk
Costs lives* warned the posters. I had no secrets

To offer, but acquired a habit of
Permanent secrecy, never admitted
How I hated the wolf-whistling lorry-loaded
Soldiers, passing me *en route* to D-day.

WASHING-UP

(*for Hilda Cotterill*)

Our mother, hater of parties and occasions,
Made much of the washing-up after. It became an exorcising,
A celebration. Outsiders gone, the kitchen choked
With leftovers, disordered courses, mucky fiddly forks,
The alarming best glasses. She worked a system,
A competition. First we stacked the mess
In regular order: glasses, cutlery, plates
(Each in their kind); saucepans and base things last.

Then we began. She washed, I wiped; to the first to finish,
The prize of *putting-away*. A wiper-up
Should finish first. I never did, for mother
Slaved in a bacchic frenzy, scattering Vim
And purity, splashing new libations
Of suds and scalding water, piling with exquisite fingers
(Unringed for the occasion) the china in ranks,

Knives all together. I was made slow by her passion.
And as we worked she sang. My doughty mother –
Who lived through wars and took life seriously,
Never read fiction, seldom laughed at jokes –
My sorcerer-mother sang grand opera,
Parodied makeshift words and proper music.
Softly awoke her heart, without too much bathos,
But *Samso-o-o-n* got her going, and she never
Took *Trovatore* seriously: *Ah, I have sighed to rest me*

Deep in the quiet grave she'd serenade
The carving-knife, from that a short step
To saucepans and the Jewel Song: *Marguerita, this is not I*
High-born maiden I must be, high-born maiden . . .
Her mezzo skidding along coloratura country,
My laughter rattling the stacks. The men
Came down to hear. And as she nipped
Between cupboards (having won), she added the footwork
Of humbler songs: *Home James, and don't spare*
The horses. This night has been ruin for me. Home James,
And don't spare the horses. I'm ruined as ruined can be
With a pert little mime. She liked these ruined maids,
Or about to be. *No! No! A thousand times no!*
You cannot buy my caress. No! No! A thousand times no!
I'd rather die than say yes. But her feet denied it.

Lastly when all was done, her party-piece
True to the self she seldom let us see:
I feel so silly when the moon comes out . . .
Then, everything purged and placed, we'd go to bed.

O I remember my magical mother dancing
And singing after the party, under the airer
With the used tea towels hanging up to dry.

EATING OUT

Adventures into rehearsed but unknown living,
Table napkin tucked conscientiously under chin.

Choice of cutlery supervised, menu explained.
So much good behaviour was indigestible;

Mother took me outside to recover. Later,
Father introduced London cuisine:

How to handle *moules marinière*, not
To eat all the *petits fours*, or pocket them for later.

When the proper time came, he initiated me
Into the ritual consumption of lobster.

My last outing with him: teacakes in
A Petworth teashop. He leaned heavy on my arm,

But did the ordering. Mother died older, later;
I never accustomed myself to this autocrat's

Humble *I'll have whatever you're having, dear.*

7301

Learning to read you, twenty years ago,
Over the pub lunch cheese-and-onion rolls.

Learning you eat raw onions; learning your taste
For obscurity, how you encode teachers and classrooms

As *the hands, the shop-floor;* learning to hide
The sudden shining naked looks of love. And thinking

The rest of our lives, the rest of our lives
Doing perfectly ordinary things together – riding

In buses, walking in Sainsbury's, sitting
In pubs eating cheese-and-onion rolls,

All those tomorrows. Now twenty years after,
We've had seventy-three hundred of them, and

(If your arithmetic's right, and our luck) we may
Fairly reckon on seventy-three hundred more.

I hold them crammed in my arms, colossal crops
Of shining tomorrows that may never happen,

But may they! Still learning to read you,
To hear what it is you're saying, to master the code.

OLD MAN, OLD MAN

He lives in a world of small recalcitrant
Things in bottles, with tacky labels. He was always
A man who did-it-himself.

Now his hands shamble among clues
He left for himself when he saw better,
And small things distress: *I've lost the hammer.*

Lifelong adjuster of environments,
Lord once of shed, garage and garden,
Each with its proper complement of tackle,

World authority on twelve different
Sorts of glue, connoisseur of nuts
And bolts, not good with daughters

But a dab hand with the Black and Decker,
Self-demoted in your nineties to washing-up
After supper, and missing crusted streaks

Of food on plates; have you forgotten
The jokes you no longer tell, as you forget
If you've smoked your timetabled cigarette?

Now television has no power to arouse
Your surliness; your wife could replace on the walls
Those pictures of disinherited children,

And you wouldn't know. Now you ramble
In your talk around London districts, fretting
At how to find your way from Holborn to Soho,

And where is Drury Lane? Old man, old man,
So obdurate in your contracted world,
Living in almost-dark, *I can see you,*

You said to me, *but only as a cloud.*
When I left, you tried not to cry. I love
Your helplessness, you who hate being helpless.

Let me find your hammer. Let me
Walk with you to Drury Lane. I am only a cloud.

QUEUEING OUTSIDE THE JEU DE PAUME IN LIGHT RAIN

If you were here
I'd ask the smiling African
In my slow-motion French what makes his birds
Rattle their paper wings, and fly, and fall
Beside his hand. *Gilly-gilly-gilly,* he woos us all,
Very good, very nice. For you he'd laugh,
And tell.

If you were here
Something profound about his airy art,
The art we queue for under our umbrellas,
Would bounce between us, jokily. You'd note

The grace of our neighbours' passing-the-time conversation
(*Mind you, Muriel says it's always raining in Paris,*
And she lives here).

I have grown expert on your absences. I know
How things would differ, how the resolute
Mock-bird would tangle frailly with my feet,
And how you'd buy it, just because it did,
And you were there.

DIFFICILIOR LECTIO

'thaes ofereode, thisses swa maeg'
(*Deor*)

Absence is incontinent. It leaves
Shaming wet patches in obvious places.
Some people cry easily. I am one.

Not you.

Study of Old English, under legendary masters,
I took to be an advantage. So many years later
That all I can safely remember is a *hwaet* or so,
I can't eliminate the aura of authority,

Claim to understand the ancestral mind,
How it was always defeat that moved them; how, if the hero
Killed a dragon or two, there was always
A final one coming; how to be on the winning side

Was dull, and also misleading. You, who read translations,
Speak humbly of their world. I catch you
House-training the dragon, my absence, with small

Jokes, diet of liver and onions, digging
A vegetable patch, reading my old books.

Why, I ask, *why the Anglo Saxons?*

Because, you said, *they understand exile.*

LOOKING FOR JORVIK

Veterans swap yarns about how long they queued
In the rain to see Tutankhamun.

Sweet summer York is nothing. They dip alertly
Into the dark, the time capsule. (*No dogs,*

Smoking, ice-cream, cameras.) History
Breathes them in, past *Pack up your troubles,*

Puffing billies, factory acts, perukes, Marston Moor,
(*Have you got a sweety, Geoffrey love?*)

Mendicant friars, the Black Death, through the one
Date everybody knows, to the ancestral

Mutter and reek. This is then, now. We are
Where it was, it is. *(There's a man as big*

As a troll at the door.) Here the foundations are,
Pit, mud, stumps, the endless tons of bones,

Tiny dark plum stones of Viking York.
(And he said *I dabbled my blade in*

Bloodaxe's boy.) At this level the appalling
Icelander Egil who must not be killed at night

(Night-killings are murder) saved his neck by his
Head-Ransom song next day. And got off.

As we do, in the souvenir shop. *That wouldn't*
Interest me. But for someone like Barbara,

Who's a real intellectual . . . She was an English teacher,
You know. T shirts, baseball caps, keyrings, tapestry kits,

Activity packs proclaim *Eric Bloodaxe Rules OK.* And I
Have unearthed my own past under Jorvik's shaft,

Changing trains twenty years ago on York station at midnight
Among kit-bagged soldiers, on my way to you, thinking suddenly:

I am on my way to life.

Note: In 948, Egil had been shipwrecked off the Yorkshire coast, and knew
he could expect no mercy from Eric Bloodaxe, who ruled York, because he
had killed Eric's son. The rules of that society prevented Eric from having
Egil put to death at once, because he had arrived after dark, so Egil was
given the chance of composing overnight his Head-Ransom song
(20 stanzas in praise of Eric). This, because it was so brilliant, forced Eric to
grant Egil his life.

DEAR TRUE LOVE

Leaping and dancing
Means to-ing and fro-ing;
Drummers and pipers –
Loud banging and blowing;
Even a pear-tree
Needs room to grow in.

Goose eggs and gold top
When I'm trying to slim?
And seven swans swimming?
Where could they swim?

Mine is a small house,
Your gifts are grand;
One ring at a time
Is enough for this hand.

Hens, colly birds, doves –
A gastronome's treat.
But love, I did tell you,
I've given up meat.

Your fairy-tale presents
Are wasted on me.
Just send me your love
And set all the birds free.

CONFESSIO AMANTIS

Because I know who you are
Up to a point: – you are
Martha, who feels ashamed
Of merely doing; Atlas
Who uncomplaining keeps off the fearful
Skies from the cringing earth
With the palms of his hands
For ever, without mentioning it, so that he appears
To be a mountain rather than a man;
Martha, the handyman of the Lord,
Up to a point;
              therefore to you
I will confess my own name. I am Dog
Who loves mankind but must also
Bark at the gate; I am Dragon,
Mythical, absurd, with wings; I am also

Watchman, who waketh, generally without a clue
Of what he waketh for; and I am Spy,
Watchman's other self, the double agent,
The fifth column who has lost touch
With the other four. And I am the fifth column
(Which is unnecessary) who is the Fool,
Full of wise saws and modern instances,
Babbling away irrelevant, incoherent,
In the world's apocalyptic thunderstorm

Up to a point.

HOMING IN

Somewhere overseas England are struggling
On a sticky wicket; somewhere in Europe
An elder statesman is dying *adagio*; and here,
Nowhere precisely, I slip to pips and bens
Through the occupied air.

Somewhere along this road an invisible ditch
Signals tribe's end, an important mutation of [Λ];
Somewhere among these implacable place-names
People are living coherent lives. For me the unfocused
Landscape of exile.

Somewhere along this watershed weather
Will assert itself, swap wet for dry,
Scribble or flare on windscreens, send freak gusts
Sneaking round juggernauts, ravel traffic with
A long foggy finger.

Home starts at Birmingham. Places
Where I have walked are my auguries:
The stagey Malverns, watery sharp Bredon,
May Hill's arboreal quiff. These as I pass
Will bring me luck if they look my way.

I should be rehearsing contingencies,
Making resolutions, allowing for change
In the tricky minor modes of love. But,
Absorbed by nearly-home names,
Dear absurd Saul, Framilode, Frampton-on-Severn,

I drop, unprepared, into one particular
Parish, one street, one house, one you,
Exact, ignorant and faithful as swallows commuting
From Sahara to garage shelf.

TEACHER'S CHRISTMAS

It's not so much the ones whose cards don't come,
Friends of one's parents, old distinguished colleagues
Who taught the colonies and, retiring home,
Did a spot of dignified coaching. Their sudden silence
Is a well-bred withdrawing, not unexpected.

But those who move from address to more sheltered address,
Whose writing gutters gently year by year,
Whose *still hoping to see you again* after *love*
Is bluff; or those who write after Christmas
Because *cards are so expensive now.* Ah those, how those

Punctiliously chart their long decline.
The stages grow familiar, like disease.
First it's *my dauntless Mini, less staunch now,*
But I could come by bus, with sandwiches.
I shall enjoy the jaunt.

WEA classes go. Then television
Becomes remote, and radio's
Hard for the hard of hearing. Still they write,
They write at Christmas. Prithee, good death's-heads,
Bid me not remember mine end.

Season as well of cards from brilliant girls,
A little less incisive every year,
Reporting comings, goings: another Hannah,
Another Jamie; another husband going off; and
Writing my thesis is like digging a well with a pin.

You, the storm-troopers of a newer, better world.

Down with you, holly. Come down, ivy.

S. MARTIN'S COLLEGE, LANCASTER

(for Robert Clayton)

Sword into felt-tip, Mars into Martin
The Oxfam saint. It's true about plough-shares:
Almost anything warlike, kept long enough,

Rusts into use. Armoury was where library is,
Since books are dangerous as bayonets,
And keep their point longer. Where officers

And gentlemen once toasted *The King the Duke*,
Bragged about whores and horses, the soft
Uncritical hum of the photocopier, plans

For peaceful teaching practice manoeuvres
In Morecambe. Inside the compound the urgent
Dilatory promenade of study, irregular presence

Of willow and flowering crab, where other ranks
Stamped their exact angles, angled their eyes
As the sergeant told them. Gone, all gone.

Now on the barrack square the chapel's shaft,
Collecting eyes like an after-dinner hostess,
Suggests a move elsewhere; in the keep now

TV's inhuman eye invigilates. Only the dumb
Dangling ghost of the suicidal batman
Still persists, and the guard-room dogs,

Nab de Cordova and Bob, unfailing garrison,
In their regimental graves, in the old tradition.
Two chiselled Lancashire roses. No flag; not a drum.

IN RESIDENCE

(for Anita Mason)

Watcher by the wordhoard, waiting
Alone for the lightning, the long night
When patterns show plain as parsley
And pen knows its way along paper;

Sentry over old songs and nothing-special,
Exiled to not-explaining, expected to do well,
Sentenced to endless hospitality of the innocent,
Trying not to bite, to be human;

Envier of other lives, evenly earthed
In mothers-in-law, milkmen, catchment areas,
Of their open fires, elderly cats, allotments,
So solidly dictated by the district;

Alien uncamouflaged and only,
Constant odd number at the kindly tables,
Idle, inquisitive, untrustworthy;

The writer wriggles inside the residence.

GOING DOWN

(for Kate Macher)

Who in the library dump books and stand as if waiting.
Ten minutes later still standing, still as if waiting.

Ending's an art. In symphonies, those slamming
Incontrovertible chords cue in the cheers.

Three years' Top Twenties will always conjure up
This place, these no-more selves. Initiation

Would make it easier: clowning in fancy dress,
Vigil, carnival, balloons going up and away.

Instead, a formal dinner: bare backs, bow ties,
I pray you be upstanding . . . comic speech by the Bursar.

A disco, too loud for truth, too bright for facing eyes.
Swapping addresses with friends they won't be writing to.

Tutors are no help. Hands clasped guiltily, knowing
How much failure lies in the sweat between palms.

A heatwave now is inexcusable. Buildings
Preen in the sun, and first years sprawl on lawns.

No, I haven't exactly got a job . . . *to find myself* . . .
We're neither of us sure . . . Cloud nine should be close,

But all that's heard is a quiet voice saying
I think I ought to go and get a bottle of wine,

And parents are waiting at home with questions:
Well, what is it you've got? What's a Two-One, then?

OFF SICK

Regime of the house: the sun's morning
Tour, his unsuspected finger on a dim corner.

The house is not primed for my presence. I intrude
On its private life. Forgive me, house,

My excuse is fever. You can disregard me.
If I were myself I should not be here.

My true world is dancing to its own
Metronome: mail, first clinic, coffee-break,

FEM's letters. Someone there is being me,
Not perfectly, I hope. I sweat to think

They imagine me malingering, may fancy
I enjoy this fretting leisure, place of estrangement.

RESIGNATION LETTER

I am cartographer of the dull incline
Which all who visit choose to leave and forget.

I am on nodding terms with explorers of
The Rolandic Fissure, the Optic Chiasm, the Island of Reil.

I can guide the helpless to the lavatory,
The patients' canteen, the bus back to the centre.

I can interpret the hieroglyphs of initiates.
In the R 1/2 sphere the 9–10 Hz alpha rhythm

At 30–60 uv in amp. means nothing to me,
But I can decode it. My name is Pomp.

Circumstance is what I am paid to prevent.
It's all very well for you. Your sex life

Is probably all right is the sort of thing patients want
To shout at consultants. My job: to ensure that they don't.

I am keeper of keys and secrets. I am familiar
With high IQs and low grade mental defectives.

I am acquainted with the smells of grief,
Panic, obsession, incontinence, apathy.

I understand the meaning of expensive florists' bouquets
On patients' birthdays, and no visitors.

I know how to speak to ambulance men:
Flattery, gratitude, abject femininity. Never cap their jokes.

I have composed a full scale commination service
For those who interrupt receptionists' coffee breaks,

Or say *Easy for some*. It is not easy.
I know too much, remember too much. It is time to go.

TRAVELLING MAN

Wonderful where you can go nowadays
(He says). Where you can go,
What you can learn. It wer Portugal
This year for us (he says).

Now the wife, she gets a bit bored like
Wi' culture. But me,
I wanted to see Wellington's campaign
Int' flesh, you might say.

'Course, being a package tour, we only
Went where they took us.
But magic places, magic. Porto, now,
And Jerez. I liked Jerez.

Last year it wer Italy. Vesuvius
(All that lava, y'know) and Pompey,
And Rome. Wonderful, wonderful!
And Sorrento. What a name!

I couldn't lie about on beaches
(He says). I like to see t'sights.
But I feel guilty about th'owd uns.
They din't ave these chances.

Me grandparents, y'know. I feel guilty
They din't see this,
They din't gerrabout. Me grandmother,
When she cum from Blackpool to see us,

She allus said *I have to be ome at night*
To get t'meat (cheap cuts, that were, y'know).
She wouldn't ave wanted. And me mother,
She just laughs at me feelin guilty.

She says *Your father ud never*
Sleep in a strange bed.

SUNDERLAND POINT AND RIBCHESTER

Sunderland Point, where sea, wind, sky
Dispute dominion, on a spur of land
So bitter that you'd think no one would take
The trouble to go there.

Here SAMBO lies,
A faithful NEGRO, who (attending his Mafter
From the Weft Indies) DIED
On his Arrival at Sunderland.

It is, of course, unconsecrated ground.

Now children stagger here on pilgrimage,
Their offerings the sort of things you'd find
On a pet's grave: a cross of driftwood, lashed
With binder-twine; a Woolworth vase,
Chocked up with grit and pebbles, crammed
With dead wild flowers.

                    Sam lies very low.
You can allow him any voice you like.
Despair, pneumonia, exile, love, are variously
Thought to have killed him. A good place
To bring the kids in summer at weekends.

Ribchester had a stone, now lost.
Camden preserved the proper idiom:
By this earth is covered she who was once
Aelia Matrona, who lived 28 years, 2 months,
And 8 days, and Marcus Julius Maximus,
Her son, who lived 6 years, 3 months,
And 20 days.

                  A place to bring the kids.

Children are the most authentic
Pilgrims, having farthest to go, and knowing
Least the way.

                The Romans understood
The use and pathos of arithmetic.
And the Ribble bites its banks, and the sea gnaws at the shore.
So many patterns gone, the *faithful slave,* the *son*
Most dutiful to his father. The word
Strives to be faithful, but the elements
Are against it.

                We are all exiles, Sam,
From the almost-forgotten country
Before the divorce, before the failed exam,
Before the accident, before the white man came.

Your situation's more extreme than most,
But we all of us, all of us seek
That country. And you, who so clearly were not
Your own man, lying in no man's land,
A journey's end for children, seem in your muteness
To be meaning something.
Alternative:
The massive Roman formulas: *the century*
Of Titius built 27 feet . . .
. . . According to the reply of the god.

FIRST FLIGHT

Plane moves. I don't like the feel of it.
In a car I'd suspect low tyre pressure.

A sudden swiftness, earth slithers
Off at an angle. The experienced solidly

    This is rather a short hop for me

Read *Guardians*, discuss secretaries,
Business lunches. I crane for the last of dear

    I'm doing it just to say I've done it

Familiar England, motorways, reservoir,
Building sites. Nimble tiny disc, a sun

    Tell us when we get to water

Runs up the porthole and vanishes.
Under us the broad meringue kingdom

    The next lot of water'll be the Med

Of cumulus, bearing the crinkled tangerine stain
That light spreads on an evening sea at home.

> *You don't need an overcoat, but*
> *It's the sort of place where you need*
> *A pullover. Know what I mean?*

We have come too high for history.
Where we are now deals only with tomorrow,
Confounds the forecasters, dismisses clocks.

> *My last trip was Beijing. Know where that is?*
> *Beijing. Peking, you'd say. Three weeks there, I was.*
> *Peking is wrong. If you've been there*
> *You call it Beijing, like me. Go on, say it.*

Mackerel wigs dispense the justice of air.
At this height nothing lives. Too cold. Too near the sun.

CARTHAGE: AN HISTORICAL GUIDE

'Dux femina facti' (Aeneid 1, 264)
'A woman led the exploit' (tr. C. Day Lewis)

Respect the time! she cautions, *respect the time!*
In all my years as guide, I lose only one person.
Now you must synchronise your watches.

Wheat grows between oranges. Massive lemon trees
Bow under yellow heavyweights. Vines in March,
Pruned grasping gnarls.

Story of Dido and the bullhide.
She was intelligent! (meaning – almost French).
The Romans emerge without credit,

Irrational, short-memoried. *They hated this place!*
The ten-day holocaust, the sowing with salt,
The solemn imprecations,

And then they went and rebuilt it. *Next came the Vandals,*
And you can forget those people for history.
As for today, we should notice

Very wild driving what the Tunisians do.
They have the mirror to look at the hair,
Not at the car behind.

They are poor, we must understand. *You have money,*
You can live. If not, it is for you
Bread and olives.

The Phoenicians she approves. Child sacrifice, certainly,
But only in the best families, and
It was for the Commerce.

We are to read *Salammbô*, distinguished work
Of Flaubert, celebrated novelist
(Who was, of course, French).

Now at La Goulette we must notice flamingos,
Men trawling snails, the Turkish fort where Christians
Scorched until sold,

And finally, Dido's headland, where she flared
Into legend. Not, we are glad to learn,
For frail Aeneas' sake,

But prudently, as a true Frenchwoman would,
For the Commerce, so that her people might be briefly sure
Of olives, freedom, bread.

TERMINAL FEELINGS

Like coming late to a tough public schooL
They all know the rules except me,
And watch my mistakes coldly, knowingly.

I am body-searched. Judiciously she avoids
My erogenous zones, takes my word

That the bulge in my pocket is four pens:
Even as a terrorist not taken seriously.

I will not ask my way to the Ladies
Of blackhaired silent women or smiling brown men.

A prefect takes pity on me in the Duty Free,
Where expert hands clutch Harrods carriers,

Cases of Glenfiddich, smoked salmon sandwiches.
I emerge with a film, a blush, an orange juice.

Authority intones a lesson of boarding tickets and gates.
The native language sounds kinder in French:
Priez vous présenter . . .

Everyone approachable proves incomprehensible.
Why does no one want my passport?

Surely the air-hostesses will be
Miss Temples of the air, gentle, wise,

Offering me toilet facilities and hot
Buttered toast, cut small? But no,

They are sweet-centred Tunisian dates,
Smilers only at men.

RAG TRADE

(for Diana Hendry)

Winter is exclusive. Such shape-defining whiteness
Can be worn only by the fine-boned, the unsoiled.

Spring is proverbially cruel. That special yellow
Kills all but the most invincible complexions.

And the variations on green that summer
Unendingly designs. Redheads alone can live with them.

But autumn, with her Blood-and-Bile range,
Her crêpy textures. We all gravitate to her house.

OF MUTABILITY

(for Meg)

Granted the fragility of Maran chicks,
New goslings, a twelve-year-old willing dog,
An arthritic right hand; granted the staying power

Of dock, cow-parsley, slurry; of this world's weather,
The helm wind. There is also a knack
Of enduring. This house was built because of it.
And since vocation hauled you unceremoniously
Here, from all the usual sweet concerns of life,
To breathe among curlews, between limestone and sandstone,
I see that something is expected of you here.

Cats will kill swallows; the finite scenes
Of birth and death recur. But things done,
Meals cooked, fires lit, trees planted, words said,

Poems observed, have their own posterity,
Though dreams may deny it. In such cold harbours
What's done is meant, and being meant, it stays.

M.S.

There is a small dead tree in the aviary
For them to perch on. But the aviary's closed.
(*Too cold yet, I suppose,* she says, though we're drinking
Tea in the garden.) Two and a half pair,

Dippers, rollers, a single red canary, waiting
To be found a mate; they have all chosen
To sing in their cage. From three in the morning
They're at it: opera, jazz, chorale –

Better, he says, *than yer nightingale, any day.*
I'd set 'em free, she tells me quietly, *only I know*
They wouldn't live. She sees I find her hard
To understand. Precise control has left
Her lips and tongue. She pitches as she lumbers

The deck of her world, the trim new stairless house.
The canaries are nesting, their young are hatched.
She tells me she can't bear to look at them.
I watch her lifting her *stupid* left leg

Into a new position. He spends
A lot of time in the garden. The new small pond
Is his work, where the fine fat red fish swim.
Evening: the birds are chanting a sort of requiem.

BRONWEN

Not an exacting shopping-list: lambs,
Birds, wildflowers, a walk, a whiff
Of Gloucestershire's April. She'd scraped together
A day for it, came provided
With entrance fee: whisky she couldn't afford,

We guessed. Not little Nell, remotely pathetic,
But tough Aussie Bron from her Brixton squat,
Wasting her wits in a clerical dead-end,
Horizon the push-bike's two-mile circuit,
Her calling the comrades, the Party, the Trots.

So we walked. She played childhood,
Mystified lambs with human bleating,
Frisked a hill-top folly, scaled drystone walls
(Sorting out the wool trade, of course, quick to note
Capitalist mansions; but cryptic violets too).

Bit short on graffiti round here?
Shot all the vandals, have they?

I introduced dog's mercury. Germander speedwell
She found for herself. How did she know it?
None grows in Brisbane, not much in Brixton.

'Speedwell, shy blue flower of the hedgerow
With the white eye,' she said. I just knew it.
Spent most of my life reading Brontës and that lot.
They're always on about your countryside, your flowers,
Sorta thing you don't forget, she said.

UNAUTHORISED VERSION

(*for Elma Mitchell*)

'Martha was cumbered about much serving, and came to him, and
said, Lord, dost thou not care that my sister hath left me to serve
alone? bid her therefore that she help me. And Jesus answered and
said unto her, Martha, Martha, thou art careful and troubled about
many things: but one thing is needful: and Mary hath chosen that
good part.' St Luke 10, vv. 38-42

Of course he meant it kindly. I know that.
I know Josh – as well as anyone can know
The Son of God. All the same, he slipped up
Over this one. After all, a Son is only a son
When you come to think about it. And this
Was between sisters. Marty and me,
We understand each other. For instance, when Lazzie died,
We didn't need to spell it out between us,
Just knew how to fix the scenario
So Josh could do his bit – raising Lazzie, I mean,
From the dead. He has his own way of doing things,
Has to muddle people first, so then the miracle
Comes as a miracle. If he'd just walked in
When Lazzie was ill, and said *OK, Lazzie,
You're off the sick list now* – that'd have lacked *impact.*
But all this weeping, and groaning, and moving of stones,
And praying in public, and Mart saying *I believe etcetera,*
Then *Lazarus, come forth!* and out comes Lazzie
In his shroud. Well, even a halfwit could see
Something out of the ordinary was going on.
But this *was* just ordinary. A lot of company,
A lot of hungry men, not many helpers,
And Mart had a go at me in front of Josh,
Saying *I'm all on my own out there. Can't you
Tell that sister of mine to take her finger out,*

And lend a hand? Well, the thing about men is,
They don't realise how *temperamental* good cooks are.
And Mart is very good. Believe you me.
She was just blowing her top. No harm in it.
I knew that. But then Josh gives her
This monumental dressing-down, and really,
It wasn't fair. The trouble with theology is, it features
Too much miraculous catering. Those ravens feeding Elijah,
For instance. I ask you! They'd have been far more likely
To *eat* him. And all those heaven-sent fast-food take-aways –
Quail, and manna, and that. And Josh himself –
The famous fish-butty picnic, and that miraculous
Draught of fishes. What poor old Mart could have done with
Was a miraculous draught of coffee and sandwiches
Instead of a ticking-off. And the men weren't much help.
Not a *thank you* among them, and never a thought
Of help with the washing-up.

Don't get me wrong. Of course I love Josh,
Wonder, admire, believe. He knows I do.
But to give Marty such a rocket
As if she was a Pharisee, or that sort of type,
The ones he has it in for. It wasn't right.
Still, Josh himself, as I said – well, he *is* only
The Son of God, not the Daughter; so how could he know?
And when it comes to the truth, I'm Marty's sister.
I was there; I heard what was said, and
I knew what was meant. The men will write it up later
From their angle, of course. But this is me, Mary,
Setting the record straight.

GAUDY LADIES

The pianist is young, appassionata. She has anarchist's hair.
She flings bright splinters of music, she glitters with promise.

They sit, dazed by *saumon, contrefilet,*
Vacherine aux fraises, delicacies their post-war non-youth

Never imagined, sit tired, the kind faces ready but blurred.
Were they once bright, savage? Was the easily manageable hair

Once eloquent? Did it get kissed in the bike sheds
At 11.15 curfew? Will her face acquire

Their lined sockets, their patient bones,
Their willingness to try to understand? O once they were

Rash, lovely, courted; I wondered at their verve,
Their Bodleian love-letters, unsolicited roses, the skeletons

They hung as knockers on their doors.

NATIVITIES

Godlings are born racily.

They are excavated
Into life by the strong licks
Of the world-cow, suckled
By goats, mares, wolves.

Blossom of oak, blossom of broom,
Blossom of meadowsweet
Go to their making.

They erupt through the paternal
Skull fully armed, hatch from an egg,
Or appear, foam-born,
In Cyprus, in a shell,
Wearing a great deal of hair

And nothing else.
This one arrived
At the time of the early lambs
By means of the usual channels.

GARDEN PLANNING

The garden seeds itself, and weaves and spins
A web, a maze, a snare.

Below becomes the way in, where hunting
Buttercups throttle with

Claw feet, and bindweed is biding its time,
Dangling slack as a noose.

More civilized mint advances neatly,
Pawn by indigo pawn.

Violent foxgloves gang up in crannies;
They have rape in their heads.

Limp goosegrass forces its mucous kisses
On more upright neighbours,

And nettle, straightforward barbarian,
Blots opposition

With a wag of green beards. Only tulips
Counter-attack, steadfast

And stiff as the Old Guard at Waterloo,
Erect, correct, scarlet,

Stalking above the delinquent chaos
With their formal statement

That somebody once created this garden,
And there was a design.

UNFINISHED CHRONICLE

(for Mick North and Janni Howker)

1. 1938
A slack year on the estate, the men
Hanging about idle. Mrs Pretty set them
To dig the heathy tumps outside the garden.

> In this year the Germans marched
> Into Austria, and they held it.

Basil, the one with the gift, *had a profound feeling*
(Says authority) *for the local soil.* Grew wedded to it.
If e'd ad is bed (says gardener Jack), *e'd ave slept
Out there in the trench.*

> In this year also wise rulers in Europe
> Met at Munich and spoke for peace.

Three mounds opened. Strange things found
In a boatgrave. *I was a green hand*
(Says Jack), *didn't rightly understand*
The value of the things.

2. 1939
      In this year Adolf the leader sent men
      Into Bohemia, and they held it.

They trenched the highest barrow, found
The bows of a great ship. Experts came,
Under the darkening skies of the world, to see
What hid at Sutton Hoo.

      In this year also the men of Italy
      Marched into Albania, and they held it.

The archaeologist spoke. *We might*
As well have a bash (said he, being young),
So a bash was what we had.

In the Bull pub at Woodbridge they stayed,
Clever, lanky young men with pre-war haircuts;
Eminent, emeritus now, with their pasts behind them,

Retired, superseded, dead. And the gold
Came out of the earth bright and shining
As the day it went in.

      In this year also Adolf the leader
      And Benedict the leader swore to keep faith.
      Men called it the pact of steel.

The winds of that year blew Redwald's flaked bones
Over the fields of his kingdom. Gold leaf also

Floated away in that weather.
Potent treasures were packed in boxes and tins
Scrounged from chemists and grocers. It was all borne
From the great ship by an elderly Ford
Which ran out of petrol outside the gates
Of the British Museum.

In this year also the men of Russia swore
That they would not fight against the Germans.
Both sides set their hands to it.

Learned clerks counted and cossetted
The awesome things, and they were stacked
In Aldwych underground for the duration.

In this year also the men of Germany
Marched into Poland, and they held it.
Then the rulers of England and France,
Who were handfast, defied the Germans,
And there was open war.

Long enough ago.

Now Mrs Pretty is dead, who loyally gave
The royal lot to the nation. Gardener Jack
And brown-fingered Basil died too, no doubt;
We have no records of them. But high to this day
In Londonchester looms the High King's regalia,
Sword, sceptre, shield, helm, drinking horns and harp,
Patched and polished, explained, made innocent, aimless.

Behind glass, air-conditioned, they wait in their own way
For what comes next:
                another inhumation?
                        another finding?
                                another year?

NECK-VERSE

1992

AS WELL AS THE BIBLE AND SHAKESPEARE ... ?

You are what   I would choose

      for companion in the desert.
      You would know the way out,
      think providently about water.

      in the solicitor's office.
      You would have generous answers
      for disagreeable contingencies.

      on the motorway.
      In your presence
      I shouldn't notice tailbacks.

      at the picnic.
      You would have remembered matches,
      have brought a surprise for the greedy.

      at the funeral.
      You would speak gently with mourners,
      but your hands would be warm with life.

BRAUNEBERG ON THE RIVER MOSEL

A place born with a vocation
Should accept with grace, and not be curious.

Long-headed Romans recognized the gift:
Earth, water, wood, fire, frost and dawdling spring.

Since then names repetitive as a stammer
Have done the right things at the proper seasons,

Laid down now in their vaults under marigold and fuschia,
Licht, Zimmer, Boujong, Link. Not families, but years,

The human vintage. These bodies knew their uses:
Bend forward to dig, to harvest; lean back to swallow, to sing.

It is as easy as being a cat. A young one
Comes socially towards me, purring in German.

Perhaps he is of Roman descent; he seems untroubled
By my accent. We are person and cat. He has lemon eyes.

Yes, there is evil around. Weather is always chancy,
And blight of various sorts. The heirs

Are called away to die in other vineyards.
But endurance is here. Vocation demands it.

The mystery continues like the cat's descent,
The neatly decanted dead, the know-all river.

BACK TO THE FRONT

I remember too much here. Michaelmas daisies
Butterfly-bushed in September; ceanothus
That got above itself, the derelict caravan
Where I ate cheese and wrote on used paper.
A scorched-earth policy has scotched the lot.

Instead there are new toys, compact, intense,
User-unfriendly. The photocopier will mug me
If I face it alone. The phone is tapped

By a sharp inquisitor, who calculates my fear.
This wallpaper, with its lilt of country kitchens,
Was chosen to deceive.

O *you haven't changed!* say the ones who knew me
(Wanting not to have changed themselves).
But I have. I am older and more frightened.
Sophisticated engines run free in the kitchen,
Only the patients still huddle and fumble, and somewhere
Someone is still screaming.

And I ought to have been here yesterday,
They tell me, for six-foot Laura's language.
Words Averil had never heard before . . . We had to explain them.
The police had to come. *Yes,* they say, *yes,*
You would have enjoyed yesterday.

(Would I have ever enjoyed yesterday? Was I,
Before I went away, so good at relishing
The anger of the helpless, such an eaves-dropper
On misery? I suppose I was. I suppose that
Was how I lived, semi-attached to despair.)

And still unspoken misery slams through
Prim clinical diction. Doctors alone are still
The privileged, who *think* or *say;* patients
Are back at their old tricks, *claiming,*
Admitting, denying. Still they endure urinary urgency,
Demonstrate gait disturbance, suffer
Massive insults to the brain.

Saddest of all, the one who should remember;
The smart young man, always in and out of good jobs,
With his cavalier lovelocks, his way with women,

Slow, now, and spoiled. He doesn't like the shape
Of twenty-pence pieces. Can I change them for him?
I don't like the shape of your future, Tony.
No magician here can change the currency,
Or the fused charge in your head.

CHILDREN IMAGINING A HOSPITAL

(*for Kingswood County Primary School*)

I would like kindness, assurance,
A wide selection of books;
Lots of visitors, and a friend
To come and see me;
A bed by the window so I could look at
All the trees and fields, where I could go for a walk.
I'd like a hospital with popcorn to eat.
A place where I have my own way.

I would like HTV all to myself
And people bringing tea round on trollies;
Plenty of presents and plenty of cards
(I would like presents of food).
Things on the walls, like pictures, and things
That hang from the ceiling;
Long corridors to whizz down in wheelchairs.
Not to be left alone.

CLERICAL ERROR

My raiment stinks of the poor and the afflicted,
Of those whom healers, in a parody of you,
Have called back to mimic life.

I understand they are yours, and concern
All of us. But I am paid to do other things.
What must I do when Job and his daughters

Cram into my office where they are not allowed,
When I am typing medical reports against the clock,
When they mop and mow at me, seeking comfort?

I can tell you what I do. I address them as *love*
(Which is an insult), and say in a special soothing voice
(Which fools no one), *Go to the nurses, Judith,*

Judith, the nurses are looking for you (which is a lie).
How, Sir, am I to reconcile this with your clear
Instructions on dealing with the afflicted

And the poor? I do not seek to justify
My job description. I did not write it,
But I volunteered to live by its commandments.

THE COMFORTERS

(*for Philip Gross*)

'The night cometh, when no man can work.'
St John 9, v. 4

Because their aim was not comfort, these
Are the comforters. That we find comfort
In what they wrote is our affair,
Not theirs. They never imagined immortality,
But watched each minute instant so hard
That it broke and flowered into ever.

Samuel of London, Gilbert of Selborne,
Francis of Clyro. And many more. Their own lives

By no means easy. We could tell them
The last dates in those diaries,
The hard labour of their dying: *a nest*
Of no less than seven stones in the left kidney;
A nervous cough and a wandering gout;
Peritonitis on a delayed, delightful
Honeymoon, aged thirty-nine.

We prize them
Not for their ends, but for the light
Of their everlasting present. Like them, we wait
For our own particular doomsday. Ours
May be premature, comprehensive. In the meantime, they
Reach down centuries with their accidental
Offer of comfort.

So I choose to believe
The old lie: that we all died normally
Ever after: *suddenly, following*
A road accident; after a long illness
Patiently borne. Not in the monstrous
Nuclear glare, but in the moderate
Darkness and light, darkness and light
That were the evening and the morning
Of the first ever day.

COSTA GERIATRICA

Evening quarters; land
Of the tranquil solo deckchair,
Of the early Ovaltine nightcap.

Here patient shop-assistants
Pick the right change from freckled
Trembling hands, and wrap

Single rashers tenderly. Here gardening
Is dangerous as bull-fights.
Dogs are dwarfish,

Coddled and lethal.
Here sagas are recited
Of long-dead husbands,

Varicose veins, comforting ministers,
Scarcity of large-print library books,
And endless hands of photographs

Of the happily-ever-after children
They make believe they have:
A nice son in the police force

And two lovely children.
Marriages are made in heaven,
For Mr Right not only exists

But arrives on cue. Tragedy
Is reduced to a foot-note: *The husband?*
Oh, he went wrong, or died,

Or something. They have all
Had what they wanted:
A *lovely little square family,*

And now, comforting morticians:
That's the man I want at my funeral,
If anything ever happens to me.

DEAR SIR

(in memory of Dr H. J. Crow)

Body prescribed a comic part for you,
Denied the pallor of those inchless, touchy men
Who terrorise worlds into taking them seriously,

Refused too the surgeon's histrionic profile,
Noble silver forelock, hairless fiddler's fingers.
Made you a shy Scot, haggis-shaped.

Laughter skirts the need for small-talk,
So you made yourself droll. Materialised
Tiptoeing round corners as Quack-in-the-box

(*Aha! Gotcher!*) short stout explosion
Cued to blast off in muffled thuds of laughter,
Your warning note down corridors a drone.

Gracefully at Christmas you accepted your vocation,
Assumed kilt, sporran, funny hat, the lot.
Little Lord Mis-Rule, whose considerate war-whoops

Shrouded your morbid clinical conscience.

But Sir, I accuse you of worrying about patients
After hours; of not sleeping; of irrational fears
For your children; of concealing your DFC courage;
Of inconspicuous valour on behalf of underdogs;
Of exploring humanity's dark places,
And not letting on; of making us all believe
We were curable; of mixing the genres,
Of playing Quixote in Sancho Panza's clothes.

And, Sir, I accuse you of losing heart,
Of not curing that endless queue of incurables,

Blight of Thursday afternoons; of believing they'd vanish
If you shut your eyes and wished.

O Sir, I accuse you of dying at home,
In bed, asleep, without a hint of impaired
Cortical integrity; of failing to present
An interesting case; of leaving no heir

To that florid prose style, to that susceptibility
To *Limehouse Blues* late on Fridays
In a subordinate's subtle hum.
       Dear Sir,
I accuse you of being irreplaceable. By God,
You had a crack at those windmills!

DESCENT

Some unremembered ancestor handed down to me
The practice of walking in darkness.

I didn't ask for it. I didn't want it.
Would choose to be without, if choice could move

The hard *fiat* of genes. I don't like darkness,
Its arbitrary swoops of stairs, its tunnel vaults,

Black bristly air, its emptiness. Others speak
Of the shining end of the tunnel. I haven't seen it.

This is my black. I alone
Am the authority, and I know no further

Than I've got, if that be anywhere.
I inherited no maps. A feckless line.

So I choose you, intransigent old Roman,
As ancestor; who at the City's

Most sinister hour, fathomed the riddle;
Who faced the *it*; who, a man in arms and mounted,

Willingly entered the dark; who worked, however blindly,
However strangely, for good, under the earth. Who worked.

Note: 'Old Roman'. Mettus Curtius. In BC 362 the earth in the Roman forum
gave way. A chasm appeared, and soothsayers said it could only be filled by
throwing in the city's greatest treasure. Mettus Curtius armed himself,
mounted his horse, and leaped in. The earth closed over him.

DIGLIS LOCK

Image of something unknown: dank walls
Where nothing grows but chains; moody
Unreadable water; dog howling near;
Keeper unseen; but we are scrutinized
From above. Then the great gates open
To let us through, and in the half-darkness
I hardly see you, but I know you are smiling.

DOUBLES

Since they're not made to tell truth,
They tell it squintingly. But tell it
They do. Curious beauty's mirror shows her
What the cameraman will never let fans see:
The dark side of the moon.

Light bends in its tracks, and the incompetent
Eye in its orbit walks upside down.

Inside the tunnel the traveller meets
Self not the same in the shadow that mimics
His place in the carriage. Those blurred angles
Are his double, waiting in the wings
Of a parallel but unscheduled journey.

North and south under the great mountains
Lights fizz, picks ferret, men fumble
In the random dark. First they will hear,
Then see, finally touch. *Is that you, brother?* they will say
In a different language.

ELEGY FOR A CAT

'Cats being the least moveable of all animals because of their strong
local predilections; they are indeed in a domesticated state the serfs
of the animal creation, and properly attached to the soil.'
(Southey: *Memoir of the Cats of Greta Hall*)

Yours was the needlework, precise and painful
As claws on a loved naked shoulder, that sewed us
Back into that Merthyr morning, when, terrorised by toddlers,
You mined under our alien gateway, claimed sanctuary
In a jacket pocket.

You were the first to join our outlandish outfit
On that hilltop housing estate, with the garage-in-name-only,
Invisible agog neighbours, rhubarb corms from Aberfan;
You the first source of our logged jokes, with
Your ears akimbo,

Eyes so excited they retreated behind their withers,
Living a paw-to-mouth existence, elbowing your way

Up bodies like a midshipman up rigging
Your whiskers wet with passion, sitting with one ear
In a human mouth, to keep warm.

I was never sure that English was your language,
Though you were probably just as dim in Welsh,
Vague about status, doglike coming to a whistle,
Running on white bandy-legs with a
Welcoming cluck.

You never took offence, were always ready
With an Eskimo kiss of your pink plebeian nose;
Set records for slow learning when we installed
The cat-flap; had no idea of the gravitas
Proper to cats.

Exiled in Gloucestershire, you domesticated
It for us, materialised on preoccupied laps, and,
Mozart-addict, rushed in filthy-footed from
Uprooting lupins, to settle yourself round Primo's collar
When duets began.

Now the heir's installed, she colonises
The outposts (both next-doors, and one further)
Where she's feasted and fêted. Such cunning
Is natural to your prudent race, in case
Of catastrophe,

And I see, dear dead one, how we severed you
From your own earth, how you chose us to be
Your territory. You are there quite often,
Dear tabby blur, in my bad eye's corner. We left you
Nothing to haunt but ourselves.

Haunt us still, dear first-footer,
First to live with us, first to confirm
Us as livers-together, you who took us so simply
For granted, translator of life into
The vernacular of love.

You who saw love, where innocent others
Saw only convenience.

ESCAPING

You were the reader in the family,
Leading me on, through Pooh and Pimpernel,
To Swallows, Amazons, men in boats.

A good pupil, I devoured
My volume a day, *Willows* to *Wuthering,*
Enlisted at the public library, grew

Up to despise your straightbat lending
Library world, where quiet women in cardigans,
Prey to your serious charm, smuggled you

The latest of *your sort.* Thirty years later
I rumble at last your quirky taste
For quiet workers who one day absent-mindedly

Walk out of offices and discover
England. Was this your secret, surfacing only
In books we didn't discuss? While you waited

For death in Worthing, condescendingly I
Played the system for you, collected the ripping
Good yarns by gentlemanly pen-names –

Taffrail, Sapper, Bartimaeus – but drew
My sanctimonious teenage line at Ian Fleming.
Tell me, father, why you chose him for deathbed reading?

And tell me, did you want to walk out of our world?

FAMILIARS

There are two of them. The one that thinks it's a cat
comes at me widdershins, out of the dark,
inches along my spine, claw by implacable claw,
knots itself round my neck, croons in my ear
of things done wrong, of things bound to go wrong,
of the four last things. Seduced by its attentions,
its intimacy, its hoarse plausible cry,
I submit to darkness.

The other's imaginary too. It runs ahead,
as dogs do, stopping sometimes
to check on me. It would like me to throw sticks,
to give it a name. If I did, it would come at my call.
It rubs its silly head against my knees.
Almost I think it loves me,
would show me the way out. I haven't yet decided
what colour it shall be.

GOING UNDER

I turn over pages, you say,
Louder than any woman in Europe.

But reading's my specific for keeping
Reality at bay; my lullaby.

You slip into sleep as fast
And neat as a dipper.
You lie there breathing, breathing.

My language is turn over
Over and over again. I am a fish
Netted on a giveaway mattress,
Urgent to be out of the air.

Reading would help; or pills.
But light would wake you from your resolute
Progress through night.

The dreams waiting for me twitter and bleat.
All the things I ever did wrong
Queue by the bed in order of precedence,
Worst last.

Exhausted by guilt, I nuzzle
Your shoulder. Out lobs
A casual, heavy arm. You anchor me
In your own easy sound.

HALF-PAST TWO

Once upon a schooltime
He did Something Very Wrong
(I forget what it was).

And She said he'd done
Something Very Wrong, and must
Stay in the school-room till half-past two.

(Being cross, she'd forgotten
She hadn't taught him Time.
He was too scared at being wicked to remind her.)

He knew a lot of time: he knew
Gettinguptime, timeyouwereofftime,
Timetogohomenowtime, TVtime,

Timeformykisstime (that was Grantime).
All the important times he knew,
But not half-past two.

He knew the clockface, the little eyes
And two long legs for walking,
But he couldn't click its language,

So he waited, beyond onceupona,
Out of reach of all the timefors,
And knew he'd escaped for ever

Into the smell of old chrysanthemums on Her desk,
Into the silent noise his hangnail made,
Into the air outside the window, into ever.

And then, *My goodness*, she said,
Scuttling in, *I forgot all about you.*
Run along or you'll be late.

So she slotted him back into schooltime,
And he got home in time for teatime,
Nexttime, notimeforthatnowtime,

But he never forget how once by not knowing time,
He escaped into the clockless land of ever,
Where time hides tick-less waiting to be born.

IDYLL

Not knowing even that we're on the way,
Until suddenly we're there. How shall we know?

There will be blackbirds, in a late March evening,
Blur of woodsmoke, whisky in grand glasses,

A poem of yours, waiting to be read; and one of mine;
A reflective bitch, a cat materialized

On a knee. All fears of present and future
Will be over, all guilts forgiven.

Maybe, heaven. Or maybe
We can get so far in this world. I'll believe we can.

KING EDWARD'S FLORA

Your mind commandeers an island.
It seems simple. The neighbours
Are fish, not Christian fretful kings.

But in my halflight rear hulking trees,
Sulky, indigenous. Their names crack
Like an enemy's laugh. Short words, long trees.

It is not simple, cousin. I am the heir.
In me shines the clear claim of Wessex.
But the trees were before. Their roots run back

Below Grendel's forest. Ash was earliest.
Odin carved man from him; then alder,
The spirit tree, whose blood breaks red

Like ours. Alder is old. And guilty aspen,
Our Saviour's hangman, that chronicles Calvary
By a fine tremor in sweet summer air.

Then the holy ones: oak, many-fingered;
Holly, that fights for us against darkness,
And never fades; holy thorn that is quick

In the dead of the year, at birth-time; yew
Slow and sacred, that nothing grows under;
Red-berried rowan, that warns off witches.

Cut-and-come again bushes, hazel and willow;
And walnut the wanderer, tramping north
In the legions' brown fists.

All the bright welter of things
That maim, detain, deceive: bramble and briar,
Furze, moss, reed, rush, sedge; thistle the spearman.

These are my shieldwall. Take them, cousin,
You or Harold. Settle it between you,
For I choose ending: Edward the heirless,

My children the stone forest
At the West Minster. These are the trees
That I make holy. You, I can see,

Will be William of the Wastes.
My woods will not content you.

But take care, cousin. Trees are unchancy.
I say more than I know, being the last –
Son of Bad Counsel, Edward the healer –

You will plant your dynasty, if Harold lets you,
But the trees will not endure it. Your saplings totter
Under my trees. A red man sprawls, a white ship founders.

The boy from the gorse-bush will snaffle the lot.

A LIFE

I never saw the judge
Who sentenced me.

Foreign, I think. Some curt
Three-letter name

Suggesting deserts. No
Jury, no press,

No public interest.
Court officers,

Professionally kind,
Explained the law

Regarding benefit,
Remission, drugs.

I didn't take it in,
The nightmared don't

Study the science of
Dreaming, just wait

For release. Those having
Nothing to wait

For go on waiting (their
Syntax deranged

As their dreams). My prison
Soon smelt of me,

Became familiar as
A bed. I could

Weep in all its corners.
Books, food, were what

You might expect. No view
From the shutters;

That was fitting. Music
Stabbed me; silence

Was offered. The chaplain
Visited, but

Had been gagged. I was glad.
I saw only

The hand of the warder,
Holding my dish.

Looked no further, knowing
If I explored

From wrist up arm to face
What I should find:

The proud, unalterable
Eyes of love.

MAY 8TH: HOW TO RECOGNIZE IT

The tulips have finished their showy conversation.
Night's officers came briefly to report,
And took their heads off.

The limes have the look of someone
Who has been silent a long time,
And is about to say a very good thing.

Roses grow taller, leafier,
Duller. They have star parts;
Like great actors, they hang about humbly in the wings.

On the lawn, daisies sustain their candid
Childish shout. Hippy dandelions are stoned
Out of their golden minds. And always

The rub-a-dub-dub recapitulation
Of grass blades growing. The plum tree is resting
Between blossom and fruit. Like a poker-player,

She doesn't show her hand. Daffodils
Are a matter of graceless brown leaves and rubber bands.
Wallflowers have turned bony.

This is not the shining childhood of spring,
But its homely adolescence, angular, hypothetical.
How one regrets the blue fingertips staggering
Up from the still dank earth.

NEIGHBOURS

The Collared couple lived at number one,
In the guttering. They were good neighbours,
Kept an orderly house, the missus was always home.
They might have been R.C. Her tender nape
Bent over her brood was slightly Madonna-ish,
And the three notes they chanted all day, all day,
Some kind of psalm?

Ivy made the gable a high-rise ghetto;
The Blackies at 1 b were a racketty lot.
Kept odd hours, zoomed home like motorbikes revving,
Tried to mug the Collareds, at the least excuse
Would scream blue murder, threaten to call the cops.
It was because of them the cat left home.

Our next-door neighbours keep themselves to themselves.
We swap small talk and seedlings over the fence
Sometimes, but not too often. You have to keep
A certain distance.

Two terrorists at large in our neighbourhood
Must have holed up somewhere close. We haven't seen them.
Our neighbours have. *Her*, with her kill,
Standing as if at home on the compost heap,
One foot upraised to pluck. She didn't move,
Outstared them till they backed into the house.

They talk of her yellow eyes, her butcher's poise,
The pigeon bleeding in her taloned fist.

To be a sparrowhawk's neighbour is an honour,
And yet the harmless squabs and fledgling blacks
(Her prey) are neighbours too. We let them be,
And then she guts them for the fluffy brood
She nurtures with the awesome tenderness
We see on television.
                              We don't say this
To our human neighbours, not-quite-friends,
In case they think we're soft. You have to keep
A certain distance.

THE OLD LADY AND THE WEATHER

Raining? Oh dear, you say.
The farmers want it, I correct you,
Look at the garden.
Yes, you say.

Is it fine outside? you ask.

Foggy, I tell you. *There'll be pile-ups*
On motor-ways today.
Oh dear, you say.

Lovely day! you say,
And I, *Rain on the way.*

Why can't you have your own fine indoors weather?
Why must I bring these chills into the house,
When that shape-changer on the other channel
Will have you sooner than you think, you think but never say,
Out in all weathers, ever?

THE POET'S COMPANION

Must be in mint condition, not disposed
To hayfever, headaches, hangovers, hysteria, these being
The Poet's prerogative.

Typing and shorthand desirable. Ability
To function on long walks and in fast trains an advantage.
Must be visible/invisible

At the drop of a dactyl. Should be either
A mobile dictionary, thesaurus and encyclopaedia,
Or have instant access to same.

Cordon bleu and accountancy skills essential,
Also cooking of figures and instant recall of names
Of once-met strangers.

Should keep a good address book. In public will lead
The laughter, applause, the unbearably moving silence.
Must sustain with grace

The role of Muse, with even more grace the existence
Of another eight or so, also camera's curious peeping
When the Poet is reading a particularly

Randy poem about her, or (worse) about someone else.
Ability to endure reproaches for forgetfulness, lack of interest,
Heart, is looked for,

Also instant invention of convincing excuses for what the Poet
Does not want to do, and long-term ability to remember
Precise detail of each.

Must be personable, not beautiful. The Poet
Is not expected to waste time supervising
The Companion. She will bear

Charming, enchanted children, all of them
Variations on the Poet theme, and
Impossibly gifted.

Must travel well, be fluent in the more aesthetic
European languages; must be a Finder
Of nasty scraps of paper

And the miscellany of junk the Poet loses
And needs *this minute, now.* Must be well-read,
Well-earthed, well able

To forget her childhood's grand trajectory,
And sustain with undiminished poise
That saddest dedication: *lastly my wife,*

Who did the typing.

THE RECEPTIONIST TO HER WATCH

Your job: to wake me with your tiny chime
(*De Camptown Racetrack*) at the proper time.
So what possessed you, that Outpatients day,
While I was holding a shaky hand, to come butting in with your
                      endless, heartless *doo dah doo dah dey?*

SUPERANNUATED PSYCHIATRIST

Old scallywag scapegoat has skedaddled,
Retired at last to bridge and both kinds of bird-watching.
No more suspect phone calls from shady acquaintances,
Anonymous ladies and flush-faced Rotarians.

He could always be blamed when case-notes strayed.
(His MG boot? His mistress's bed? We enjoyed guessing.)
How we shall miss his reliable shiftiness,
Wow and flutter on tape, Wimbledon-fortnight illness,

Dr Macavity life. Dear foxy quack,
I relished your idleness, your improvisations,
Your faith in my powers of you-preservation.
Who will shoulder our errors now?

What of your replacement, the new high flyer,
Smelling of aftershave and ambition? Is that tic
Telling us something his mind will arrive at later?
Meantime, I watch his parentheses. A man so much given

To brackets is hedging his bets.

FRIENDS' MEETING HOUSE, FRENCHAY, BRISTOL

When the doors of the house are shut,
Eyes lidded, mouth closed, nose and ears
Doing their best to idle, fingers allowed out
Only on parole; when the lovely holy distractions,
Safe scaffolding of much-loved formulae,
Have been rubbed away; then the plant
Begins to grow. It is hard to rear,

Rare herb of silence, through which the Word comes.
Three centuries of reticent, meticulous lives
Have naturalised it on this ground.

And the herb is the Vine, savage marauder,
That spreads and climbs unstoppably,
Filling the house, the people, with massing insistent shoots
That leaf through windows and doors, that rocket through
                                        chimneys,
Till flesh melts into walking forms of green,
Trained to the wildness of Vine, which exacts
Such difficult witness; whose work is done
In hopeless places, prisons, workhouses,
In countinghouses of respectable merchants,
In barracks, collieries, sweatshops, in hovels
Of driven and desperate men.

                              It begins here
In the ground of silence.

THE MIDDLE PASSAGE

. . . and the sombre absent presences
Of the Middle Passage, of those
Who never saw Bristol; who were sold
On the Guinea Coast for cloth,
Jet, beads, muskets, spirits, trinkets
And other things accepted by the Moors;
Who were shipped like cattle, the Males
Kept apart from the Females, and handcuffed
(Bristol ships triple such as are sturdy,
With Chains round their Necks);
Who never saw Bristol; who were sold

In Jamaica, Barbados, Antigua, St Kitts,
Virginia, Carolina, to the plantations.

And scudding shipshape back they came,
The little slavers of the Middle Passage,
Marlborough, Tryal, Greyhound, Laughing Sally,
Home to Bristol with their innocent burdens,
Sugar, rum, tobacco, supplied
By the sombre absent presences
Of the Middle Passage, by those
Whom Bristol never saw . . .

RECEPTION IN BRISTOL

These men are rich; they buy
Pictures before asking prices.

Their shirts are exquisite; I know instinctively
I must not say so.

Conversations are precisely timed,
Costing so much per word per minute.

Wives are worn small this year, soberly dressed.
Their eyes are wild, but there is no exit.

Schools that encourage music, says the chairman,
Have no hooligans. No one replies.

The photographer is our memento mori.
He takes two sandwiches at once

From the curtseying waitress. There is a crumb
At the corner of his mouth, and he has

To go on somewhere else. He is here to remind us
That in this city Savage died, a prisoner;

That Chatterton poisoned himself in his London garret
Rather than creep back here.

TITANIA TO BOTTOM

(*for Alistair and Becky*)

You had all the best lines. I
Was the butt, too immortal
To be taken seriously. I don't grudge you
That understated donkey dignity.
It belongs to your condition. Only,
Privately, you should know my passion
Wasn't the hallucination they imagined,
Meddling king and sniggering fairy.

You, Bottom, are what I love. That nose,
Supple, aware; that muzzle, planted out
With stiff, scratchable hairs; those ears,
Lofty as bulrushes, smelling of hay harvest,
Twitching to each subtle electric
Flutter of the brain! Oberon's loving
Was like eating myself – appropriate,
Tasteless, rather debilitating.

But holding you I held the whole
Perishable world, rainfall and nightjar,
Tides, excrement, dandelions, the first foot,
The last pint, high blood pressure, accident, prose.

The sad mechanical drone of enchantment
Finished my dream. I knew what was proper,
Reverted to fairyland's style.

                              But Bottom, Bottom,
How I shook to the shuffle of your mortal heart.

A TOY

(*for Selima Hill*)

Someone made me,
Clothed me, forbade me
To stand, dance, sing,
Do anything
But strut rat-a-tat with my drum

                              Dum-dum

Someone made my monkey-body
Ape his look. I cannot move
Until he turns my key

                              Rub-a-dub

Uncrucify my stiff bones, someone.
Strip me, free me, let me stand,
Dance, sing

                              Rat-a-tat

Play my own tune,
Do my own thing

                              Dum

THE TWO

His are the shifty promise and the sack,
Forcer of entries through chimney and window.

His household cavalry the Horned Ones, and he
The blood-wearer, whose crew runs the night-sky,

Exact and awful as Exocet. Toddlers taste
His sweet bright lips in urban grottoes

Where he distributes his hard-edged toys.
Eat is his name; Eat or Be Eaten.

She is nameless; green her colour,
Green of new grass, or a starling's freckle.
No ceremony calls her. She comes of herself
And no one celebrates. She is
Her own midnight mass.

WAITING

The porter blows his nose with two fingers
In a clinical way.

The nurses giggle when they meet. They have permission to do this.
That is how we know they are nurses.

The receptionist addresses the telephone by its Christian name.
She too is part of the inner circle.

There are two consultants. Occasionally they walk the room.
They are never able to speak.

A great many bit-part players, the outpatients
Have come unprepared. No one has told them
That this is a serious play, they have major parts.
They chat about floods in the Severn valley, softly they practise
breathing.

The worst of all, the man on the stretcher, the woman who
cannot walk,
Are the most at ease. They are the ones
Whom the nurses already know. Who smile, and tease,
Knowing they have reached the last act.

WORD GAMES

1. *Comfortable Words*

"'Never mind,' he said, "we'll get the solution tomorrow."'
(Elma Mitchell: 'Winter in Lodgings', from *People Etcetera*)

When you understand that a river is a flower
You have begun. Friday, of course, is a man,
And a duck means nothing. Victim of gin
Is not an alcoholic, nor revolutionary
Political. Cardinals, favourite standbys,
Are always news. The Mayfair Railway's wiry,
And the 6.50's found in the first three villains.
Night's a dark deranged thing. Possibly, we hear,
Perhaps, can be, are warnings; damaged isn't serious.

      He doesn't have to make dying
      As hard as this. I've seen how easy-going
      He is with the old, the infirm, letting them drift

Unbothered away, like a bleached leaf dropping.
If he can be so kind, why must he prise
My baby's body apart like butcher's meat?
I mustn't think too much. The doctor said so.
But she is broken by successive spasms,
Changed to this thing, squinting, deranged.

The words are not really cross,
Only pretending. The answer will come
In tomorrow's paper. There is nothing here
That won't in the end be solved. (The answer to a mix-up (8): *solution*.)
But here is also where my little boy

Strains hardly back to me, and my baby
Leaves me for ever. There can be nothing
Worse than this, and this is now,
And I am here inside it. I shall never
Leave this place. (The final exit? (6,4):
Death's door.)

This one's hard.
I am familiar with his usual clues,
I know his mind, as if we danced
Kindly together. I think of him
As a friend, tweedy, pipe-smoking,
With a faithful sort of dog – retriever,
Labrador, perhaps. When he's contrived
Some tricky pun I'll just manage to crack
He smiles in my mind: *There, Sweetheart,
I put that in for you*. (Castle I'd reconstruct
To discover local languages (8):

Dialects.) My baby's local language
Is anguish. Shrieks are all she says.
I pray, Frank pays; neither does any good.
Only the reliable riddle that comes each morning,

Its answer the day after. (More
And more cavalry casualties? (8,6)
Mounting losses.) Although it comforts,
Each answer bears my darling's dying too.
Money is nothing, Frank said. Second opinion,
Trained nurse night and day, whatever
Does any good. He is so good to me.
Always the gentleman, knowing I don't much fancy
That sort of thing.

(Wormwood that can bring joy
To a maiden's heart? (4,4):
Lad's love.) A hard game, yes, but
A fair one. No syllable is meaningless,
The coding is consistent. Down is easier,
Always; helps with Across, is necessary
For working out the pattern. I couldn't crochet
This crossword comforter without my Down.
(Implement satisfied consumer demand,
But not in time (3,4).) I'll need a while
To puzzle that one out.
                                        And meantime
Down, down she goes, my darling.

Note: Answer to last clue – *too late.*

2. *Neck-Verse*

Armour of phrase disarms despair;
Ancestral patchwork plasters. Someone else
Was wounded here and stitched a turn to fit
The later maimed. I cherish
A cat's cradle of country proverbs,
Homely as singin' hinnies, handy as hankies.

Not hard equivocal wisdom for grand folk,
But reassuring halloos from the past:
We have been here before you, pet!

My kitchen prescriptions:
For Resignation:
You can't get feathers off the cat.

To take the ache out of Age:
He's seen a few Easter Sundays.

For the different ways menfolk are difficult:
Cross-grained: *He's got his braces twisted.*
Stingy: *He'd kill a louse for the hide and tallow.*
Impossible, like mine: *Awkward as Dick's hatband.*
Went three times round the crown
And wouldn't tie a bow.

Hysteria has many cues; its bubble
Needs pricking. After Effort:
It's all over now, and the child's name's Anthony.
To bypass weepy Thanks: *That'll be ninepence,*
Or *Keep your seats, there's no collection.*

For Last Ditch Stands: *That's me,*
And my dog's at Tow Law.

And O, for how it should be, could have been,
I have two simples: *As easy*
As me granny's old shoe, and
All in together, like the folks at Shields.

Too often, though, just the longing
For freedom, a fresh start:
I wish I was married and living at Jarrow.

I know what they'll say of me: *she brought*
Her pigs to a poor market in the end. Yes,
That'll be what it'll be. And to comfort me,
Cheer up, hinny, it's nobody's neck.

But that's not true. It is some body's neck.
It's mine.

Note: Neck-Verse: the first verse of Psalm 51, so called because it was
the trial verse of those who claimed Benefit of Clergy. If a condemned
person was able to read this verse (thus originally showing that he
was ordained, and therefore exempt from trial by a secular court), he
had saved his neck. This privilege was later extended to anyone who
could read and write, or even who knew the psalm's first verse by
heart. It was abolished in 1827.

AWKWARD SUBJECT

The light is wonderful, he says. Not light
For house-agents, certainly. They avoid
November shots, when wisped and bony trees
Throw a disturbing shade on property.

Stand there. Just a bit further. Don't look at the dog.
My casual adaptation to the place
(One hand in pocket, right knee slightly bent)
May not be what I mean, but is in danger
Of immortality.

       I feel my teeth support me
Against my inner lip; face him with all my skin.
Sensing my misery, *Would you rather smile?*
He asks. And break the lens, I hope. Words are my element.
Photograph them.

PROGRAMMED

Their idea of truth is yesterday's weather.
They track it through slots in clouds
Down a freezing hospital garden.

His idea of truth is what was said
Before, in unscripted rehearsal. But the words he wants
Weren't mine. He committed them.

My truth is the one that really was
(I think). The chair goes here, not here.
And those distressful lights, do they represent

The just understatement of daylight?
I try to pin down the homely fact
Of what happened, was felt.

The reproachful murmur of poems reminds me
They are not compromised. But at each take
Something diminishes.

Only body, with its helpless accuracy,
When the phone rings, recovers unprompted
The hunch and duck of slavery,
Remembers the words.

NOTES AT A PHOTOGRAPHIC EXHIBITION

Julia Margaret Cameron: Call and I Follow,
I Follow – Let Me Die (c. 1867)

I see in women's faces the desire
For sacrifice. The unprotected eye,
Hair rippling helplessly, the mouth
In glowing readiness to take what comes
A death, a kiss.

Tony Ray-Jones: Ernie Cagnolatti and Grandson, 1971

This, I guess, is what a jazzman
Wants in the end. Kid with a sax,
Grandson, more of a black than me,
With a tear in his pants, but plays
A bigger instrument, going my way,
But gonna go way way further . . .

Tony Ray-Jones: Billie Pierce, New Orleans, 1971

My shoulder-straps show. I don't care.
My age shows. I don't care.
Sadness shows. I don't care.

I am what I am: old woman
Tired, glad to sit down, weepy-eyed.
Worked hard, sung hard, lived hard.
Make what you can of it. You're welcome.

Edward Weston: On Route US 61, Mississippi (1941)

One day this truck'll be out of date,
These gas pumps too. Shell
Will probably stick around, maybe

There'll still be Toastmasters. But Ole Missus
Won't stay under this Toastmaster, nor will you
Be able to take this swollen me, smiling, black,
Offering you something, with a hopeful look,
And a door in my skirt.

Edward Weston: Farm House in New Jersey, 1941

Look close. This is not comfortable country.
For the folk who live here, depression
Is not a state of mind.
Nothing here is picturesque, neither trees,
Nor boarded windows, nor the shack
In the yard. The invisible people
Are avoiding each other's eyes. We could tell them
That hope is on its way. Its name is War.

Agnes B Warburg: Ou Sont Les Neiges d'Antan?

It's a matter of angles and implications.
Why, mademoiselle, do you choose not to reveal
My face? Because it might be smiling?
Why do you emphasise the empty chairs?
As it happens, I like to sit by myself.
Does anyone want snow
To last for ever?

Frederick H Evans: Frederick Holland Day

This is the me you might see in the street,
Taken by my friend, another
Photographer Fred. Closed mouth, lensed eyes,
Reticent beard. You can't be sure of me,
Or anything. That is my message;
At least, it's what I told Fred my message is.

Frederick Holland Day: The Crucifixion

I am the man who was lifted up,
And came down again on the same day,
Getting ahead of Christ. Don't suppose it was easy.
I starved six months for this
Skeletal effect, grew my hair, planned
My crucifixion to the last painted detail.
The nails are counterfeit, but as you see my arms
Are genuine. I took the photograph, too,
Making it easy for the world to believe in me.

Roger Fenton (Waterfall in Wood)

I gave this piece no name. As barrister
And man of words, I had my silent reasons.
De minimis non curat lex. It is the trifles here,
Too small for words, that matter.
So many leaves, more leaves than any painter
Could ever show, all witness to themselves.
The light stalks through the air and catches water,
And growing things. The rule of law
Has been here, interposed a bridge, and left
A world of wildness, world not needing word.

SAFE AS HOUSES
1995

HAUNTING

The ancestors. The shadow people,
Who now and then lean softly from the dark
And stroke on chin or thumb the new generation.

Mothers fear them, and their gifts,
Guessing half what they fear. *Who knows what you'll find
If you look. Wreckers. And swindlers.*

Daredevil grans and presumptuous children
Ransack the archives. No treasure
But outlandish Christian names: Ephraim, Mercy.

And tanned gigantic offspring from far-off
Hoping, in holiday mood, for the Old Country,
For village blacksmiths, village greens and thatch,
Sadden to find in faded sepia
The unpretending minutes of bleak lives.

Even the noble, under his courtier's tiptoe,
Admits some fearful Berserk or Spreadeagler
As line-founder, and waits, tight-lipped,
For the claw to poke out from the lordly cradle.

THE SILENCE

(*for Jane Grenville*)

I suppose it was always there, the strangeness.
Once on a patterned floor there was a god
With ears like lobster claws.

And those vast savage roads, stabbing
Like swords into distance. You could see how they
Hated the landscape.

Still there, but other things are taking root;
And still at times, through stripes of sun and shadow,
The stiff dead legions striding back.

Some of it I liked. The big town arch, those
Tall confident letters, the docked words,
Imp. Tit. Caes. Div. Aug.,

And so forth. Nonsense now. And toppled, I daresay.
Nobody goes there. One thing I remember
Of all their words.

A slave told me the yarn: some man, on his way
From losing a kingdom to finding another, gave
A friendly queen his story,

And her people stopped talking, and listened. *Conticuere omnes,*
Something like that. Stuck in my mind, somehow:
They all fell silent.

Nobody goes there now. Once it was full
Of tax-men, and gods, and experts
In this and that,

And the endless stone walls, sneering down,
Keeping out or keeping in? We'll never know.
And their magic unbudgeable mortar.

Strange beyond telling. They did so much,
Then turned their backs and left it. We, of course,
Can't keep it going,

No longer know their ways with central heating,
Water supply, and sewage,
And sickly babies.

They came too near the dark, for all their know-how.
Those curses they scratched widdershins on lead –
Asking for trouble.

We withdrew into the old places, that are easier
To believe in. Once we waited
For someone to come back,

But now it's clear they won't. Here we stand,
Between *Caes. Div. Aug.* and the next lot, expert only
At unspeakable things,

Stranded between history and history, vague in-between people.
What we know will not be handed on.
Conticuere omnes.

Conticuere omnes. (Aeneid II). Aeneas tells the story of the fall of Troy
and his escape to Queen Dido and her court at Carthage. These words
describe the response of his listeners. They were found scratched on a
tile by excavators at Silchester, in north Hampshire.

THE ROOM WHERE EVERYONE GOES

(*Mount Grace Priory*)

God's humour: uncouth helmet of silence;
God's blessing: hard cold water;
God's nursery: frigid stone.

His curriculum: spinning wheel; loom;
The word; and God, fidgety partner,
Fills the cell, or vacates it, at a whim.

Here we come, the inheritors, girt about with guidebooks.
Fast, prayer, solitude, face us like whips.
We try to imagine foot's curt patrol
Down each midget cloister; garden breath
Of mint and chives; the dished up smell
Of dinner the lay-brother left in the dog-leg hatch;
Holy sting of Latin in cold teeth
On dark mornings. Here, the monk's chair and bed,
Where we can sit or lie. Here, his window;
We can look out of it. How alien it all seems,
But for one spot, in the north wall,
At the end of the covered way. – *Ooh, look!*
The loo/the toilet/the bog! We run to see,
Take turns at sitting, feel (of course) at home.

Such cold, clean men.

The King's curriculum: ten monks from the London house
Chained hand and foot to Newgate posts
And left to rot (*Despatched by the hand of God,*
Said a careful cleric). Daily, a woman bribed her way in
With a bucket of meat, and fed them like fledglings;
(*Which having done, she afterwards took from them*
Their natural filth). In the end the gaoler panicked,
In the end (of course) they died.

They were always on sentry-go, never on leave.
Drill, practice, training never stopped.
One way or other, they knew, God's inspection was coming.

They are out of reach. We can walk where they did,
But the guts and the goodness are beyond us.

Cold and godliness alienate.
The scent of the commonplace brings them home.

NOTES

1. 'The Room Where Everyone Goes': I've borrowed this from
W. H. Auden's 'The Geography of the House':
> . . . this white-tiled cabin
> Arabs call *the House where*
> *Everybody goes.*

2. The London house, i.e., the London Charterhouse. Founded in 1371, suppressed in 1538.

3. A woman: Margaret Clement (née Gigs), adopted daughter of Sir Thomas More. When she was prevented, she climbed to the roof and tried to let food down in a basket.

TYNDALE IN DARKNESS

(*for Michael Foot*)

'Almost every good translation of the Bible . . . has been undertaken by a single highly gifted zealot. Tyndale was executed before he could complete his task, but he set the English style . . . which lives on in the King James Version (1611). A sacred book must be all of a piece, as though written by the hand of God Himself; and this can hardly happen unless a man of strong character, wide knowledge, and natural eloquence, working only for the love of God – perhaps under threat of death – sets his seal on it.'
Robert Graves: *The Crane Bag*

'St Jerome also translated the Bible into his mother tongue: why may not we also?'
William Tyndale

TUESDAY

Defecerunt sicut fumus dies mei et ossa mea sicut gremium aruerunt.
(My days are consumed like smoke, and my bones are burned
as an hearth) Ps 102, v. 3

The Old isn't as easy as the New.
Greek's nothing, but I needed Germany
To teach me Hebrew. Then the endless trail
That drags from Genesis to Malachi!
Now the New's finished, printed, launched on the world,
Doing its work in England, in plain English,
All clinched and Bristol fashion. But I
Not there to see it. Flushed out
From Gloucestershire first by a rout of clownish priests

Who, because they are unlearned, when they come together
to the ale-house, which is their preaching place, they affirm
that my sayings are heresy.

Then in London, bluffed, swindled, bullied,
Hounded at last abroad.
                            Well, God's work
Can be done here too, though I miss the rough sweetness
Of English. But on the run always, always I need more time,
Space, books and peace to do things properly.
And light, and warmth. These I miss here
In my palatial jail, the Emperor's guest.
Still, I can get things done. But how I grieve
The watery deathbed of my Pentateuch
In the deep roadsteads off Holland. Back to the start
Again. I did them all again. All five.
But it held me back. Here I am now
Still toiling through the waste of Chronicles,
When I could be at the Psalms, dealing with hope,
Injury, loss, despair, treachery, joy,
Not endless histories, churned out by some

294

Dull priest with a long memory. Only five books to go
But how long have I? I get used to Death
Leaning over my shoulder, with his noose and brand,
Breathing at each sentence end. I know he waits his day,
But not the day itself. I doubt I'll ever reach
So far as the happy man who's like a tree
Planted by water, that brings forth his fruit in its season,
And look, whatsoever he doeth, it shall prosper.
Well, Miles gets the Psalms. My heir. He'll bring forth his fruit,
The happy man. But I too was planted by water,
Born with the tune of Gloucestershire in my head,
Knowing our English as much the language of heaven
As Jerome's tawdry Latin, pagan patter,
That Jesus and His fishers never spoke.

They say it cannot be translated into our tongue it is so rude.
It is not so rude as they are false liars. For the Greek tongue
agreeeth more with the English than with the Latin. And the
properties of the Hebrew tongue agreeeth a thousand times
more with the English than with the Latin.

Not many days left me, not many days.
They keep my working books, my Hebrew Bible,
Grammar and dictionary. I'd get on faster
If I had them, and light to work in the dark.
Sicut fumus dies mei, my days are consumed –
Consumed? An empty word. Eaten is better.
Defecerunt. Bloodless Latin! But English lives!
Will Miles be up to it? – yes, eaten
Like smoke, and smoke will finish me
Here, in the marketplace at Vilvorde. *Et ossa mea –*
And my bones burned up like a hearth.
That too. But here, while I live, in the cold and the dark,
I long for a whole shirt, and a lamp at night.

I suffer greatly from cold in the head, and am afflicted by a perpetual catarrh . . . My overcoat is worn out; my shirts are also worn out . . . And I ask to be allowed to have a lamp in the evening; it is indeed wearisome sitting alone in the dark.

WEDNESDAY

Vigilavi et factus sum sicut passer solitarius in tecto
(I watch, and am as a sparrow alone upon the house top) Ps 102, v. 7

He is the sparrow, the Friday lord.
I hoped to be the watcher on the rooftop,
But He was first. I'm flake of His fire,
Leaf-tip on His world-tree.
                            But I watch too,
As once I stood on Nibley Knoll and looked
Out over moody Severn across the Forest
To the strangeness of Wales, Malvern's blue bony hills,
And down on the dear preoccupied people
Inching along to Gloucester, the trows with their sopping decks
Running from Bristol with the weather behind them,
And none of them knowing God's meaning, what He said to them,
Save filtered through bookish lips that never learnt
To splice a rope or fill a bucket. So I watched,
And saw the souls on the road, the souls on the river,
Were the ones Jesus loved. I saw that. Now I see
The landscape of my life, and how that seeing
Has brought me to this place, and what comes after.
So He saw the history of us, His people,
From Olivet. And told His men to watch.
Vigilate ergo (nescitis enim quando dominus domus veniat; sero,
an media nocte, an galli canto, an mane), ne cum venerit repente,
inveniat vos dormientes.

They couldn't keep their eyes open, poor souls.
Vigilate. As well tell them to stand on their heads.
Erant enim oculi eorum gravati. For their eyes were heavy.
I doubt I'd have done much better.
It must have been a hard day for them,
And they weren't used to late nights, the disciples,
But to early mornings, when the shoals come in.
Hard-headed men with blisters on their palms
From the nets. Why did He ask them to stay awake
When He knew they couldn't? Because He always does.
He picks the amateurs who follow Him
For love, not devout professionals
With a safe pair of hands. Look at Peter,
A man permanently in hot water, chosen,
Perhaps, for that very thing. God sets His mark
On us all. You start, and it's easy:
I heard the ploughboy whistling under Coombe Hill,
And I thought, *I could do that.* Give him God's word,
I mean, in his own workaday words. And I did,
But it got so difficult: exile, hardship, shipwreck,
Spies everywhere. Then prison, and the fire.
God's mark on me, as on Peter. I would have slept, too.

THURSDAY

Principes persecuti sunt me gratis.
(Princes have persecuted me without a cause)
Ps 119, v. 161

What can you do with power except misuse it?
Being so mighty makes these men afraid
That we, their subjects, might guess they're men too.
That I can understand. It's the followers
Who turn my stomach. The glib climbers

Greedy for money, land, influence, jobs for the boys.
They're drawn by the power and the glory,
And kings aren't fastidious. Consider Henry's men –
Cuthbert the cloth-eared Bishop of London;
Wolsey the Suffolk wolf; and foul-mouthed More,
The bitterest tongue in England. Consider also
Their noble master Henry, the subject-harrier,
Who drove me here. Well then, consider them.
They fear me. So they should. I plan
The invasion of England by the word of God.
And it will come. Just now, they burn my books.
An easy step from that to burning clerks,
Burning this clerk for doing what God wants,
Turning God's word to King's English.

                                    But not the King's;
The people's; England's English. That's where Christ is.
Not a king to do business with Popes and chancellors,
But a servant, a man beneath us, who washes our feet,
Who goes before to try out the hard things first,
Who opens gates so we can go easily through,
That is the king, one and only, who speaks our own words.
The powerlessness and the glory.

Princes have persecuted me. Perhaps they have a cause.

FRIDAY

Scribantur haec in generationem alteram et populus qui creabitur laudabit Dominum. (This shall be written for those that come after: and the people which shall be born shall praise the Lord) Ps 102, v. 18

The powerlessness. This is the day He dies,
Jesus, the Friday sparrow, the watcher on the cross
Who forgives those who put Him there. He's dying now,
And His world is dying too. I made this world twice
After God; twice I translated Genesis. I know

The deep places in it. And God said,
Let there be light, and there was light.
The accurate voice of God. And after Him, me;
Tyndale of Nibley. The human small-scale words
For the unimagined thing. And as Jesus hangs dying,
That same immense familiar light, that shines
Over Nibley and Bristol, London and Flanders,
Over all the countries we know glancingly of,
Goes out, as the world, more faithful than its people,
Mourns for its maker. The world itself dies.

God says, Let there be no light.
And when the sixth hour was come, there was darkness over the
                              whole land until the ninth hour.
Starlings think it night, celandines shut their petals,
Trees in Westridge Wood stand frostily waiting.
No light. No light. God said, Let there be no light,
While Jesus is dying.
                              I want to die like that,
Brave and forgiving. I may not be able.
The grace is not in us. We have to ask.

We must also desire God day and night instantly to open our eyes.

So little time. We have to hustle God
Who, in His unhorizoned sphere of time,
Can hardly know how short our seasons are.
And I pray too for resurrection in the word.
This shall be written for those who come after.
And still, these tedious Chronicles waiting for me,
These kings and priests and rulers of this world,
These Jeroboams and Jehoiakims,
Between me and *beatus vir*, the happy man,
Whose leaf shall not wither. Unlike mine.
And look, whatsoever he doeth it shall prosper.

Et omnia quaecumque faciet prosperabuntur.
Prosperabuntur? God's teeth, what a word
For Christian tongues to wrestle with. Language for liars!
Our dear and patient English shall rip out
The rubbish Jerome stuffed in the Church's mouth.
I must get on. Day and night. Instantly.
The Psalms are waiting. So are the English.
Vile the place is, but still my Father's house.
Lampless or not, He lights it.

NOTES

Who, because . . . are heresy: Tyndale, quoted in Demaus, *William Tindale,* London, 1886.

The Emperor: Charles V. My Pentateuch: Tyndale's first translation of this was lost when his boat sank.

The happy man: Ps 1, v. 1: *Blessed is the man that walketh not in the counsel of the ungodly . . . he shall be like a tree planted by the rivers of water.*

Miles: Miles Coverdale, who worked with Tyndale and took over at his death. *The Book of Common Prayer* Psalms are Coverdale's.

Jerome: Translated the Old and New Testaments from Hebrew and Greek into Latin (the Vulgate). *They say . . . with the Latin:* From Tyndale's *The Obedience of a Christian Man.*

Vilvorde: Where, in 1536, Tyndale was strangled and burned. *I suffer . . . in the dark:* Letter from Tyndale, imprisoned in Vilvorde Castle.

Nibley Knoll: in Gloucestershire, where the Tyndale Monument now stands.

Trows: Severn barges.

Vigilate ergo . . . dormientes: St Matthew 24, v. 42: *Watch ye therefore, for ye know not when the master of the house cometh, at even, or at midnight, or at the cockcrowing, or in the morning: lest coming suddenly he find you sleeping.*

Erant . . . gravati: St Matthew 26, v. 43. Cuthbert: Cuthbert Tunstall, Bishop of London.

More: Sir Thomas More was more vituperative in polemic even than Tyndale – which is saying something!

Twice . . . Genesis: The first translation was lost in the Rhine shipwreck.

And when . . . ninth hour: St Mark 15, v. 33.

Westridge Wood: On the ridge above North Nibley.

We must also . . . our eyes: From Tyndale's *A Prologue.*

THE DOLL'S CHILDREN

I have been your doll wife, just as at home I was Daddy's doll child.
And the children in turn have been my dolls. (Ibsen, *A Doll's House*)

We are the children of the doll,
Our mother plays sweetly with our toys,
She is better at childhood than we are.
O mother! with your little feet and your little fingers,
Your sweet tooth, your pretty ignorance,
Your laughing and shrieking and hiding under the table,
Your tambourine and your tarantella,
Shouldn't you have grown up by now?
We need to explore the casual ways of childhood;
You are so professional, you take up all the room.

We are the children of the Bank Manager,
Whose job it is to be master,
Who is surrounded by people
Who are softer and smaller than he is.
This is the man who understands audits,
Debit and credit and profit and loss,
Who never listens or understands,
Whose children stay babies,
Who married a skylark,
Who lives in the house that he built.
We are the children of this house.
We sit on dinky chairs, at dinky tables,
Speaking gingerbread language.
We are afraid, mother, father, we are afraid.
Some day we shall turn gawky,
Voices will break, hair and blood
Spring from unchildish places.
How will you go on loving us then, you who need us
To be younger than you?
When shall we see your faint suspicion
That we have betrayed you, becoming ourselves?

We are the children of Norah,
Who walked out of the doll's house
Into a city unfriendly to skylarks and squirrels,
Whose dance-halls were shady,
Whose cake-shops were shut;
We are the children of Norah who slammed the front door,
Who walked out alone with her courage
As the youngest son walks alone into the forest.
We were the children of the doll;
It seems there is hope for us, after all.

READING BETWEEN

'It is perfectly true, as philosophers say, that life must be understood
backwards. But they forget the other proposition, that it must be
lived forwards.' (Kierkegaard, *Journals*)

Novelists were no help. They made you think.
Mr Joyce, so difficult; Mr Lawrence, so coarse;
And Mrs Woolf, so strange. But these
Were the kindly ones, whose gift was
To immobilise memory.

So much to face: bald war-memorials;
One-armed men at stations selling matches;
Failing chicken-farms; little mad mothers
Muttering at bus-stops.

But these were the code-breakers; these gave answers.
In locked rooms, in libraries, one man
Dies for the people. Not in random shambles,
But stylishly, slugged on the left temple
With a blunt instrument.

These civilised Death. Such singular corpses
Could be coaxed into downright discourse:
Rigor mortis; finger prints; contents of stomach.
Nothing to mourn here.

The police, thick-witted, true-blue,
Are on our side; and their unlikely allies,
Foreigner, with accent; unimportant old lady
With knitting; nervy nobleman
With heirloom brains.

No doubt they guessed what was coming. They knew
History's unreliable narrators, Europe's locked room,
Poor bloody little Belgians. Identical twins, unclassified poisons –
There was no irregularity they hadn't charted.

And yet of course there was: the colossal one
On the edge of being true, Auschwitz, the Burma Road,
Hiroshima, all that followed. Perhaps they chose
Not to tell, being creators of small occasions,
Of problems with answers.

O rare little world, where a biking bobby
Is about to spot that open window; where Whitehall 1212
Is the number to ring; where golfing colonels
Are ready to say *Eh what?* and nice girls
Like being rescued,

O rare little world,
Imagined to gentle the English through war,
And Depression, and war, and peace, and anything else,
Cheap, unpretending, with your faith in solutions,
O Never-Never world, not to be read twice.

SIRENSONG

(for David)

'What song the Syrens sang . . .'
(Sir Thomas Browne, *Urne Buriall*)

I know the song they sang. I heard it,
The husky warbling, on the war's first day.
I learned the meaning, too: *Lie low, lie low.*

Gipsy women came to the door for help
With ration books they couldn't read. They gave us
Spuds from giant baskets; told no fortunes

(All fortunes were the same). Endlessly Mother
Explained about The Will, and who
Would take us on, if anything . . .

Ours had been a safe house. Safe as houses
Ever are. Built in a post-war country
It stood up straight, untroubled by rumours of war.

My baby knees crawled through it, certain of polished parquet,
Turkey carpets, quarry-tiled kitchen floor.
My knees understood this was a forever house.

The end of faith in brick. The house fluttered,
As trespassing aircraft droned life-long overhead,
Leaving the town rubble and honeycomb.

We were precocious experts on shrapnel and blast.
Things broken weren't replaced. What was the point?
Friends were lost, too. You didn't talk of it.

We knew how bombs sliced off a house's flank,
Uncovering private parts; how bedroom grates
Still stuck to walls though wallpaper flailed outside;

How baths slewed rudely, rakishly into view;
How people noted, and talked of what they saw;
How ours might be the next; and what they'd say.

Peace made no difference. Still too young to matter,
Someone still fighting somewhere, some children
Are invaded for ever, will never learn to be young.

We missed the jazz and swing of our extrovert parents,
The pyrotechnic raves of our groovy kids.
Our ground was never steady underfoot.

We had no wax to cancel the sirens' song:
Lie low, lie low.

DYING FALL

November's leaves flock ginger and stiff along the gutter,
Waiting for the wind to say.

Boots (black), shoes (brown), knee-socks (white).
Their feet speak for them:

Brownies and cubs (eyes left to grin at Mum),
WRVS, swinging arms whose baskets we know,

Guides, Scouts, Sea Scouts, all different, all tweaked
Into step by the bully band,

And the band's irresistible, dammit. I choose not to conform,
I don't want to fight, but by jingo jingo jingo . . .

Thin irregular pipe of peace, please. Not this rude
Heartbeat that fuses us all

With the bowler-hatted grey shufflers and their hulking flag,
Grasped cack-handed in a gauntlet,

And the washed dim names that no one remembers,
Who died in a muddle of bugle-calls

And the fitful drumbeat of glory,
Ending up, like the leaves, in mud,

Skulls, tongueless bells, miming their message,
Waiting for the wind to say.

COLLATERAL DAMAGE

The minor diplomat who brings terms for a ceasefire
Enters through a side-door, in the small hours,
Wearing a belted raincoat.

The children have become bold. At the first siren
They cried, and ran for their mothers.
Now they are worldly-wise,

They clamour to watch dogfights above the house,
They prefer under-the-kitchen-table to the shelter,
They play fighting games

Of reading the paper by bomblight,
Pretending to be the enemy. These children
Are no longer safe.

They have learned rash and contrary for ever. Come soon,
O minor diplomat in the belted raincoat, come
To capitulate. For the children have ack-ack nerves,
And a landmine has fallen next door.

Under the reservoir, under the wind-figured water,
Are the walls, the church, the houses,
The small human things,

That in drought rise up gaunt and dripping,
And it was once Mardale, both is and is not Mardale,
But is still there,

Like the diplomat, and the crazy fearless children
Who progress through their proper stages, and the churchbells
With their nightly riddles,

And the diplomat, and the children still running
Away from shelter, into the path of the bomb.

LAST HOUSE

Like the dead march, the beat of destruction is slow.
The crane-man stirs; the giant ball moves over;
A hum; a waver; a trickle of mortar; a pause;
A slice of wall flops over out of the sun.

This is the last performance. The Regal yaws doubtfully
As audiences do, wanting the star to fall,
But not till the last reel, at sunset, to the right music.

The crowd remembers whistling in limelit smoke,
Organist rising astride his yodelling nag,
Usherettes with torches and no-nonsense style,
Chocolates, cigarettes, trayclad girl in a spotlight,

Buckled backseat couples, gauging how far they can go,
Persistent men in macs at matinees,
Lustrous magnified eyes oozing slow motion tears,
Hi-ho-ing dwarfs, hi-yo-ing cowboys, Hitchcock.

Here once they studied poker-faced dialogue
(*Here's lookin' at ya, kid*); here they learnt
How to sing in the rain; to hamlet; to tootsie; to catch 22;
How to make passionate love to Elizabeth Taylor.

Where now the oilfields of ketchup, the acres of hair?
A shame to knock the old place down, they say,
Drifting along, *We had some good times here.*

Celluloid shades of Garbo, Garland, Groucho,
Welles, Goofy, Wayne, rise hissing in the air,
And *Hi-yo!* the call sounds high and very far off,
Let's go, big fella! Hi-yo, Silver, away!

COUNTING SONG

One man and his dog
Went to mow a meadow.

Not always the same dog,
But the man looks the same, disposable,
Scrapped. Hungerford Bridge his meadow.

This is the city we come to when we're young,
With the golden pavements. Where office-workers whisk
Like weir-water over zebras; where 15s and 77s
Snuffle down bus lanes, showy as heralds.

One woman and a baby

Probably borrowed, we say, not looking,
Moving on. We need to move on.
Our shoes are embarrassed. Our shoes are what she sees.

There's less of sky, now the great Lego thumbs
Angle their vacant heads into the gullspace,
But the saints watch us, Martin the beggars' friend,
Bride in her wedding-cake hat, and Paul,
Skywise and circumspect, sitting out centuries
Under his helmet, Thames washing past,
Refusing to run softly.

One gran and her bottle
Have given up on mowing

These are waste people, grazing in litterbins,
Sleeping in cardboard, swaddled in broadsheets
And Waitrose plastic bags, who will not be recycled,
Must lie where they fall.

These are the heirs, the true Londoners,
Who work in this stern meadow. The others
Are on their way to somewhere else:

Statesmen and filmstars, remote, chauffeur-driven;
Volatile journalists, folding themselves in taxis,
As homegoers fold themselves into introspection
And the *Evening Standard*.

Written on Hungerford Bridge in letters of chalk:
Save Our Earth. Save Twyford Down.

Save Earth. Save Twyford Down. Save every one.

DEATH ROW POETS

(*for Marie Mulvey-Roberts*)

To wait, to watch. Vocation
Of the prisoner and the poet.

Not those who choose to watch,
Chess-players, crossword-puzzlers, those who flinch

From the blazing face of Time, and focus
On small exacting things. But the poets,

The prisoners, whose stretch is finite,
Look straight in Time's face, and see

The unrepeatable marvel of each second.
Consider these prisoners, these poets.

Consider also those who are taught not to see,
To blanket violence by conditioning;

Decent men, kind to wives, who must not know
Which of them pressed the button;

Who must learn to see the dummy, not the person;
Who must be helped, by rectal plug and catheter,

Not to smell the body's final protest.
Consider these men also. And those who give them their orders.

THE UNPROFESSIONALS

When the worst thing happens,
That uproots the future,
That you must live for every hour of your future,

They come,
Unorganized, inarticulate, unprofessional;

They come sheepishly, sit with you, holding hands,
From tea to tea, from Anadin to Valium,
Sleeping on put-you-ups, answering the phone,
Coming in shifts, spontaneously,

Talking sometimes,
About wallflowers, and fishing, and why
Dealing with Kleenex and kettles,
Doing the washing up and the shopping,

Like civilians in a shelter, under bombardment,
Holding hands and sitting it out
Through the immortality of all the seconds,
Until the blunting of time.

A MAJOR ROAD FOR ROMNEY MARSH

It is a kingdom, a continent.
Nowhere is like it.
                    (Ripe for development)

It is salt, solitude, strangeness.
It is ditches, and windcurled sheep.
It is sky over sky after sky

> (It wants hard shoulders, Happy Eaters,
> Heavy breathing of HGVs)

It is obstinate hermit trees.
It is small, truculent churches
Huddling under the gale force.

> (It wants WCs, Kwiksaves,
> Artics, Ind Ests, Jnctns)

It is the Military Canal
Minding its peaceable business,
Between the Levels and the Marsh.

> (It wants *investing in roads*,
> Sgns syng T'DEN, F'STONE, C'BURY)

It is itself, and different.
> (Nt fr lng. Nt fr lng.)

DNA

'. . . and so their horses went where they would.'
(Malory: *Le Morte d'Arthur*, XXI, ch. x)

So at the end the company dissolved.
Kings died. Queens turned into nuns.
Knights came to grief, or left in symbolic boats.
They made Lancelot a priest. And those other knights
Read holy books, and holp for to sing mass,
And tinkled little bells. Then it was over.

Their horses, the noble destriers,
The lordly ones, plaited and groomed and oiled,
With their grave names and their alarming harness,

Who carried nothing, except men to war,
Stepped mildly over the brambles, tasted grass,
Cantered composedly through the forest waste
Of early England, and at last
Went where they liked, quick and shining
Through kingdoms. Time whittled them down.
They became the dwarfish ponies of now,
Shaggy and hungry, living on the edge.

Sometimes, in a foal's crest, you can see
Some long-extinguished breeding. So in us,
The high-rise people and the dispossessed,
The telly idols, fat men in fast cars,
Something sometimes reverts to the fine dangerous strain
Of Galahad the high prince, Lancelot the undefeated,
Arthur the king.

GRAND UNION

In the faintly rocking three foot of the cut
Two grey heads drowse on the permanent double.

Elsewhere, adult children wonder if they're safe,
The dog pines mildly in its boarding kennels.

They are at peace in their clean unchallenging ship,
Enfranchised from garden, telephone and friends,

Next meal a certainty at the Boatman's Arms.

The smutty water oils and clots around them,
Eavesdropping on the past: bargees' thick talk;

Snorting of horses; muffled shout of the woman
About to be raped, as the men close in on her.

Happy, old girl? he asks. *Oh, very happy.*

AT SWARKESTONE

'It is often said that Bonnie Prince Charlie got as far as Derby in his
invasion of 1745. In fact, he reached Swarkestone, some nine miles
further south.' (J. G. Collingwood, *The River Trent*)

He turned back here. Anyone would. After
The long romantic journey from the North
To be faced with this. A *so what?* sort of place,
A place that, like a mirror, makes you see.

A scrubby ridge, impassive river, and beyond,
The flats of Middle England. History waited
To absorb him. Parliaments, dynasties, empires
Lay beyond these turnip fields. Not what he wanted.

He could have done it. The German Royals
Had packed their bags, there was a run
On the Bank of England, London stood open as jelly.
Nobody could have stopped him. This place did,

And the hurricane that blew his cause from Moidart
In a bluster of kilts and claymores and bright red hair
Faded at Swarkestone as they turned their backs,
Withdrawing into battle, slaughter, song.

LOSTWITHIEL IN FEBRUARY

Civil, unfriendly, they answer
Our questions with a small pause first
As if to say *Is this an interrogation?*

We blunder aimlessly round their shops,
Exclaiming and moving on. Who wants
Walking sticks, ammonites, books about Daphne du Maurier,

This time of year? It takes the huge
Communal chumminess of August to generate
Such off-the-cuff traffic. Here, in a quiet season,

We brood on empty chairs in cafés, For Sale signs,
Open at Easter. But it's not just that,
The unmoneyed half-life of the partitioned year.

It's the unheard, unspoken comments as we pass:
We are their revenue, and so they hate us
For making them what we want. In summer

They will be different, vernacular, picturesque.
Now we can hear the authentic Cornish snarl,
Razor's edge language of the occupied.

GREENSTED CHURCH

Stone has a turn for speech.
Felled wood is silent
As mown grass at mid-day.

These sliced downright baulks
Still wear the scabbed bark

Of unconquered Epping
Though now they shore up
Stone, brick, glass, gutter
Instead of leaf or thrush.

Processing pilgrims,
The marvels that drew them –
Headless king, holy wolf –
Have all fined down to
Postcards, a guidebook,
Mattins on Sunday.

So old, it remembers
The people praying
Outside in the rain
Like football crowds. So old
Its priests flaunted tonsures
As if they were war-cries.

Odd, fugitive, like
A river's headwaters
Sliding a desultory
Course into history.

HELPSTON

This is where it happened. These are the fields,
Plain, with a Gothic augmentation of hedge.
These are the skies, high, hard, dispensing light.

The modern contributions: tight-lipped housing;
Trees pruned to the bone, leafless as winter;
The church bell's funereal bark as it deals out time.

A banshee plane roughs our hair. A detached native
Tells where you're buried. This is where
You wanted to be, what you loved. We came

Because of you. The wind comes at us,
Swearing, along the furrows.

UNDER THE MOTORWAY

There they go charging through the muck,
Lada, Lagonda and Leyland truck.
But under the motorway, what's there?
What lies in wait? Is it brown and bare
Like earth in fields? Is it rocks and stones?
Is it dead people, and dinosaurs' bones?

Something no doubt of all of these.
But more importantly, it's seeds
Waiting their time to spring to the top
When the tarmac ends and the lorries stop.
When there is no more Renault and Rover,
Roads will be thick with Cleavers and Clover.

Petrol and diesel will both dry up
But that doesn't happen to a Buttercup.
Flowers shoot upwards with mighty heaves
And sprout in a flurry of stems and leaves.
Here they come shouldering through the road,
Willowherb, Woodruff, Woundwort, Woad.

On viaduct, bypass, clearway, trunk,
Mercedes, Minis turn to junk.

But Love-in-a-Mist and Love-lies-Bleeding –
They're on our side, and they're succeeding.
Rolls Royce and Volvo, their day is done,
But Charlock and Dandelion blaze in the sun.

WHAT, IN OUR HOUSE?

'The play (*Macbeth*) is remarkably short, and it may be there has been some cutting.' (J. G. Collingwood)

Macduff	O Banquo, Banquo,
	Our royal master's murdered.
Lady Macbeth	Woe, alas!
	What, in our house?
Banquo	Too cruel anywhere.
Lady Macbeth	That's not the point. Who cares for anywhere?
	Mere woolly-minded liberals. But *here*
	Is where I am, my house, my place, my world,
	My fortress against time and dirt and things.
	Here I deploy my garrison of soap,
	And, like all housewives, just about contrive
	To outmanoeuvre chaos. Not a job
	For men. What man alive will grovel
	Scrubbing at floorboards to mop up the blood?
	(No doubt there's blood? Or if not, sick or shit
	Or other filth that women have to handle?)
Banquo	O gentle lady . . .
Lady Macbeth	Only women know
	The quantity of blood there is that waits
	To flood from bodies; how it soaks and seeps
	In wood and wool and walls, and stains for ever.
	No disinfectant, I can tell you, Banquo,
	So strong as blood. Then, the implicit slur
	Upon my hospitality. Was Duncan
	Suffocated? Something wrong with the pillows!

Was his throat cut? Check the carving knives!
Poison? Blame the cuisine. I wish to heaven,
Banquo, he'd died in *your* house. Your wife
Would tell you how I feel.

Enter Malcolm and Donalbain

Donalbain	What is amiss?
Macduff	Your royal father's murdered.
Malcolm	O, by whom?
Lady Macbeth	Such donnish syntax at so grave a moment!

How hard to frame the first and random thought
Detection snuffs at, to seem innocent
And psycholinguistically correct at once.
And my *best* bedroom, too.

AN EASY DAY FOR A LADY

1. THE CLIMBER

The Alps were right for him. Unpeopled. Snow
Affirmed no one had ever been that way.
Melchior, his honest guide, tactfully keeping
Out of sight; his Cambridge friend,
Kennedy, Taylor, some gentlemanly cleric,
Don, civil servant, slogging a long way after,
But sure to hail him at last with that fierce reliable
Cambridge facetiousness able men use.

A clean, competitive world. The great white heads
Scale one above the other, brow by brow exposing
New challenges, new hazards, a new route,
Like men from another college, suddenly known
As serious rivals for a serious prize.

As candidates are measured by degrees
(Wrangler to passman), so climbs are graded:
Inaccessible; most difficult point in the Alps;
A good hard climb, but nothing out of the way;
A perfectly straightforward bit of work;
An easy day for a lady.

She watches him. She will use this later.

2. THE FATHER

He's grounded now in a rented Cornish garden,
Stamping his Mr Carter boots over unremarkable
Borders and beds, with children bundling
In and out of the kitchen garden, cricket lawn,
Coffee garden, love garden, endless gardens,
Boxed in by hedges, cheeping everywhere
(One his, three hers, four theirs), so many
Expensive expanding mouths.

He bucks himself up with the litany
Of his Alpine firsts: Bietschhorn, Oberaarhorn,
Schreckhorn, Blümlisalphorn, Monte Disgrazia.
Then there's the work in hand, the great Biographies,
Gauging how many lines each life is worth.
Sometimes he's audible. His headful of fossil verse
Suddenly sprouts through the escallonia:
Beware the pine-tree's withered branch! Beware
The awful avalanche! Embarrassing;
But worse the sheer-drop silences in front of strangers.
Like a hole in the world.

She watches him. She will use this later.

3. THE HEIR

The heir isn't always apparent. All those fine
Upstanding boys, with their Cambridge brains; not them?
The older sisters, Stella, Laura, the Saint?
Not them, not them, but Billy the giddy goat.
She was the one to inherit the gift
And miss the education. She climbed, unsupervised,
Creating routes, perspectives, sentences,
Climbing above streets, buses, rooms, to take it all in.

He bagged the view at the top. Had to be first.
Wanted it to himself. Below, cosmopolitan cockneys –
Magnifique! Wunderschön! Simply splendid! – suburban cooings
Made Alpine sunsets stink of Baedeker.
But Billy the goat, she capered where he had trampled.
She risked the lunatic leap between feeling and sense,
And invented a syntax for it. She charted
Innominate peaks of silence, emptiness, space;
Shared what she found with all who cared to come.
When time ran out, she walked to death, prospecting
The weedy channelled Ouse, that lowland stream,
Stones in her pocket.

She watches this. Some things are never used.

NOTES
He: Sir Leslie Stephen, famous mountaineer and first editor of the
Dictionary of National Biography.

She: His younger daughter, Virginia, who became Virginia Woolf.

Rented Cornish garden: of Talland House, St Ives, celebrated in *To the
Lighthouse*. Her father's boots are also immortalised in this novel, but
I found Mr Carter's name in Sir Leslie's mountaineering writing.

The Saint: Vanessa (Bell). This was her family nickname, as Billy
was Virginia's.

Some things are never used: Virginia Woolf wrote about most
things, but not her own death.

ODYSSEUS' CAT

(for Barbara Britton)

Aged and broken, prostrate on the ground,
Neglected Argus lies, once fabled hound.
Odysseus' footsteps he alone descries,
Perceives the master through the slave's disguise;
He lifts his head, and wags his tail, and dies.
(The Corgiad, trans. J. G. Collingwood)

                        Not that I don't believe
The first part of the yarn – the ten years' war.
Ten seems quite modest for a genocide.
No, it's the ten years' journey afterwards
I boggle at, bearing in mind
The undemanding nature of the route.
Why did he take so long? One thing's for sure
Those junkies, cannibals, one-eyed aliens,
And friendly ladies living alone on islands
Well, what do you think? Of course. Exactly.

In the meantime, in another part of the archipelago,
Old Argus had been catsmeat long before.
Man's best wears out, with rushing around and barking,
And digging and wagging. Cats, on the contrary, last:
The harmonious posture, exact napping,
Judicious absences from home . . .
                            I had, of course,
Been busy. Did what I could to discourage
The mistress's unappealing Don Juans,
Lurked boldly in dark corners, slashing
Shins of passers-by; performed
Uninhibited glissades down dinner tables,
Scattering wine and olives; free fell
From rafters upon undefended necks;

Produced well-timed vomit in my lady's chamber
When a gallant went too far; and I helped
With demolishing the tapestry each night,
Having an inbred talent.
So when Odysseus came, I rubbed his legs.
He recognised me – well, he said *Puss, puss,*
Which is all you learn to expect.

                And then the liar
Concocts this monstrous calumny of me:
He leaves me out, supplants me with a dog,
A dead dog, too. And the one thing
Everyone believes is that dog's tale,
Tale of the faithful hound.

                You'll see
I've improved his version; cut out the lies,
The sex, the violence. Poor old Argus
Wouldn't have known the difference. But cats
Are civilised. I thought you'd see it my way.

HE REFUSES TO READ HIS PUBLIC'S FAVOURITE POEM

'I think Yeats hated all his early poems, and "Innisfree" most of all. One
evening I begged him to read it. A look of tortured irritation came
into his face and continued there until the reading was over.'
(Dorothy Wellesley)

They always asked for it. He knew they would.
They knew it off by heart: a b, a b,
Reliable rhymes; thoughts they could understand.
But dreams, as well. Their own, their Innisfree.

So why refuse? He knew the rest were better,
His serious bid for immortality.
What man defends the tenets of his twenties?
Who would be tied for life to Innisfree?

'Give us *Arise and go* in your Irish accent,
Give us the cabin, the glade, the beans, the bees.
Not Maud, Byzantium, Crazy Jane, Cuchulain.
We are your public. Give us more Innisfrees.'

'A poem heard twelve times in public is dead and finished.'
'Ah no! Too much of a good thing there cannot be.
Too much of Shakespeare, Wordsworth, Milton, Shelley,
There is. But not enough of Innisfree.

I will arise and go now – Senator, please!'
'I won't. I can't. I'm not him any more.
Young fool who prattles of crickets and wattles and linnets –
I hate him in the deep heart's core.'

DEUS v. ADAM AND ANOTHER

Summing up for the defence, m'lud, I must say
(In spite of my learned friend's eloquence)
I see no case to answer. Consider first
The object of the alleged theft. We have no means
Of identifying it. We may, I think,
Safely surmise that it has been consumed.
But by whom? I submit, m'lud,
That there is no evidence. Posterity
Is going to affirm it was an apple;
The document in the case refers to *fruit*.
The accused are vague: she says it was a lemon;
He thinks on the whole a raspberry.
A strange case of pilfering we have here:
It's claimed they ate it, but they don't know what it was.

Now the witness. Members of the jury,
What can one say of a witness who, it's alleged,
While the offence was being committed, had the normal
(Four) number of limbs, and an adequate, nay, a persuasive
Voice with which it addressed the female accused,
Yet which now appears in court literally legless,
And proverbially struck dumb, so that it can only
Hiss and wriggle apologetically? M'lud and members of the jury,
It is quite clear, is it not, that the serpent has been got at?
I will not exceed my brief and suggest by whom,
But we are all men of the world, are we not,
Members of the jury (except, of course, for those of us
Who are women)?

Lastly, m'lud, the very peculiar
Question of motive. The accused had been warned,
As you have heard, by the landlord, not to eat
The fruit of the tree of knowledge of good and evil;
If they did, they would die. This, m'lud,
We call a penalty clause. It is claimed they *did* eat,
Whatever it was, apple, lemon, or good red herring,
But didn't die. For here they are in court,
Mr Adam and Mrs Eve. So did they break the clause?
I see no evidence. The prosecution fail
To establish a theft. The only witness
Has been tampered with. And finally,
Do the defendants look as though knowledge of good and evil
Had come their way? Their rather pathetic ensemble
Of verdure hardly suggests it. Would such knowledge
Result in so trifling a step forward
As covering one's private parts? O no, members of the jury.
If we knew good from evil, we would know the answers
To the perennial hard questions – abortion, pacifism,
The rights of trees, euthanasia, what-about-Europe.

Do our two defendants, shivering there in the dock,
Look like creatures able to conceptualize such questions,
Let alone answer them? M'lud, I rest my case.

WOMAN IRONING

I thought I knew what was coming when he said
He wanted to do my likeness at the ironing.
I live in the city, people tell you things. Me looking at him,
It would be, across the ironing board, my hair and my eyes
In a good light, and something a bit off the shoulder.

But it wasn't. He rushed around drawing curtains.
Made it hard to iron. O yes, I had to keep ironing.
He needed to see the strength, he said. Kept on
About my dynamic right shoulder, then left it out,
Though you can see where he ought to have put it.

Come on, what's-your-name, he kept saying,
Show us that muscle-power! That's what I'm after.
I might've been an engine, not a person.
No, I didn't take to him. I'm used to rudeness,
But he was making such a sketch of me.

If someone's paying you, it isn't easy
To speak your mind. Still, *Sir,* I said,
I really don't want to see my hair like that,
All scraped back, like a hot person's hair,
And anyone can tell that under my arms I'm sweating.

Hair? Sweat? That's how it is when you iron,
Says he. *You're not here to tell me what to do.*

326

I'll make you permanent, the way you look
When you're ironing. O yes, he says, I'll show you
The way you look when no one's watching.

Note: The original title of this painting is La Repasseuse. The Walker
Art Gallery translates this as Woman Ironing, which suggests to me a
casual activity, like woman smiling. I'd think it more accurate if the
painting were known as Ironing Woman. Degas's ironers are trained
specialists.

PAINTER AND POET

Watch the painter, children.
The painter is painting himself.
Palette enfisted, aloft; brush brandished.
There are men watching the painter painting,
Children. The spectacled one with a beard
Is saying Magnificent! a touch of sfumato there!
Did you see how he gouached that bit of scumble!
O, a very good investment, gentleman. You can't go wrong,
Financially speaking, when the artist has used
So much technique. There! did you see how he stippled?
My advice is, certainly purchase. Always a market
For work of this kind. The painter listens, children,
And smiles a banker's smile. He does
A spot more impasting.

Now, children, the poet. He is less exciting.
All he brandishes is a ball-point,
Which he plays with on unastonishing paper.
See him unload his disorganised wordhoard,
Children, as he sits alone. No one comes
To admire, or commission. Having only
Himself to please, he tinkers at pleasing himself.

Watch silently now as that metaphor
Fans slowly out, like a fin from the sea.
Did you notice him then, secret and shy as an otter,
Transferring an epithet? See that artless adverb
Mutate into a pun! And now – O children,
Keep very quiet – he is inserting a verb!
A cryptic cipher, for friends' eyes only, he splices
Into his work, not guessing that what he writes
Will turn into a *text*, a *set text*,
Children; nor that you will think
He committed it deliberately to hurt you.

Invest in the painter, children; as for the poet,
Bad luck is catching. I should steer clear.

COLOPHON

'We're not going out of the book business, we're just throwing away
the paper and the print . . . Books won't disappear, they'll just become
marginalised.' (Peter Kindersley, of Dorling Kindersley)

Led by *Exchange and Mart* we came to Slough:
A nest of garages, a leaking roof,
Rain spitting into plastic buckets. Man
In overalls, cloth-capped; a Berkshire voice.

Come up the M4, didjer? Lovely job.
The great gaunt things loom round him patiently,
Hoping for work. *They come here from all over.*
Ipswich. And Leeds. There's several comes from Leeds.

How dangerous they were, the ancestors,
Whose children stand here, endlessly resold,
Iron feet in puddles; whose work was burned,
Chained, or inherited, precious as manors.

The printer's devils worked them, skinny, short-lived,
Coughing up blood like Keats; and the journeymen,
With their mirror-image eyes, masonic alphabet
Beginning ampersand k; ending at r;

Who knew how to handle f, with its double
Delicate kerns; for whom every speck and nick
Had to be right. *Founts over here*, he says.
Plantin, yerse. And Perpetua. Lovely Perpetua.

We get what we came for. Come away
With a great gape of loss, like losing one's language.
Tigers, elm trees, Perpetua, lovely Perpetua,
Sidling into extinction. No more, yerse.

We paid. He slotted the flatbed into the boot.
There you go. Cheers, lifting a hand as we left.
It felt like a blessing. Could be. We needed one.
He seemed like a man who had the power to bless.

QUEENING IT

Inside every man there lurks the Widow Twankey,
Brazen and bosomed as a figurehead,
Dressed to the tens,
Lusting to get out,

Lusting for the frou-frous and the pads,
For the wig like a fierce self-raising pudding,
For the Cupid's bow visible over a measured mile,
For the slit skirt, the rangy shaven legs,
The Pennine heels,

Snatching those parts the girls aren't really up to –
The Ladies Bracknell, Thatcher, Macbeth;
Imogen, Rosalind
(*Written for chaps, after all*)

How she holds her audience, the Widow!
The men, because she knows what they like;
And the women, sitting relaxed inside their stretchmarks,
Plugged in to their PMT and their HRT,
Their caesareans and their hysterectomies,
Their design faults, poor dears, glad to be made to laugh,
Not caring about the half-shrugged message,
This is how it's done, admiring her dash,
As the monstrous lashes flick, the colossal cleavage throbs.

These are the women men like. Not the supermarket
Slowlane crawlers, near tears, running out of cash;
Tired, with sneezing kids, in endless surgeries;

Not the women we run to in trouble, fat
Putters-on of kettles, who listen, and wait,
And hug if we want it, and are still wearing slippers;

Not the uncertain people, stared at in streets,
For whom both *Gents* and *Ladies* present problems;
Who practise belonging somewhere, but never do.

How expert, admired is Twankey, modulating midway tones,
Making the best of both sexes, the true Queen of Hearts!

But we who must wear our true hearts on our sleeve
How to do that? Tell us the answer, Widow,
If you know.

WATER EVERYWHERE

Officially they do not acknowledge this god.
Officially they honour assorted immortals
In stone buildings with pioneering roofs.

Their houses betray them. Above ceilings,
Tanks for the precious stuff. Below, a shrine
To the godhead. Here they may stand alone

In confessional boxes, or lie full length
In his hollow bed, singing. Here he sometimes speaks
In loud, disquieting, oracular tones.

Fish are considered holy; where they go
We found contemplatives, with green umbrellas,
Making symbolic gestures at the stream.

In the hot month they consecrate their gardens
With a wet rite involving children, rubber, dogs.
On Sunday mornings they lustrate the car.

They pretend to disparage the god and his rainy gift,
Using set litanies: *Lovely weather for ducks!*
Last Thursday we had our summer. Flaming June!
(Black comedy is native to this people.)

Daylong, nightlong, ministers of the god
Recite on different airways his moods and intentions.
The people claim not to believe. But they listen.

Their literature is great. They never read it.
Water, water everywhere the only
Line they can quote. Though ignorant of the context,
They reckon these words cover everything.

DAMAGE LIMITATION

Barbaric, unruly, alarming,
The power of those who would rather not;

Who, while the others are chewing or snoring
Or pondering duty-free,
Sustain, by a massive exertion of will,
The whole company in air;

Or who avert their magic eyes
From small useful shops in marginal districts,
Since if they look, the next message will be
Closing Down Sale and *Everything Must Go;*

Like the man whose son was riding
The Derby favourite. Family watched downstairs,
But he ran a bath, laid his dangerous
Body in it, earthed it in water,
Made himself harmless;
                       And those spires,
Fragile, audacious, that hover and start
To waver in air when the wrong eyes look.
Safer the country parish with its twice-a-year congregation
Whose harvest offerings come to church privately
And after dark: dogged, peculiar, warm.

ON WORMS, AND BEING LUCKY

Two kinds of sand. One heavy, gritty,
That falters moodily under your toes, like custard;
The other, shiny weedy ribs, and further,

Out of sight, the standstill sea. You tramp along
In sunbonnet and spade, summer's regalia.
You choose a grey snake's nest, slice into it,

And yes, there *are* lugworms, and you carve them out,
And he hoicks you up, your dad, to the space round his head.
You've got the knack, my princess, he says. *You're lucky.*

Then there's your turn for betting. Bored by favourites,
You always picked the unfancied outsider.
The field foundered at Becher's. Or something.

Anyway, yours won, against the odds
(*Lucky, my princess!*) since you knew it would,
And knew it into winning. (*Sweetheart. Lucky.*)

After the operation, you were sent for.
(He was propped up in bed, reeking of ether,
Possibly dying.) You held the big limp hands,

And lugged him back to life, like a cow from a bog.
He clung to your luck, and kept it
For two more years. You gave him something,
Not knowing what it was. (*The knack,* he wheezes.)

Or love, maybe. Two kinds of luck.
My luck, dear father, flashy and absurd,
A matter of long odds and stop-press news;

Yours was the gift that sees life gold side up,
So that a knack of finding worms becomes
A serious blessing.

DAFFODIL MINISTRY

One of the more difficult denominations.
No artless formula of psalm, collect,
And-now-to-God-the-father; unrelenting ministry
Of the solo conscience. Mankind's cheerless concerns
Can drop in here like friends.

And yet, the daffodils, she says.

And yettishness: a state of mind.

O yes, of course the world is harsh,
And suffering, O yes – and yet
This morning, as I walked along
And saw the daffodils, I thought –
And so forth, daffodilling on.

Easier not to meet each others' eyes.

And yet, and yes, the daffodils
Making their point, in scurfy gardens,
Beside the lake, beneath the trees,
Municipally distributed, like grit.
Wherever a bulb can lodge and multiply,
Long-legged, gape-mouthed, a yellow hop in air,
Daffodils are.
                    Homelessness, poverty,
Injustice, executions, arms trade, war
Are too.

The stillness isn't easy with itself.

And yet, and yet.

ATLAS

There is a kind of love called maintenance,
Which stores the WD40 and knows when to use it;

Which checks the insurance, and doesn't forget
The milkman; which remembers to plant bulbs;

Which answers letters; which knows the way
The money goes; which deals with dentists

And Road Fund Tax and meeting trains,
And postcards to the lonely; which upholds

The permanently ricketty elaborate
Structures of living; which is Atlas.

And maintenance is the sensible side of love,
Which knows what time and weather are doing
To my brickwork; insulates my faulty wiring;
Laughs at my dryrotten jokes; remembers
My need for gloss and grouting; which keeps
My suspect edifice upright in air,
As Atlas did the sky.

THE ABSENT-MINDED LOVER'S APOLOGY

I would like you to think I love you *warmly*
Like brown cat yawning among sheets in the linen-cupboard.

I would like you to think I love you *resourcefully*
Like rooftop starlings posting chuckles down the flue.

I would like you to think I love you *extravagantly*
Like black cat embracing the floor when you pick up the tin
                                                    opener.

I would like you to think I love you *accurately*
Like Baskerville kern that fits its place to a T.

I would like you to think I love you *with hurrahs and hallelujahs*
Like dog whippetting at you down the intricate hillside.

I would like you to think I love you *wittily*
Like pottery Cox that lurks in the fruit-bowl under the Granny
                                                    Smiths.

I would like you to think I love you *pacifically and for ever*
Like collared doves on the whitebeam's domestic branch.

I would like you to think I love you *chronically*
Like second hand solemnly circumnavigating the clock.

And O I want to love you, not in the absent tense, *but in the here
                                            and the now*
Like a present-minded lover.

SISTER

She was a success with dogs, cats, rabbits,
Small, furry, uncritical creatures.

Little afterthought, coming behind the do-no-wrong brother,
The brilliant, touchy sister, nothing left for you
But the cul-de-sac of immaturity.

Always giggling frivolously in corners
With silly friends, or husbands-of-someone-else.

Named after a road, because your mother
Hadn't really given her mind to it.

Even the gentle nuns were disappointed:
Your dear sister, always so good at . . .

Elder child of elder daughter, I inherited
You as my younger sister, little aunt

Who sniggered, and knew nothing, and rebelled
Automatically against the tyranny, the benevolence.

America gave you formulae. Returning,
Smudged with accent, *I want out* you'd say,

Looking around for admiration, like
A clever child, and *No way, no way.*

No way. You were never going to ripen
Dear little aunt, as a puppy does, or a plum,

In spite of the serious husband, godly daughter,
Yours still the horrified eyes of a creature

Trapped in a magic, unyielding world,
Child of the cul-de-sac.

CHRISTMAS PRESENTS

Christmas, very, have a merry very
A very merry Christmas, trilled the cards.
In gynae wards that means: There is a future.

I lay there, while you sorted friends and stamps.
The local wise man had come up with gold:
A benign cluster. You'll be home by Christmas.

Nothing to say. When I was tired, we held hands.

But next bed's visitors were staring.
Why us? The colour of our hair, perhaps?

You didn't notice, so I didn't tell you.

Next day (another day!) her bed was stripped.

Her lovers (husband? daughter?) hadn't cared
To watch death creeping up and down her face;
Stared at us out of tact, no doubt,
Somewhere to rest their smarting eyes, but also
(I like to think) because we were,
Of all things, human;

Human, of all things.

CAT IN THE MANGER

In the story, I'm not there.
Ox and ass, arranged at prayer:
But me? Nowhere.

Anti-cat evangelists
How on earth could you have missed
Such an obvious and able
Occupant of any stable?

Who excluded mouse and rat?
The harmless necessary cat.
Who snuggled in with the holy pair?
Me. And my purr.

Matthew, Mark and Luke and John
(Who got it wrong,
Who left out the cat)
Remember that,
Wherever He went in this great affair,
I was there.

CHRISTMAS SOUNDS

Boeings wing softly over Earth
Humming like enormous *Messiahs,*
Bringing everyone home for Christmas.

Children wailing impossible wants,
Housewives worrying in case enough isn't,
Parsons, with prevenient care, sucking Strepsils,

Telly jingling twinkling mistletoe-ing,
Cash tills recording glad tidings of profit,
Office parties munching through menus –

Crackers! Champagne corks!

At the heart of it all, in the hay,
No sound at all but the cattle
Endlessly chewing it over.

THE INVITATION

The Gloucestershire foxes' message
To the child beyond the sea:
We d'hear thee was born in a stable.
Us dreams uneasy of thee.

Us knows the pack be after thee,
Us knows how that du end,
The chase, the kill, the cheering,
Dying wi'out a friend.

So lover, us makes this suggestion
To thee and thy family tu:
Come live wi we under Westridge
Where the huntin folk be few.

Thee'll play wi cubs in the sunshine,
Sleep in our snuggest den,
And feed on – well, us'll see to that –
Forget they beastly men.

Maybe thee thinks tis too far off,
Our language strange to thee,
But remember us foxes of Westridge
When thou tires of humanity.

THE WICKED FAIRY AT THE MANGER

My gift for the child:

No wife, kids, home;
No money sense. Unemployable.
Friends, yes. But the wrong sort –
The workshy, women, wogs,
Petty infringers of the law, persons
With notifiable diseases,
Poll tax collectors, tarts,
The bottom rung.
               His end?
I think we'll make it
Public, prolonged, painful.

Right, said the baby. *That was roughly*
What we had in mind.

CONSEQUENCES

2000

CONSEQUENCES

A Note

This sequence is about, among other things, England and Leicestershire and Richard III and hope, courage and gypsies. It also touches upon war and peace, second sight, and the arms trade, and the uses of language and architecture; and, being late twentieth century, it acknowledges the part played by money in determining what is important. Shakespeare, George Fox, Richard III, Torrigiano, the Master of the Cast Shadow and Urania Boswell all have something to say on these topics. The title (the name of an old party-game) suggests that nothing happens in isolation from the past or the future.

(U.A.F.)

1. FOUND ON THE BATTLEFIELD

The moorhen slips into the water
Like a Neanderthal bird. And water
Spreads out in planes all over England.

The heiress sits in the manor garden
With her high plucked forehead and her noble bones
Thinking, will it be King Dick or King Harry
That fathers my dynasty?

The precious things, the crowns and golden chains,
Are dirtied, and the fine steel basinets
Rot in the caked and scummy ditches.
Toilet-paper standards flutter from the banks.

This landscape is not given to forgetting.

The moorhen, crabwise and odd as a man-at-arms,
Jerks in the water. A horse shouts in the night,
And a dog finds something beastly to eat
Under a hawthorn. Swans cruise, freighted with meaning,
Eloquent and ferocious as heraldry.
Their painted scowls outstare the afternoon.

It is the usual battlefield, with a hill, a wood,
A marsh, phlegmatic cows, visitors' car park,
Disused railway, battle trails. And people,
No doubt with other things on their minds.

The canal has invaded this landscape,
But it speaks the same idiom: will it be
King Dick or King Harry? Theme park or business centre?
Choose, England.

2. LOST AND LOST

Under the great gold saltcellar, the gilded moorhen
Lost for five hundred years. Lost,
Mourn the archivists, the keepers, the metal detectors.

But maybe not. Perhaps, in its own time,
It will surface. Return and delight, with its pearls
And precious stones, marvellous rich.

But Richard the King is lost for ever,
Under the weight of Leicester City Centre.
Above him trolleys, buggies, perform

Their daily quickstep. Above him workmen
Pitch and toss crates, mothers hurry and go
With cars full of kids and plastic carrier bags.

What mortal bones could resurrect from here?

Richard is lost, and his reputation.
Here lies the bunch-back'd toad, the bottled spider,
The hellhound, the abortive rooting hog,
God's enemy, and England's bloody scourge.

Fine language is one way of being remembered.
This is the best we have. This is Shakespeare.

3. THE MASTER OF THE CAST SHADOW

Some painters leave shadow out. The Master hunts it
From the source of light to where the last
Faint filigree fingertip falls,
Unthinking as a sundial.

We each inherit our shadow, our ration of darkness,
That shrivels and spreads as light walks here and there.

They don't see us, these sad mediaeval faces,
With their crosses, their rings, their daggers, their painted eyes.
They're on the watch for various ugly kinds
Of early death.
                    What they see is the weather,
For the weather warred over England,
As the roses slugged it out: fog at Barnet,
Snow at Towton, three suns at Mortimer's Cross
In the open fighting season. Red Gutters
And Bloody Meadows are sprayed over counties.
They killed and killed and killed. Thirty thousand
In a morning. Where did they find the people?
So few around, so many of them butchered.
But some live on as the Master saw them,
Praying, or holding a naked broken sword.

4. THE YOUNG PERSON'S GUIDE TO ARMS

i   Enemies come in pairs, like socks. There is no such thing
     as a single enemy.

ii   When one enemy kills the other it is called Ethnic Cleansing.
     Of course, Cleanliness is next to Godliness;
     and much easier.

iii An Eye For An Eye. This is a very old wargame called
     Retaliation. However, no one has yet worked out what to
     do with someone else's Eye.

iv   Collateral Damage. This is when Children and Ordinary
     People come between enemies and get killed. It's really
     their fault for being in the wrong place at the wrong time.

v Surgical Strike. This is when you hit One Special Thing,
like a surgeon cutting out a cancer. 'Surgical' makes it
clear that killing is a good thing.

vi Concentration Camp. Everyone enjoys camping holidays,
so people don't worry about what will happen. When
you've put the people all together in a Camp, it's much
easier to kill them.

vii Liquidate. Another way of getting rid of people. It
sounds like making soup, so no one minds.

viii Friendly Fire. This means killing someone on your own
side by mistake. Since it saves them from being killed by
an enemy, it's quite kind, really.

ix Human Shield. This is when you are very polite, and say
'After you' to women and children and people like that.
Then, if your enemy kills them because they're in front
of you and in the way, this gives you something called
The Moral High Ground.

x Enemies never forget the past, because it justifies what they
are doing. They seldom mention the future, since there
might not be any.

5. HOMILY OF THE HASSOCKS

In Leicestershire, in Sutton Cheney,
in the church where he prayed when time ran out,
not the man himself, but woolly whispers:
Remember before God Richard, remember
and those who fell . . . The whisper of hassocks
(gift of The Richard Society). This patient cross-stitch
is done for love not money, in a homely idiom.

Remember *before God* all the obliterated,
in Sutton Cheney, in Leicestershire,
all the world over, ever.

6. HATS OFF, GENTLEMEN. A GENIUS!

No. I not like the place. I detest.
What I find here to admire? I,
Artist and citizen of Firenze?

The stink of dirty beards, broccoli,
Herring, bad teeth. A celery language,
Language for ape, not man.

They not comprehend *me,* these idiot workmen,
To whom I am coming like saviour
To world-without-end their little dead English king.

I make the Pope his saints. English Henry? No trouble.
He look like Pope when I finish him,
Though nasty piece of work in life, no doubt.

These English oafs! Cut rope, spill colour,
Crack stone. *The usual accidents, signor,* they smirk.
I comprehend *them.* And I have reputation.

Who fight for Borgia? Stuff Michelangelo
Nasty nose down filthy throat like biscuit?
True, I am exile here, among the beasts,

But money, money, lotsa money! And I make
Effigy to move the heart. *Prodigioso –*
Ma doloroso! These English they so halfwit,
Too greedy to know to praise me good.

7. THE USES OF ARCHITECTURE

'For Ruskin, the hanging fan vaulting in Henry VII's chapel (1502)
was a great sham because it disguised the function of the roof
supports.' (Victor Sage)

When in disgrace with fortune and men's eyes

Distract public attention. A building puts things right.
After the massacre, a hospital
(Sports centre, university),
Anything eye-catching; red herring in stone.

Henry the tax-gatherer, Henry
Reviser of records of all the days before yesterday,
Henry who picked off all heirs but his own,

Lies here in his Henry chapel, named in his name,
In an hysteria of greyhounds and roses,
Portcullises and little red Welsh dragons,
Gilt bronze on black, cherubs at every corner,
Under a ceiling exploding with pendants and putti,
Vaulted like the hand of God. A good buy.

Don't miss that meagre, brooding head. Holy,
You'd say. Ascetic. The best buy of the lot.
Florence's best, of the best period. Torrigiano.
(Never saw Henry, of course, but knew what was wanted:
The austere look. The best, if you can afford it.)
He charged a mint. Worth ever penny, though.

Here's Henry, in a golden web of grace,
For whom the cherubim continually do cry,
And tourists edge past, wanting to get on
To Mary Queen of Scots and Bloody Mary,
But the guide thinks they oughta see this geezer, and somewhere

Out there Richard, under the trolleys, the buggies,
The lamentation of traffic

Remember before God all the obliterated.

8. MASTER SHAKESPEARE: HIS MAGGOT

(*for Brian Vickers*)

'I may do that I shall be sorry for.' (*Julius Caesar*)

Not really a good beginning. I like
An uneasy scurrying, *what country's this? who's there?*
With luck, they're hooked.
                              A solo confident voice
Telling us what he'll do before he does it?
Obvious. Obvious.

All Marlowe's doing. Burbage sees himself
As Jew or Faustus, witty, aspiring, perverse,
Poetic justice waiting in Act Five.

But reconciliation's more my line,
And a decent quota of clothcaps talking prose.

Villains are difficult. I haven't the knack.
Circumscribed citizens, without that other dimension
Of unexpectedness, something irregular.
The fans don't fancy moral cloudiness.
They like to know where they are with the criminal classes.

The future nibbles, too. Not just Burbage,
But unborn ghosts of players, Burbages to be,
Wanting this part. *Your hunchback, Will,*
They twitter. *The monster part. The hog! The hog!*

Simplifications of the acting trade:
Crook back, frozen arm, unfinished look.
Hard to refuse the future. Not much choice,
Either, with Burbage at me, moaning about the takings.

I hate predictability. Richard's a Jack-in-the-box
With his *Here we are again.* Jacks are predictable
In their Jackish way. The best bits are
The sudden, sideways turns –
This is All Souls' day, fellow, is it not?

And *They about cockshut time, from troop to troop*
Went through the army cheering up the soldiers.
Something might come of that.

I must do better. No more truck
With scapegoats, Burbage, Marlowe, groundlings,
Actors to come; and you, poor ghost,
Crippled in memory as maimed in life –
Guilt and responsibility; I know about them.

9. ASK A SILLY QUESTION

'The age of chivalry is gone. That of sophisters, economists and
calculators has succeeded.' (Burke, *Reflections on the Revolution in France*)

King Dick or King Harry? Theme park or business centre?
Choose, England.

I choose peace; I never get it.
Takeovers and overtakers, de-militarised zones,
Kings dead in ditches, displaced persons,
Class war, sex war, civil war, war. Tortures,
And other irregularities.
                                   Somewhere, all the time,

A dog is finding something beastly to eat
Under a hawthorn. Does it matter
Who it is, Harry or Dick?
What matters is that people live
The ordinary all-in-a-day's-work life of peace.

They've thought up a disinfected vocabulary
In Rwanda, Lebanon, Bosnia, Ireland, here.
I know the anodyne lexicon: Ethnic Cleansing,
Military Option, Defence Procurement, Friendly Fire –
Language of arms dealers to shareholders
At a safe distance. With a nice feeling
For euphemisms, you can get away with murder.

This was the battlefield. Birds, hedges, sheep,
And long November shadows. *Hedge laying*
On Saturday. Strong clothes, please,
And bring a packed lunch. Remember,
This is a haven for wildlife with a variety
Of wild flowers and different species
Of butterflies. Please do not pick or harm.

Far off, the inveterate voice of battle:

> *Who's 'im, Bill?*
> *– A stranger.*
> *'Eave 'alf a brick at 'im.*

This is all there is.
No Andes, no Outback. There's no more than this,
And the sea chews away at Suffolk.

10. HUNDREDS AND THOUSANDS

(at Brinklow)

The seesaw rattle of goods trains in the night
Watery quiet observations of duck
The moorhen's morning gurgle

This century excels at calculation
Thirty-five hundred thousand at Dresden,
Seventy-eight hundred thousand at Hiroshima,
The first hundred thousand, the second hundred thousand,
Eight hundred thousand starved at Stalingrad,
Six million in the camps. And other,
Less famous headcounts. This is an age
In serious debt to statistics.
                                    One death
Is enough to convince. We don't need crowds
To remind us how precious we all of us are.
Marvellous rich. An offer not to be repeated.

11. FOX UNEARTHED

(*for Nick Large*)

He is eleven. God is after him.
But what's it mean? What's he supposed to do?

Nineteen now. He ditches job and home.
Hears God saying *Thou must be
A stranger with all.*

                    Takes to walking,
A Baedeker journey, from Drayton-in-the-Clay
(Which is the beginning) to Bosworth, Barnet,
Lutterworth, Leicester, through

The muddy muddled middle of Middle England,
Through a world turned upside down.

Where's ta going, George?
God knows.

Thrashing it out with any who seem
To know an answer. Sad adolescent dropout
Unable to settle. Marriage? *Ah no,*
I am but a lad. Not how God sees him.

Treading the water lanes, mouth stuffed with silence,
Eyes re-reading a not-yet-written book,
His shoes in pieces again.

                              He hears
What was coming, always. Now it comes:
All things were new, and all the creation
Gave another smell unto me than before.
The smell of God.

Now he can run up the length of England,
To Pendle Hill, the bare unfriendly ridge.

Up wi' thee, George, says God. And being up,
He saw the Lancashire sea, and God's people,
Waiting to be found. So shins up further Firbank,
Drinks water, preaches to a thousand. The beginning
Of the beginning.
                              The high moments
On the high places. Fox runs free.

But Fox also trapped in the prisons of England,
Carlisle, Derby, Lancaster, Launceston, Leicester,
Nottingham, Scarborough, Worcester,
In the dark, the cold, the wet, alone.

This is where the chase leads, to the stopped earths
As well as the fell tops. And, dying,
After so much cross-country work, in London, telling friends
I am glad I was here.
                    The smell of God
In the muddy, the high, the beastly places.

12. THE FORTUNE-TELLER'S FUNERAL

The seeing has been my life. Handed down
Like silver. No use here, in Farnborough,
Where they know my proper name. But Easter-time
Sees me off on my way to Margate.
A good place to mystify. Westgate sometimes,
Or Broadstairs. All gainful addresses.

Vardo, curtains, crystal ball –
They draw the people. I'd do better in the sun,
In my big chair, holding damp gorgio hands,
Say just as true a future. But they need hocus-pocus,
The lamp, reflections, shadows, me in pearlies,
Queen Gypsy Rose Lee on the posters.

I find the future. They giggle and stare,
Helpless at belief. I muzzle what I know:
How many young women will marry twice,
How many lads die young, in sand or air.
I speak riddles: *Many will love you.*
Beware of high places, of fire and steel.
They can unravel it if they like.

My own death's different. I've planned it.
Picked my undertaker, Mister Owen,
Who did so well by Levi. The procession,
He'll see to it: six jet horses

(My Levi's pals should find a proper match),
Outrider, coachman, flowers and flowers and flowers,
Great wreath in the shape of my special chair,
Romanies walking, three hundred or so,
  Twenty thousand, I say, twenty thousand
Some in mourning, some not
  Black triangles, the gypsy Z
  They are marched through. The see-saw rattle
  Of goods trains in the night.
  Whose death is this? I will not see it.
  What country's this? A world turned upside down.
  I refuse the seeing.

The mourners go
From Willow Walk to Crofton Road,
By the Park to Farnborough Common.
Traffic jams. The Deputy Mayor
Of Margate, he'll be there to show respect.
A proper Romany funeral. Like an old queen's.
  The ash tree, I say, the birch tree.
Such things need to be thought about before.
  And the Devouring.
  I refuse the seeing.

My death, I know it well:
The April day in nineteen thirty-three; the weather, rainy,
And cold; the missel-thrush singing all day
By the vardo, till I die. I am Urania,
Friend of the skies, the one who knows the future.

  I will not hear the gypsies playing in the lager.
  I will not hear it when the music stops.

13. AT STAUNTON HAROLD

> [He] founded this church
> Whose singular praise it is,
> to have done the best things in ye worst times,
> and
> hoped them in the most callamitous.

> (over the west door at Staunton Harold church)

Many churches speak,
But this, in its despair, more eloquent than most.

The craftsmen who built it were looked after:
Shepheard artifex, the mason, who remembered
The tricks of the old trade; Smith the joiner;
Sam and Zachary, brothers, who created
Their own cloudy Creation overhead.

I'll see you safe, lads, he must have said,
No paperwork, no names, no packdrill.
I'll pay in cash. Money can't talk.

The church was unlawful, built doggedly
In the old proscribed fashion. But the founder's name
Runs clear as an indictment inside and out.
He didn't trouble to protect himself. Cromwell
Had him six times in the Tower, for weeks,
For months, suddenly for ever. He was twenty-seven,
And he died.

> the best things

> ye worst times

> callamitous

> hope.

NOTES

1. 'Found on the Battlefield': Bosworth Field, in Leicestershire, where Richard III was defeated by Henry VII in 1485. *The canal has invaded . . .* : The Ashby Canal, created much later.

2. 'Lost and Lost': *Under the great gold saltcellar . . .* : This was described in a document as worth £66.12.4d. *Leicester City Centre . . .* : Richard was ultimately buried in Grey Friars Church; this was destroyed at the Dissolution. The site is now covered by banks, shops and a car park.

3. 'The Master of the Cast Shadow': Portraits of this school show a combination of cast shadow and flat colour background. *The Master* was probably of German origin. Barnet (1471), Towton (1461), Mortimer's Cross (1461) were battles fought during the Wars of the Roses. *Red Gutters . . .* : Such names are often given where battles have been fought.

4. 'Homily of the Hassocks': Sutton Cheney is a Leicestershire village on Richard's route from Leicester to Ambion Hill, where the Battle of Bosworth took place. Tradition says that St James's Church in Sutton Cheney was where Richard heard Mass for the last time, on 22 August.

5. 'Hats off, Gentlemen, a Genius': Pietro Torrigiano (1472–1522) was responsible for the monument of Henry VII in Westminster Abbey.

6. 'The Uses of Architecture': Victor Sage, 'Gothic Revival' in *The Handbook to Gothic Literature*, ed. M. Mulvey-Roberts (Macmillan, 1988).

7. 'Master Shakespeare: His Maggot': *Burbage* Richard Burbage, actor-manager.

8. 'Ask a Silly Question': *Who's 'im . . .* : old Punch joke.

9. 'Hundreds and Thousands': Brinklow, Warwickshire, is on the Oxford Canal.

10. 'Fox unearthed': George Fox (1624–1691), the founder of Quakerism, was born at Drayton-in-the-Clay, Leicestershire (now Fenny Drayton), not far from the site of Richard's death at Bosworth Field. His youth coincided with the Civil War. Quotations and other material from George Fox's *Journal*.

11. 'The Fortune-Teller's Funeral': see *The Kentish Times, 5.5.1933;* Isabel Fonseca, *Bury Me Standing* (Vintage, 1996); Brian Vesey-FitzGerald, *Gypsies of Britain* (David & Charles, 1973). *The gypsy* Z: tattoo mark (for Zigeuner, meaning gypsy) used in Auschwitz-Birkenau. *Proper name:* Urania Boswell, wife of Levi. *Vardo:* Romany word for van. *Gorgio:* non-gypsy. *The Devouring:* gypsy word for the Holocaust.

12. 'At Staunton Harold': Staunton Harold is in Leicestershire. The church was given to the National Trust in 1954; the Hall is leased to The Sue Ryder Foundation. Sir Robert Shirley (1629–1656) was the founder, and the unnamed hero of this section.

NÉE

She had strong views on Mrs Humphry Ward,
The Brontës, poor souls, women called George,
Novelists known as A Lady.

                    There was always
An edginess. Whenever we went too far,
Children or parent, she'd flare *O you Fanthorpes!*
As if at some foreign breed.

She lost some magic when she married us.
Not race or class, but a sense of being her.
Red hair was part of it, and the surname
That gave her the convent's nickname, *Reddy*.

Marriage turned her *Ginger*, and unsettled her.
We knew the men who might have been our father,
Doctor, diplomat, soldier. We understood
They'd have had better, smarter children.

The way she said *My* family left us standing.
Racier than anything we knew, her father,
The seventh son, who wouldn't marry the heiress,
Walked from Devon to London, his flute in his pocket;

Her handsome mother, lover of dogs, not children,
Descendant of the gentle Tudor scholar,
Who never used a fullstop in her life.

She did everything well. Had a head for figures,
Understood the Married Women's Property Act.
Created faultless parcels, Fs and Ps flamboyant,
Converted the exile of marriage into art.

Vaguely we knew we'd missed something by happening.
We were the children of Mrs Humphry Ward.
Marriage is burial, she used to say.

I could have written novels, or played the french horn.

KINCH & LACK

(Boys' Outfitters)

Elderly man with a tape-measure.
Pedantic; a shade arch
(I don't see this at the time),
Treats my brother like a bride.

My mother not at ease
(I feel, but don't know why);
My brother, flattered, diffident,
Somehow aware of destiny.

Youngest son faces his kingdom
And his trousseau, socks, cap, scarf,
Wreathed in official colours
For unimagined deeds,

Greek, rugger, chemistry, things
He will do and I shan't,
Though I am two years older,
Taller, have read more books.

He's rehearsed for a special future
By a man with pins in his mouth;
Seven-year Dante, whose Vergil
Salutes his inches with respectful craft.

Mother stands restlessly by,
The cheque-book in her bag

(And I know, without being told,
There's a world enlisting him
That hasn't a place for me.

OK. I'll make my own).

MOTHER SCRUBBING THE FLOOR

She had a dancer's feet, elegant, witty.
We had our father's, maverick spreaders of dirt.

Dirt from London, dirt from Kent,
Mud, dust, grass, droppings, wetness, things,
Dirt barefaced, dirt stinking, dirt invisible.

Whatever it was, she was ready:
The rubber kneeler, clanking galvanised bucket,
The Lifebuoy, the hard hot water.

Let me! we'd say, meaning *Hate to see you do this.*
Too old. Too resentful. Besides, you'll blame us
That you had to do it.

She never yielded. We couldn't do it right,
Lacking her hatred of filth, her fine strong hands.

Don't want you to do this, she said   *Don't want you to have to.*
Just remember this: love isn't sex
But the dreary things you do for the people you love.
Home is the girl's prison
The woman's workhouse, she said
Not me, she said. *Shaw.*

I do remember. I stand where she knelt.

AGAINST SPEECH

Harpo's the wittiest Marx. Words are only
For what can be said; silence
Has a better vocabulary.

Disposable the expensive eloquence
Of QCs, DJs, MPs,
Hairdressers, headmasters, hot gospellers, humorists,
Ball-by-ball cricket commentators, consultants,
Voice recognition software from IBM.

O for a tongue-tied muse to celebrate
The steadfast dumbness of dissidents under torture,
The hangdog faces of children who won't perform,
Quakers, clever as fish in a soundless dimension,
Lovers in crowded trains.

But something must be said for the unemphatic
Chat of World Service at four o'clock in the morning,
Of nurses checking at midnight in drowsy wards,
Of parents talking things over together downstairs
When everyone else is in bed. These are
The great protectors; their half-heard patter
Signals *All's well; all's well; so far, all's well.*

WORDS FOR MONTHS

Their names in this country
Wore out, though the weather
Is still what they charted:

After-Yule; Mud-month; Mad
(The one that wants to knock
You down and plant a tree

On top of you); Easter
(Her month, the spring lady);
Three-milkings-a-day month

(Everyone smelling of
Cow); First-nice-month; Second-
Nice month (our fathers had no

Word for spade but spade); Weed;
Holy; Leaf-fall; Shambles
(Cattle-culling month); and

Here-we-are-again Yule.

Someone has overlaid
This tired chronicle
Of endless days, thin lives

With shoddy Roman goods –
War, doorways, emperors,
Even the numbers wrong.

They fit better, the dull
Words for difficult things:
Mud. Milk. Weeds. Leaf-fall. Cull.

(Se aeftera Geola; Sol-monath; Hreth-monath; Easter-monath;
Thrimylce; Se aerra Litha; Se aeftera Litha; Weod-monath:
Halig-monath; Winter-fylleth; Blot-monath; Se aerra Geola)
(from W. W. Skeat, *A Student's Pastime*, 1896)

STRONG LANGUAGE IN SOUTH GLOUCESTERSHIRE

Vocabulary of earth, names

Tough and diehard as crypts,
Cathedrals perched on their shoulders.

No committee okayed them.
They happened, like grass,

Written down all anyhow
By cosmopolitan clerks in a hurry.

Ramshackle riddles, their meaning
Deconstructed in aloof universities,

Their proper stresses a password
Known only to cautious locals.

Now, inscribed on steel, they confront drivers,
Looming on roads by the restriction signs,

Unreel their quirks along the prim
Mensuration of Ordnance Survey,

Still hard at it, still proclaiming
Here are Soppa's tinpot two acres,

Something holy, a good place for blackbirds,
Duck farm, bridge over mud,

The strangers' bright city.

(Various Sodburys; Nympsfield; Ozleworth; Doughton; Slimbridge;
Gloucester. These are all places in Gloucestershire.)

THREE POEMS FOR AMY COOK (1909–1998)

1. Amy Sits for Her Portrait

(*for Peter and Victoria*)

Like a pre-Cambrian hill, she looks down
Mildly at our callow landscape.
We stare, we ask. She endures, having learned
Over years to perform herself.

Her part is *racy rustic;* which she isn't.
Her standards are her own, so clearly better
She never explains them. We have to guess
Why she's brought her private shepherd's pie,

Solid among the pâtés and lasagne; why,
As we slop about in the sun, in shorts and sneakers,
She's upright in straw hat and floral print;
Why she takes posing seriously; why she sings,

Recites, talks about education; why the dogs
Revere her, lying in the shade behind her chair;
Why she never tells her age; why she's always saying
Rome wasn't built in a day. So old,

So many dead-end jobs, so clever, now
She lives in a different country, translates
Patiently into our language, knows how to tell her life
As if it were a story. She has the poise

Of one who never had a chance,
And yet is always listened to.
Not a *turn,* though that's how she plays it.

The speechless portrait speaks the truth.
Don't listen. Look.

2. *Amy Tells Us*

Why she brings her private shepherd's pie:

I d'like bacon. Don't like brown bread.
The chips was lovely. Piece of fish
I ad were cremated. I gave they
To the fowls.

Why she takes posing seriously:

I only ave to sit yur and
See the scenery. Whatever you want,
Love, don't be afraid to move it.
You can fiddle as much as you like.
There's sittens, and there's fidgets.
If e ain't right, say so.

Why she sings:

I d'know a few ditties.
Some o they modern songs be all right.

and recites:

'Behold, a giant am I! Aloft here in my tower . . .'
(Moving her arms as they taught her at school.
Gets to the end, without flaw.)

and talks about education:

At school, they did teach we to remember.
When I did learn the alphabet, I did learn it
Frontards and backards. (And does it.)
Teachers wasn't afraid of kids in they days.
I did like Grimms' Tales. I know

'Tis only imagination, but I did like en.
They did turn out good scholars in they days.

She won't tell her age. But she will tell you

I wasn't built in a day.

3. *A Touch of Eclair*

A golden day for our dog when, passing that Coombe cottage,
She was given a chocolate eclair. Ever after,
Our dog appalled Long Street drivers, bounding over to Amy.

Old and straight like Westridge beeches,
We see her now in paintings, not as she was,
Waiting outside the Co-op with her shopping.

Swift and surprising, like the road from Nibley,
Her wit and her way with words. Gloucester
Has an archive; they study her vowels in Birmingham.

The endless bone-weary work she did on roads round Wotton
To clean them for us. Fish and chip paper,
Toffee papers, sweet papers, *all the ruddy lot.*

Something grand, something gold about Amy. Thin, old, poor,
She blessed us all with her blunt presence. A touch of eclair
At her funeral, when the Silver Band played her out.

FOR OS 759934: 14.2.96. A LOVE-POEM

She is my Corinna, my Lucasta,
Whose name, for courtesy, I will not say.

Like a tomboy, she sprawls among sharp small hills;
Like a sibyl, she drifts into silences and fog.

She has her own way with birds and flowers;
Is given to minor fierce festivals without much notice.

Her speech is like a mouthful of hot chestnuts.
Extra hs and ls give her vowels grace.

Her lovely highborn sisters over the hill
With their suitors and reputations look down on her.

She doesn't care, preferring her laidback cronies,
Symn, Bradley, Haw, Bear, Ragnall and Shinbone.

Her favourite scent: a dab of woodsmoke behind the ears.
Haute couture and haute cuisine are not her style.

She is an early riser, watery and echoing;
I love her then. And in the evening, when blackbirds call it a day.
In all the seasons of every year I love her.
And this seems as good a day as any to say so.

CONYGRE WOOD AND HYAKINTHOIDES NON-SCRIPTUS

(for Libby Houston)

This is how it is, here:
Native halflight. Rain off the Atlantic.
Rack of blue like sky growing
A foot above ground. Hush. Birdcalls.
Small puckered beech leaves, and earth,
Its muscles showing, hurdling up limestone,
With acres of blue on its back.

Disappointment to the early masters,
Dons, doctors, name-givers,
Like getting a girl when you wanted a boy.
They hoped for Hyakinthos, the beautiful,
Whose literate petals say *AI AI*
Sorry Sorry, inscribed by divine Apollo,
Who killed the lovely creature by mistake.

But our island gets this lot, illiterate
Non-scriptus flowers. Growing along with garlic,
Smelling of honey, careless of Latin snubs.
Blue and blue and blue and free
Of an invented grief, free
To come and go, to multiply, to chant
The noiseless bluebell anthem: *Here we are.*

THE OFFSHORE TRIP

It's not far really.
The by-laws will be the same,
And the flora. Language will be banal
In familiar ways. And yet

This small elementary act of crossing the water
Implies another chance, a different world.

(We crossed in an open boat.)

Safety announcements about dressing warmly,
Remaining calm in an emergency.
How far are we going?   What shipwrecks underlie
This modest channel?

(It was a still November evening.)

Gulls cry prosaically. The galley
Smells of bacon. Look! we are never
Out of sight of land. Two ferries
Edge past each other in the seaway
Like ceremonious topheavy tea-cosies.

(One dark heron flew over the Solent
Backed by a daffodil sky.)

We have artless designs. Mr Tennyson
Is looking for a house; a holiday, a visit –
That's about it. But inscrutable dark doings
Fidget us somewhere. Without knowing how we know,
We know of the dead great king, the open boat
Stuffed with gold and swords, ice on the thwarts,

Give way, and the people wailing,
Their luck-bringer gone. They let the sea take him,
Not knowing where that cargo would fetch up.

This we know and don't know as we board the ferry.

The parentheses indicate quotations from the diary of Emily Tennyson.
The dead king is Scyld, king of the Danes, whose ship-burial is
described at the beginning of *Beowulf.*

THE BURREN

Undomesticated. A great grey
Migrainous cramp of rock,
Squeezed, compressed and scoured
To treeless dryness, and in the air,
The noise of waters underground.

Bloody-minded sort of place, it looks,
Where old faiths shrivel, old names are defaced.
But out of these barren flags, this crazed landscape,
Jut the resilient heads of a melting-pot
Of flowers from the high and cold, the low and hot,
The wet, wet places. All at ease on this rockface.

Like finding love in someone disliked at first.

And the boy out shooting rabbits put his fingers
In a rocky crack, touched the smoothness
Of a king's gold breastplate left behind
At Gleninsheen. These flybynight findings
Wait within gunshot in unpromising places –
Gold breastplates, gentians, happiness-ever-after.

SEVEN TYPES OF SHADOW

1.
I have an item, Chair, under Any Other Business.
We ghosts have become creatures of habit, with our
Bloody shrouds, bloody footprints, blood. Some of us,
I believe, still hold our heads under our arms.

The agenda is stale, gentleghosts. Midnight. The temperature drops.
Dogs' hackles rise. Tawny owls provide

The continuo. A chain rattles. A floorboard creaks.
We know the repertoire. *So do the living.*

You see how it is, fellow-ghosts. We are fossilized.
Something unconventional's needed; the ghost, perhaps,
Of a happy moment. Try this: wraith of a spectral grandee,
Whose horse has just won the Derby. A lady might like that.

He throws his topper in the air, a champagne shade.
Or a musical ghost, ghost of divine Handel,
Scribbling down the final *Hallelujah,*
Thinking he's just seen heaven. How about that?

2.
Furthermore, ghosts, the matter of dialogue.
A surplus of vowels is ours – all those *ooos* and *aaas.*
Think of the vital things we could be saying,
Like *I've finished the Pope's ceiling! All of it!*

Or *One hundred and fifty-four sonnets! Not bad, Ben?*
Or, in the mist and snow, *I fancy this might be the top,*
Or *I tried it on the dairymaid, and it worked.*
Or – surprisingly – *We are a grandmother!*

3.
This is a country of ghosts. Down the eastern shore
Lie the drowned villages, drowned luggers, drowned sailors.

After a hot summer, fields grow talkative.
Wheat speaks in crop marks, grasses in parch marks.

Wheat or grass, what they tell is the truth
Of things that lay underneath five thousand years ago,

The forts, the barrows, the barns, the shrines, the walls.
These are the native ghosts. After a hot summer.

No haunting. No rattle of chains. They just lie there
In their rigid truthfulness, the ghosts of things.

4.
We carry our human ghosts around with us.
As we grow we face the mirrors, and see

The spectre of a great-aunt, a vague look
Known only from sepia snapshots. The hands we're used to –

Yes, these – their contours came by way of a long retinue
Of dust. We are photofits of the past,

And the future eyes us sideways as we eye ourselves.
We are the ghosts of great-aunts and grand-nephews.

We are ghosts of what is dead and not yet born.

5.
And here's a man as near a ghost
As you can be, and not be dead.
He haunts his world from love,
Before his world's awake.

His personal early morning. He moves with it,
Shredding the nightshift behind. World Service
Croons *Lillibullero* in his ear, and confides
What no one yet knows: a statesman disgraced;
Bomb in the Paris Metro; goal after extra time
In Argentina. He notes the emergency windows, bright and busy
With midwives, students, bankrupts, lovers, thieves.

These are the pinched hours, scrounged from blackout,
Too soon for milk or mail. Even the cocks
Not alerted yet. Engine silenced, he coasts
The inhabited yards to home, shuts and opens and shuts
As if doors were silk. The sleepers sprawl
In their private zigzags. He walks *sotto voce*,
As if they were all sick children. *Lillibullero*.

He has perverse cravings, to mow the lawn, to sing,
Or hoover, or run a bath. Smell's risky as sound.
No bacon. Not even the modest tang of toast.
Conscious of power, knowing he could shatter
The tenuous fringes of sleep, like a small
Insignificant god, he bestows on them quiet, peace,
The useful dreams that come at the edge of morning.

Passive, he waits for the world to move his way,
To want to know who won after extra time
In Argentina. *Lillibullero*.

6.
Ghosts of past, present, future.
But the ones the living would like to meet are the echoes
Of moments of small dead joys still quick in the streets,

Voices calling *I've passed/We won/QED/*
It didn't hurt much, Mum/They've given me the job/
I have decided to name this apple Bramley;

And the women convicts singing their Holloway march,
While Ethel Smyth conducts from her cell with a toothbrush.

7.

These are the ghosts the living would prefer,
Ghosts who'd improve our ratings. Ghosts
Of the great innocent songs of freedom
That shoulder their way round the world like humpback whales,

Ghosts of the singers, the dancers, the liberated,
Holding hands and cheering in parks, while the tanks
Squat immobilised. Ghosts of the women on the fish quay
Hugging each other when at last the boats come in.

Ghosts of the last night of the Proms. And ghosts of lovers,
Wandering round London, so happy that they could
Have danced danced danced all night.

NEW HIGHGATE CEMETERY: 4 APRIL 1996

(i.m. Tom Wakefield)

Passover. And the rabbi's taking a risk
(Somebody hints) to be at a gentile funeral
On the holiest day.* After the general amens,
In a low voice, moved, he speaks the prayer for the dead.

Maundy Thursday. The glamorous vicar, stripped
To a showy scarlet cassock, circulates
After the burial. Embraces shoulders,
Rubs his face against other wet faces. Borrows a hanky.

From Tottenham to Arsenal, Chelsea to Crystal Palace,
Florists have been picked clean. All flowers are here,
Banked up, as if honouring murdered babies,
Taking their chance of the April frosts with Tom.

Aintree week. So Tom should have been laying
His arcane bets. But death, the rank outsider,
Chose a different winning-post, and here,
In a recklessness of flowers, Tom lies, the right

Place at last, among comrades, campaigners, jokers,
Near the surly shadow of Marx. His heart gave out,
As we might have expected, used too much
For loving whoever, whatever would let him love.

We have lost his teacher's searchlight eye, that located
Not back-row trouble, but goodness all over; his novelist's ear,
That listened to the vague, the stumbling,
And knew what they meant; we have lost

His running-to-meet-you heart, that ignored
The tactics of learning and power, but cared so much
About being simply human. This over-the-top
Stuff would embarrass him. Stop. Say *Sorry, Tom*.

*In fact, the Sabbath is the 'holiest day' for Jews while Passover is
regarded as a Jewish festival.

UNDERGROUND

(Henry Moore's *A Shelter Sketchbook*)

They have come as far as there is,
Under the tree-roots, the sewers,
Under drains, cables, flood-plains.

They sprawl, wrapped in blankets,
Waiting like tubers for spring, the all-clear.
At Belsize Park, Cricklewood,

The Liverpool Street Extension,
Londoners lie under London, incubating
A difficult energy, a different life.

Round the corner the artist watches,
Jotting notes on an envelope.
To have drawn from life would be like

Sketching in the hold of a slave ship.
Not the Cockney wags of legend, but huge
Muffled forms, trussed and bandaged

Like Lazarus. Wood and stone,
As well as bones and veins, wait inside
These vast vulnerabilities.

From their coding, we can construe
Houses falling, bridges falling, London falling,
Civilisations falling down. The artist

Must show this without saying. Just
His sketchbook's sotto-voce: *Abstractish figures shelter background,*
And *Try white again then scramble dryish grey over.*

Also he shows the women knitting,
People holding hands, sleeping,
And thinking. Particularly thinking.

From these rhizomes the future will rise,
Equivocal, chancy. Crowned stones
On a northern moor, too big for houses,

And paper-shrouded Cardboard Citizens,
Sleeping in Strand doorways, neighbours to rubbish,
And all stations between. As Cabot

Aimed for Japan, got Newfoundland instead,
These monstrous eggs may hatch surprisingly.

Above them, paving stones and tarmac sag,
Windows taped into resistance, the hunched
Apprehensive roofs of Cricklewood

And Belsize Park, the Liverpool Street Extension,
Guns, smoke, cloud, fighters, bombers, fire, air,

Under the City, in the sky, pitched
Between heaven and humanity, as we are,
The tube trains shuttling between,

And the artist taking notes round the corner.

WIDENING THE WESTWAY

Torched, they might have been, in another country
Because the wrong people lived in them;
Or, in quieter times, in homelier places,
Left to slither modestly back to earth.

But this is London. There are guide-lines.
Houses are groomed for a protracted ending.

Some house-man has been on his rounds, diagnosing
The slow-motion stages of a terminal event.
Amputate, he prescribed. First went the more portable shrubs,
The carpets, fittings. Lastly, the people.

Then experts came. They blinded each window
With hardboard, extracted knockers and bells like teeth;

As nurses raise screens in wards to island the dying,
They erected eight-foot boards to segregate.

(And someone has aerosoled *Save us* and *Help*,
Help and *Save us*, along the new wood.)

An avenue-full of confident thirties semis,
Twin-gabled, porched, with double mock-Tudor chimneys,
Who shopped at the Army and Navy, golfed in Ealing,
Dentists, dog-walkers, Dry Fly drinkers – that sort of house.

Now they tremble together, W12 Samsons;
Rooftops flayed of tiles are all you can see.
Tomorrow men in heavy duty yellow jackets
With JCBs will rubbish the garlanded plaster.

(And the forsythia gamely still in flower,
And the houses opposite watching speechless
Like aristos brought too soon in their tumbrils,
Watching the load before them.)

This was the way the world marched on.
This may be how it starts. *Atrocity*
Is what we haven't got used to yet.

MAUD SPEAKING

When I came to the gate alone
    You were making eyes at a lily,
Conversing in such an intimate tone
    That I felt remarkably silly.
Your grotesque behaviour I cannot condone.
    Your welcome I found chilly.

A poet, I know, may be queer.
    One learns to be dignified.
One would rather not interfere.
    One has one's feminine pride.
That very long poem about Mr Arthur Henry Hallam
    One took in one's stride.

But a man who talks all night
    To a larkspur and a rose –
Is something wrong with your sight?
    I thought you meant to propose,
But when I arrived you ignored me quite.
    I might as well have been prose.

And I didn't care for the stuff
    You wrote about my head;
Little head, like a light-minded bit of fluff;
    But I'm tolerably well read,
Would have studied at Newnham, under Miss Clough,
    If Papa hadn't sworn *better dead*.

Away, melancholy!
    Lord Tennyson, goodbye.
I'm up to here with botany,
    I want someone streetwise and spry.
There are plenty of suitable fish in the sea.
    Poets need not apply.

GOSPEL TRUTH

(for Matt Simpson)

I am the one who sees,
    Whose eyes out-eye the sun.
Who flies beyond the mind
    Who knows all that is done.
All words, all theories
    For me spell out the One.
I am the eye that sees;
    I am the eagle, John.

I am the one who tells
    The dreadful descent of man:
Adam, Attila, Gandhi,
    Hero and hooligan.
We all inherit beastliness
    Some of us light on grace;
I am Mark, the archivist,
    Mark with the lion's face.

I learned my art in hospitals
    Where life begins and ends;
Where some refuse and some consent
    And nobody much attends.
And some are called to be sacrificed,
    The lobster, the lamb, the fox;
I honour the One who consents to death,
    Luke stands for the ox.

This is the one who walks,
    Who knows the people's names,
The shops, the cinemas, the docks,
    The pubs, the children's games;

Who loves the living and the dead
   Of the place where he began,
The holy city, Liverpool.
   Matthew celebrates man.

OVERHEARD AT LUMB BANK

(two tutors consult)

E D:

Let's toss for it. Shall it be you
Or shall it be me that speaks
To Emily about her punctuation?

W W:

There's been a complaint from Heptonstall
About Bill. He's asking kids questions.
Not exactly *accosting*, no. But odd things, like
How many in family? Are they stepping westward?
Might lead to something. You can't be too careful.
You'd better watch it, Bill, I said to him.
I'd rather you stuck to daffodils while you're here.

The Visitor:

The tall one? She isn't on my list. Seems
To have just walked in. Don't know
About her stuff. It seems
Familiar, somehow. *Rialto*, would you say,
Or *Outposts*? I get the impression
She might be local.

A T:

Well, I can see you've worked really hard at this.
All these rough drafts you've kindly brought along.
I respect your dedication. But I don't know
If anybody's going to publish it.

Friendship. Bit of a coy word, wouldn't you say
In this day and age? Come clean about *in* or *out*,
Alfred, then we'll know who your readers are.
And while we're at it, all these Greeks or whatever
– Gods, sorry – really, they won't do.
This one. Tithonus? Never heard of her.
How d'you pronounce it? How many readers know that?
And this rhyme scheme of yours, *abba*,
It really does go on, you know. Monotonous.
Depressing, too. Sorry to be so tough,
But you've come here for help; that's what you're getting.

PETITION OF THE CATS CONCERNING
MR PETER PORTER

This from the congregation of the cats:
Our candidate is house-trained; endures
Fur on his trousers, fishbreath up his nose,
Sick on the carpet, dead mice in dark places.

Though of a migratory nature, he's exact
About returning home to your deponents.
Here he communes with gods called Bark and Persil,
Speaks on paper, air and the electrics

Of things unknown to cats, but in tones we trust.
He reads in books, is globally learned.
Your excellencies know of course that Mr P
Is a major poet. Cats, though they dance, sing and skylark,

Have not mastered this craft, but we understand
Certain of our tribe have been celebrated in it,
Namely one Jeoffry, several Practicals, and a small
One singing on a train. Mr Porter speaks well of cats,

And all small harried things. He minds
About myxomatosis; spit-roasting chickens
Spit *Auschwitz*, to him; he sees *the unbending
Seriousness of small creatures.*

Remember this, excellencies: the learning,
Pity, wisdom (considering too the recent incumbent's
Taste for beaks, claws, hooks, teeth and other ungentle things),
We present our candidate as Poet Laureate (Creatures).

Thank you for your attention.

POSTCARDS

(*for Christine Wells*)

The walkabout postman studies his handful
Before he slots them home. What do they say?

Public as T-shirts, coded like
A mole's correspondence, designed to be enigmatic.

Having a wonderful they say. *Oh boy
This is the life!* or *Cooler now. Had to put*

Our *cardies on,* they say, or *Natives friendly,*
Or just *Wish you were here.* He knows, the postman,

They don't say what they mean, mean what they say.
Extraordinary too, he thinks, the cards they send:

Of opera houses; owls; folk being ethnic;
Fish; teapots; *eucryphia milleganii*

(What'll she make of that? he thinks, popping it in).
Each picture sends a message – proud, witty, wise –

But not enough for him to understand.
(*Super day yesterday sorry I missed the post.*)

O postman, postman, endlessly chivvied by cliché,
This freakish correspondence that teases you so
Is a minor rehearsal for the final take-off.

Look in the graveyard, as you make your round;
There are the ultimate postcards, trite as ever,
Stylised as runes, with a subtext intricate

As a crossword puzzle clue, or house-agent's blurb,
Delivering the last message of stay-at-homes
To those who have left on a journey beyond deliveries:

Gone, not forgotten; Sadly missed; Wish you were here.

LOOK, NO HANDS

(*Lala at the Fernando Circus,* by Edgar Degas. National Gallery, London)

He:
It was hard doing this. I had to go up near the roof,
Among the girders and dusty bits. And I had to keep
On trying till I found the right place to be –
Left, and in front; not very far below her
So I could make you see how hard it is.

You have to imagine the audience. I didn't
Bother with them, they're always the same,
Ooh-ing, aah-ing, clapping, some of them
Shutting their eyes. And the smells. You have
To imagine them too: people, horses, sawdust, sweat.

You're lucky. I'm showing you what the audience
Can't really see. Far off, up in the roof,
Something between a bird and an angel, using
Arms like wings. Hovering, you could say;
Not holding on. See how she does it?
Neither a bird nor an angel, she flies.

She:
All right, I suppose. Doesn't look much like me,
But it's me all right, my act. He's better
Than the usual gawpers. *How much d'you weigh?* they say,
Or *Are your teeth your own?* He painted my boots OK.
I told him they cost a bomb.

THE WITNESS

Picturesque as Raskolnikov,
The accused in the dock,
Probing the metaphysic of offence.

Apprentice, uncomfortable, the jury
Cranes towards every opening mouth,
Knowing that sooner or later there will be a verdict,
And they will be guilty of it.

Solicitors, counsel, clerk, have a place,
And are easy there. At home, they remember,
A separate life of hugging, smoking,
Solving the crossword, asking what's for dinner.

The judge sits above, like a tennis umpire;
Now and then he mentions the rules of the game.
He is accustomed to scarlet, horsehair, ermine.
Intimidation is not his intention,
But what he achieves. Let us now

Examine the witness. He is the outsider,
He belongs to another court, pursuing
A different code. He is messenger
Of what happened, expert without diploma,
Suspect as a prisoner, innocent as a judge.

All he can say is what he saw,
And that's an old story. Cross-examined,
He flounders. His vigilance is fishy,
His ignorance shady. Truth is hard to translate
When our only machinery is words.

POPULAR FALLACIES

that snow is somehow holy; that bleak midwinters
are commonplace events in Palestine;

that snow is snow-white (wrong. It's eyelid colour,
colour of blood at the farthest end of the wound);

that it blesses (it doesn't; its spiteful tally of wrens,
explorers, old people sitting in chairs,

kingfishers, match-girls, gives it away). Affable thug, that
has it in for the poor, small, brave, bluffing

the rest of us with your rubber-stamping sameness; snuffer-
out of difference, hypocrite white-out,

landhungry dictator with your whiteshirts, your overnight putsch,
your doubletalk about absolution,

watch it! under your white sepulchre the fifth column of
the future is waiting, new, particular,

bright green.

SIGHTINGS

1
It was there all the time, the dark planet
That no one saw. Mathematicians nagged,
Convinced it was there by the frolic
Detours of the others. Such heavenly high jinks
Offended their neat minds. A flurry

Of sums across Europe, and lo! Neptune
Exists (official). Fireworks. National pride. Letters
In learned journals. Unmoved, the great
Green gassy planet perseveringly
Coasts its majestic journey through the dark.

2
The town's there all the time, under the mist.
Well, of course it is. I walked up from it,
Alone with the dog, the early birds
And a sun so private all it could achieve
Was a bar of light on hawthorn
And the crocketed tips of the church tower
Springing up from the meadow of fog below
Chanting *glory glory* in thin gold voices.
Beneath the haze a town's work is hatching,
Quick, bright, smelling of herbs and bread.

3
There's two of each of us, I think he thinks,
But indistinguishable. There's one from Ephesus
And one from Syracuse. The audience knows,
But we don't. That's the point; the strangeness
Of the other who is the same.
Twins pop up everywhere. King Claudius, King Hamlet,
Goneril and Regan, Falstaff and the King,
Hoping to be part of the last act magic
Moment of revelation, when yes, there are two,
But also one, joined by something darker than love.

AFTERWARDS

The principalities, the powers, the politicians,
The ones who pose in the spotlight
Centre-stage, and magnetise us as they stalk
Towards bankruptcy, murder, betrayal, suicide,
And other traditional exits

The audience leaves, discussing nuances.
A scatter of sweet-papers, ash,
Smells hanging around behind. The audience leaves.

And in they come, rolling up their sleeves,
With hoovers and mops, buckets and brushes and Brasso,
Making it ready for the next time, nobody watching,
With small uncompetitive jokes, with backchat
About coach-trips, soaps, old men,
And a great sloshing of water.

This is where we ought to be. Not
Up on the stage with the rich and the Richards,
Rehearsing already their entry for the next house,
The precise strut that registers power,

But down on our hands and knees,
Laughing, and mopping up.

ANOTHER SWAN POEM

This swan knows too much poetry.
It came knocking at the window

Importunate, drumming Tap-Tap
Like a midnight lover. This is

Early morning for us, Swan. It
Takes not a blind bit of. It stands

On water, wings spreadeagling,
Neck rampant, mouthing *Me. You. Now.*

Eat. Now. You. Me. No magic shirt,
No ducal coronet, just bare

Swan, mouthing *Me. Eat. You.* Nervous,
We fetch the brown sliced. The snake-neck

Lunges as we cast Hovis on
The water. Vindictively it

Dunks, drowns, swallows. Rears up again.
Romance is what it wants. Savage

Black eyes peer close. We can number
The brownish forehead feathers. Far

Too near. The long beak opens, long
And oval-ended, containing

A sharp active tongue. The creature
Seeks to be seductive. Wants us

To slot our bread inside its beak.
We do it, gingerly, trying

Not to touch. It accepts the slice,
Dips it, comes back, until the last

Scatter of crumbs. Reluctantly
It navigates away. A faint

Me. You. comes sighing down the water.

This is not a good poem about a swan,
But it might be the bravest. It is also true.

OLIVE

Generosity: the gift of the gods. This one
Is famous for giving Athens a singular tree.

We met in my office door. She'd jammed
Her hoover in it. *Sorry, my lover,* she said.

Don't like to leave it in the passage.
Patients fall over things. Daily thereafter

She'd hail me: *Still yur, then?* And once,
Thassa funny name you got. Latin, ennit? I'm Olive.

Now you know. Her first gift, drink. A cup of tea (hot)
By my phone every day when I came to work.

Thought you could do with it. All that way
Yew as to come. No kettle, ave yer?

Thought not. Not like they nurses,
Always at the Tetleys. Next came food

(A Welsh cake) on Fridays. *Nice recipe, ennit?*
Our Nan's. From the Forest, she wuz. After that, learning

(She was famous for it). *Bit ignorant about Bristol,*
Aren't yer? Ave a read of me book.

Later, understanding. *Yer won't learn much about patients*
From doctors and nurses. Yew as to get to like em.

We're in there ages doing them toilets. It all adds up.

She decided I needed laughter. Every day
Was waiting in my office with a joke,

Selected specially, just right for me –
Not rude or stale or obvious. Not easy, either.

She watched me like a suspect. Had I got there?
Or was my laugh just half a bar too late?

Her final gift was cryptic. She put
Three flaky bulbs in my hand when I left,

And *See what comes of they,* she said.
What came was lilies. Came, and keep on coming,

Tall and immortal in a mortal garden.

Note: Athene, the wise goddess, presented Athens with the olive tree,
the gift most useful to mortals.

POST-OP

Artists are wrong about light. They strew it
Tastefully across landscapes, let it focus
Thoughtfully on a forehead or a cabbage,
Self-consciously walk down a reach of water.

Artists are wrong.

Light comes storming out of its corner
Dealing dazzling uppercuts to the eyes.

See, says Light, *It's like this and like this,*
Injecting the whole national grid into one lens;

This is what you were missing, says Light,
Grinning like a mouthful of American teeth;

Fizzing and raucous, like the mixture
In Dr Jekyll's retort; importunate, like the tune

A child has just acquired for one finger.
That's good, says Light, *I knew you'd like it,*

And demonstrates
The unexpected awfulness of the tiles on the kitchen floor.

AUTUMN OFFER

Vacancies available now
For the next millennium's consumers, investors,
And personnel. We supply
State-of-the-art instruction – the leaner, fitter curriculum
Your youngster needs. Already
We have axed from our course the modules that clearly
Have long passed their sell-by-date:
Art, music, history, literature, religion.
Currently we are phasing out language,
But retaining Japanese and German,
For obvious reasons.

(*Season of timetables, and uniform* . . .)

Up-to-the-minute hard/software is
Our speciality, thanks to the funding of
Our sponsors, whose logo you will notice. In view of
Such high-tech resources, we're talking
Economies of scale staff-wise. We're sure
Parents will appreciate the forward nature of this move.

(Season of texts, and learning what to think . . .)

Due to our expertise in counselling we guarantee
To painlessly re-program, and remove
All juvenile addictions: drugs,
Cloudsofglory, sex, humour,
Imagination, cheating, hope,
Etc. Research tells us these
No longer enjoy street cred.

(Season of learning to be like the rest . . .)

Our youngsters must learn to grow up
Aggressive, acquisitive, mean. We put them in teams
And train them to slog it out
According to the rules (union, league,
Whatever). Most of life's problems can be solved
By running fast and kicking something.

THE GARDENER AT CHRISTMAS

He has done all that needs to be done.

Rake, fork, spade, cleaned and oiled,
Idle indoors; seeds, knotty with destiny, rattle
Inside their paper jackets. The travelling birds

Have left; predictable locals
Mooch in the early dusk.

He dreams of a future in apples,
Of three white lilies in flower,
Of a tree that could bear a man.

He sits back and waits
For it all to happen.

CHRISTMAS TRAFFIC

Three, two, one, zero, liftoff
Signals Mission Control. And off they go
To the dark parts of the planets
In their pressurised spacesuits,
Cocooned in technology, the astronauts.

Mission control whispers in someone's ear.
Yes, she says, *I will.* And in due time
A different traveller makes a quieter journey,
Arriving hungry, naked, but true to instructions,
Docking on Earth, taking the one small step.

BIRD PSALM

The Swallow said,
He comes like me,
Longed-for; unexpectedly.

The superficial eye
Will pass him by,
Said the Wren.

The best singer ever heard.
No one will take much notice,
Said the Blackbird.

The Owl said,
He is who, who is he
Who enters the heart as soft
As my soundless wings, as me.

CHRISTMAS IN ENVELOPES

Monks are at it again, quaffing, carousing;
And stage-coaches, cantering straight out of Merrie England,
In a flurry of whips and fetlocks, sacks and Santas.

Raphael has been roped in, and Botticelli;
Experts predict a vintage year for Virgins.

From the theologically challenged, Richmond Bridge,
Giverny, a lugger by moonlight, doves. Ours

Costs less than these in money, more in time;
Like them, is hopelessly irrelevant,
But brings, like them, the eternal message

love

CHRISTMAS POEMS

2002

THE SUN CAPERS

The sun capers
Down the goat's short sky.

Nothing fruits but
Holly, flowers but ivy.

Ephemeral
Tinsel, glass balls, whisky,

Crackers, signal
The birth of the god.

MERRY CHRISTMAS!

WHAT THE DONKEY SAW

No room in the inn, of course,
And not that much in the stable,
What with the shepherds, Magi, Mary,
Joseph, the heavenly host –
Not to mention the baby
Using our manger as a cot.
You couldn't have squeezed another cherub in
For love nor money.

Still, in spite of the overcrowding,
I did my best to make them feel wanted.
I could see the baby and I
Would be going places together.

I AM JOSEPH

I am Joseph, carpenter
Of David's kingly line,
I wanted an heir; discovered
My wife's son wasn't mine.

I am an obstinate lover,
Loved Mary for better or worse.
Wouldn't stop loving when I found
Someone Else came first.

Mine was the likeness I hoped for
When the first-born man-child came.
But nothing of him was me. I couldn't
Even choose his name.

I am Joseph, who wanted
To teach my own boy how to live.
My lesson for my foster son:
Endure. Love. Give.

LULLABY: SANCTUS DEUS

(for Jessica Weeks)

The Angels

Sanctus deus, sleep.
Careful angels keep
Watch from sky's vast sweep.
Nothing moves but sheep.
Lord of heaven, sanctus deus,
Now's the time for sleep.

Mary and Joseph

Baby Jesus, dream
Of some happy theme.
Toothless darling, beam;
Here's no cause to scream.
Mary, Joseph, novice parents,
Whisper: *Baby, dream.*

The Ox

Little man-calf, grow.
You have far to go.
I, the patient, slow,
Stable ox, say so.
Lord of heaven, little calf-man,
My advice is: *Grow.*

THE WISE MAN AND THE STAR

The proper place for stars is in the sky,
Lighting the whole world, but negotiating only
With the highly qualified – master mariners, astro-physicists,
Professionals like ourselves.

This one came unscheduled, nudged us roughly
Out of routine, led us a wild-goose chase,
And perching here, above unspeakable rafters,
Common as a starling on a washing line,
Whistles to every callow Dick and Harry,
Idling amazed around: 'OK pals, I've done my bit.
Over to you now, Earth.'

THE TREE

In the wood I am one of many.
I am felled, sold, chosen
To be sole tree of a house.
I am throned in a gold bucket.
Light is sewn through my branches,
Precious gifts wrapped in silver
Depend on my twigs. Star-crowned,
I am adored by children, cordially hated
By hoovering housewives, distrusted
By Health and Safety Officers, who name me
Fire Hazard. I reign for twelve days,
Then am sacrificed among rubbish,
Where I wither, age, decay.

But every year I rise again indoors,
Hazardous fire of love.

NOW

After the frantic shopping
The anxious road
After the office parties
The crowded inn

Before the quarterly bills
The stones gathered
Before the January sales
And Stephen, broken

After the carols and lessons
The psalms, the prophets

After the gifts are wrapped
The swaddling clothes

Before the Queen's Speech
A baby's cry
Across the morning suburbs
The Light of the World

OPEN HOUSE

Queen Ivy and King Holly
Wait at the door to enter
Lord of dark hills, the fir tree
Reigns in the Garden Centre
And the changeling Mistletoe
        Come into the house
        Whoever you are.

Dangerous padded parcels
A red man's chancy load,
With riddled cores of crackers
Watch for their hour to explode
And the changeling Mistletoe
        Come into the house
        Whoever you are.

Black heart of the pudding,
Stuffed heart of the bird,
Green hearts of the brussels sprouts
Signal the holy word
Of ancestral Mistletoe
        Come into the house
        Whoever you are.

NOT THE MILLENNIUM

Wise men are busy being computer-literate.

There should be a law against confusing
Religion with mathematics.
There was a baby. Born where?
And when? The sources mention
Massacres, prophecies, stars;
They tell a good story, but they don't agree.

So we celebrate at the wrong midnight.
Does it matter? Only dull science expects
An accurate audit. The economy of heaven
Looks for fiestas and fireworks every day,
Every day.
               Be realistic, says heaven:
Expect a miracle.

QUEUEING FOR THE SUN

2003

QUEUEING FOR THE SUN IN WALBROOK

(for John Shepherd, and in honour of W. F. Grimes and A. Williams)

The first great London queue.
Not trivial, like the countdown to Harrods sales,
Or charter-flights stacking above Heathrow.
BIG CROWDS AT ROMAN RUIN. MANY
UNABLE TO ENTER. First
Of the serious patient processions: Mithras;
Tutankhamun; Cézanne; Monet.

The only one unearthed in London.
Bull-slayer's temple. His head, with its far-seeing
Merciful eyes, his huge right hand closed on the hilt,
Ready for sacrifice; other bits and pieces,
Gods of all sorts, the usual bones, coins,
Lamps, a hairpin, endless scraps of pots, a candlestick.
MORE FINDS . . . LATEST FINDS . . . CHANCE OF MORE
        DISCOVERIES.

Bombing resurrected the god. A full moon,
Thames at low tide, bringing blitzkrieg
Through the air. Worst raid of the war.
They suffered, Tower, Abbey, Mint,
Westminster Hall, the Commons. London's burning.
But he was still safe, the little foreigner,
DEO INVICTO SOLI MITHRAE
Though Walbrook, Budge Row, Bucklersbury
Fractured on top of him.

After the war, the man,
Grimes, in search of a river. Archaeology,
As usual, against the clock. The builders
Had their blueprints, the developers
Had secured the funding. Some of the unbuilt units
Already let. And Grimes and his little team,

Responsible for all wrecked London, unravelling rubble,
Storing things in paper bags.

On the dig's last day, the god's head,
Decapitated, dirty, alien, moving.
Photographers stalked it, the people came unflagging
To queue, as war had taught them, to see
Something outlandish, risen from London earth,
Wearing their waiting like medals.
CROWDS SEE EIGHTEEN-HUNDRED-YEAR-OLD
ROMAN GOD DUG UP.

The endless orderly march cowed the Cabinet.
Professors wrote letters. Ministers went to see,
Proposed *A week or two more digging?*
His neck materialised. Queues, and more queues,
From Cheapside, the Bank of England, down Walbrook,
Great hungry demonstrations. STILL HOPE
OF REPRIEVE FOR ROMAN TEMPLE.
But of course there wasn't. Money speaks
Louder than Mithras. *I doubt,* said a spokesman,
If this public interest will last.
This is tax-payers' money, after all.

It's still there, and it isn't. Bucklersbury House
Has cornered the holy ground. What you see of the temple,
Re-invented in Queen Victoria Street,
Is in the wrong place, not far enough down,
Looking the wrong way. SOLI INVICTO
AB ORIENTE AD OCCIDENTEM. But the sun
Remains unconquered.

Notes to *Queueing for the Sun in Walbrook*

Mithras, the god of light and the sun among the Persians, was specially venerated by the Roman army. The Roman temple of Mithras, in the City of London, was probably built AD 240–250; subsequently all traces of it were lost. It began to surface in 1941, during the war, on one of the worst nights of the Blitz. No excavation could be done at that time, but in 1954, which is where the poem begins, the digging was well under way. Professor W. F. Grimes was in charge of all archaeological excavation in the City. He was in fact tracking the course of the River Walbrook when he came across the temple.

There is a chorus: the headlines of London's evening papers (*the Star, News* and *Standard*); the Latin of the inscriptions; and the voices of civil servants and politicians.

Deo invicto soli Mithrae: to the unconquered sun

Soli invicto ab oriente ad occidentem: the invincible sun from east to west

THE GAOLER'S STORY

A string of names as long as your arm.
One of those quietish voices, you can tell
He's never had to raise it in his life.

The old school toga, probably descended
From that wolf they all go on about.
Cream de la cream. But I liked him. Really did.

Educated, of course, to the hilt. Only once
I saw him put out. They duffed him up a bit
When they bring him in. He just wiped off the blood –

Knew how to take it. No, but when
He got the message, no more books for him –
Well, then he *was* upset. Covered his head.

I think he was crying. Books, you see, books.
He could face most things with them. Now, take His Kingship
(Theo, we call him, but not to his face),

Brilliant man, brilliant, but books are something
He wouldn't thank you for. Why bother, if you're a king?
Always someone there to read 'em for you

If that's what you want. Bit of a handicap, mind,
For a king not to sign his name. Laws and that
Need signing. He has this gold stencil thing,

And pokes a pen through the holes. Well, it works.
And he's such a superpower he can get away
With murder. Unfortunate phrase. Forget it.

Anyway, make you laugh to see the grandees,
Magisters this and that, Referendariums, Praetorian whatsits
(I don't know what they do) agawp

When Theo gets out his stencil and signs
Laws that'll change their lives. And all us Goths
Sniggering up our sleeves. But quietly. He likes us

To get on. Us and the Romans. They're citizens, we're not.
Separate, but equal, says Theo. Well, not quite.
They have the thinking parts, we do the rough.

But yeah, it works. Why, I can't say, unless it's him.
He's strong. Won't take nothing from nobody.
Just as well, with all the gatecrashers we have

Hanging around on the borders. And he minds
About the Stone Age Roman junk. Ruins
That Julius Caesar knocked about a bit

(Or someone). Theatres, walls, drains, aqueducts,
He's seen to 'em all. In Rome and places,
Not just here. You should see the new work in Verona.

Not my cuppa. We're tent-men, as you know.
He's made us comfy here. But there are times
When there's a sort of edginess. This business of B –

I don't want to talk about it. But I wasn't happy,
The sort of man B was, things that went on.
My hands are clean. But whether that's enough

I'll never know. Could I have done something
More than I did to help? He was good to me,
He spared me pain. Odd for a gaolbird

To do that for a gaoler, but he did.

You have to understand, there's always been
This wild streak in His Kingship. Not battle-wildness –
That's reasonable. But stabbing a man at a feast

(Twice he's done that) when peace is declared and all.
Had the bodyguard eliminated, killed the brother,
Wife locked up (she died of hunger), kids

Eradicated. For some it's a way of life,
But not for him. Just blows a gasket sometimes.
Daresay he had to do it. We mightn't be here

If he hadn't. And really he's civilized
In the Roman way, apart from not reading and writing,
And these little accidents.

<pre>
                    civilised accidents
       see   what happened
                                      I don't want

                  it isn't easy
</pre>

B was the one who knew about everything:
Music, the stars, the gods, philosophy
(His word. He taught me it. I didn't know it),

Poetry (he wrote it), logic (never grasped that),
Sums of all sorts, how to make clocks,
Not a thing but he understood its workings.

It's curtains for our world, he'd say to me,
I'm saving what I can, to smuggle through the darkness,
So people after'll know about Plato and Arry

(Two Greek geezers. He'd translated them before.
He thought the world of them. He put them in Latin,
In case Greek didn't last. Languages don't, he said.)

In prison, of course, he hadn't got his books,
All that, *finito*. He started a new thing
(A man you couldn't stop), called Consolation.

Now that's a queer thing. Who'd console you,
In jug, everything lost, disgraced? Wife, child, maybe,
But for him it was this philosophy, a high-class dame

Who ticks him off for being in the blues,
For listening to Poetry and all that stuff
(*Shop-soiled tarts* she called them) and tells him

Listen to her and *she'll* make him
Snap out of it. So she does. All rather above my head,
But she does. And then he couldn't finish it.

He knew what was coming. How, I don't know.
One morning gave me what he had, and the papers
(*Hand 'em to the future,* he said. The old joke),

And put through his last request to Theo. Wouldn't say
What it was. I supposed wife, kids, as aforesaid.
But it wasn't that. It was me. He wanted me out

When it came to doing him in. Thinking it over after,
I guess he knew I couldn't take it. Not enough Philosophy.
And he was right. I think he liked me. Even, in a way, loved.

He knew so much, he saw so much. He was rare.
I still can't bear it. Couldn't have borne to see
The executioners coming in. The way they did it,

Cords twisted round his head, and jerked
Until his eyes came out. Then clubbed to death.
He saved me this, and died his beastly death

Alone, as in a way he always was. With Plato,
And Arry, and Philosophy.

                        When I go out
And see the stars at night, I think of him.

Notes: *These notes are for those who like notes. Please don't feel you have to read them.*

The events took place at the beginning of mediaeval history. The last Roman Emperor of the West (Romulus) was deposed in 476 AD. Theodoric was born in *c.* 454, Boethius in *c.* 480.

Theodoric ruled the Western Empire from Ravenna, having led the Ostrogoths into Italy. They didn't count as Roman citizens, and Theodoric himself didn't claim the title of Imperator; he was officially a sort of viceroy, using the title *Rex*. He allowed his Goths one third of his lands; the Romans had the rest. The Goths retained their own laws and customs, but Theodoric followed the Roman administrative system and used officials trained in the Imperial services. He was a great restorer of Roman remains. His achievement in reconciling Romans and Goths was amazing, but there were occasional outbursts of ferocity on his part. He ruled Italy for thirty years, dying in 526 AD.

B: Anicius Manlius Severinus Boethius (*c.* 480–524 AD). Roman scholar, philosopher, statesman. Consul in 510 under King Theodoric. Eventually Boethius lost favour, was accused of treason and magic, and was executed. He wrote his great work *De Consolatione Philosophiae* while in prison in Tichenum (now Pavia), waiting for death. He wanted to translate the whole of Aristotle's works and Plato's *Dialogues* into Latin, and explain them – a life's work. He failed in this, but what he did translate was vital; only through Boethius's translation of *Logic* did knowledge of Aristotle survive in the west, and his work made the whole of mediaeval (and subsequent) learning possible. That *De Consolatione Philosophiae* was translated into English by King Alfred, Chaucer and Queen Elizabeth gives some indication of its importance.

B's Translations: Knowledge of the Greek language was dying out in the West, hence Boethius's hurry to translate Greek thought into Latin. He correctly anticipated centuries of ignorance in the future, and wanted to make sure the best things lasted.

Plato and Arry: Plato and Aristotle.

MORNING AFTER

The bass, crowing voices of women
Who have cried all night. Men blowing vengeance
Sulkily into their moustaches. The legions
Keeping an eye on the natives, of course,
But rather huffed about demarcation rights,
Drily comparing blisters. And himself,
Aloofly ticking off another milestone
On immortality's Roman Road.

And the wood not a wood at all,
But a mouth after extraction. The oozing
Stumps, the pale grass which had never
Seen daylight, the smashed long bodies
Of trees. Proper woodcutters work primly,
Leave clean piles of timber behind them, delight
In bunches of kindling, the smell of resin,
Know the uses of bark. This wood was holy,
So it was butchered by frightened soldiers.
Sacred birds and severed heads had nested
In its hollow places. Now strange creakings
Happened, strange pools opened, and strange
Wicked smells. Lumps underfoot
Were sometimes only dead birds, and sometimes
Something nastier. There was a space of a kind
Where had always been trees. Even the sky
Looked surprised and odd, as if no one
Had seen that piece before.

You can't blame Caesar. Being
A top Roman, he naturally did
The Roman thing. Trees aren't citizens,
At least, not this sort, only
The tapering ones with classical profiles.

These were undisciplined, scattering
Acorns and magic with barbarian
Abandon. Also they lacked *gravitas,*
Or perhaps they had too much
Of the wrong sort. Anyway, Caesar
Gave them the chop. The soldiers
Were hanging fire, discussing hylophobia's
Fancier symptoms, so he made the first
Nick himself, yelling *OK chaps,*
Me for scapegoat. Now take your
Fingers out. *

What had he done? He didn't
Wait to find out. Being, as usual,
In a hurry to get on, *dux tamen impatiens,*
He was off to Spain while oaks, yews, alders
Were still toppling. Don't, by the way, suppose
He had the wood down for reasons
Of superstition. The only magic he believed in
Was his own luck. He just needed planks
For besieging Marseilles, and these were handy.

But the wood caught up with him; woods do.
He died with naked swords in his face,
Like a wild beast taken by hunters,
Among the Senate-house's marble pillars.

Iam ne quis vestrum dubitet subvertere silvam,
Credite me fecisse nefas.
(Lucan, *The Civil War* III, 436-7)

AT GUNTHORP, NOVEMBER 2000

(The defeat of the Roman IX Legion by Boudicca's forces may
have taken place at Gunthorp)

Once it was after the battle. The beaten
Lay choked in their litter.

Now is after the storms. The weir groans
Like all-night city traffic.

The next field in, said the dog-walker.
Unless it's the kingfisher you're after:
He's based by the sluice.

Plastic, shattered branches,
Rags, paper, binliners,
Dislodged from their lurking places,
Muffle the staggering bushes,

Like the fallout after battle,
Like the Ninth when it was over.

Fields seem to be river, and
The unbanked river has
Lost patience with its own logic.

It was the herons we were after,
And there they were, in the lee of the hedge,
Hunched, patient, deadly.
Their killer's beaks. Their raucous shouts
Echoing after.

SPRUNG

(Acts 12, vv. 3-11)

Imprisoned for the third time, knowing
Death is tomorrow. You get used to these things.
There have been my shameful sleeps
In the past. So now, shackled between
Two monstrous guards, squads at all doors
Throughout the prison, I said my prayers:
To Him, and Him my friend, then nodded off.
You'd sleep through Armageddon
My mother used to say.

A ghastly dream: cocks crowing round me;
A man called Malchus showing me his ear;
I never met the man; fall into fishy water;
Cocks, *Never!* ears, water. Me asleep.

Something rather like a prod woke me.
I sat up. The guards snored on. Even
The ones at the doors had their heads down.
Light blinked from nowhere. My chains fell off,
Left blackened scars behind. A hint, a hint
From somewhere. *Must get going.* Almost I heard
Someone say *Clothes! shoes! coat!* but no one
Was there, just me doing these things,
All thumbs.
                    I didn't know my way down
The prison corridors, but my way found me.
Guards motionless (drunk to the world, no doubt).
Still I moved dimly, a man in a dream,
As far as the vast impenetrable gates.

Now I could smell sweet freedom's city smells,
Dust, fishheads, carrion, shit, muck, man,
Felt the city wind blowing on my cheek.
                              No exit.
Nothing could get past *them*. Might as well
Go back to my chains.
                    Hard to explain.
But as I stood, the gates, the impenetrable gates,
Opened themselves to me. Gracious, as if I were
A lord coming home. It seemed a dream still, but
It wasn't. There was wet on the ground, from
Yesterday's rain. A voice I knew (it seemed like His voice)
Seemed to say *Follow me.* So I walked through
The mannerly gates, into the street.
                              Someone was with me.
Had he been there all the time? *He* thought he had.
Hugging me round the shoulders (and I hugged him),
Saying *We've done it, Pete!* and – hey presto! – vanished.
Me, looking up and down and sideways after him,
And just a clutch of feathers in my fist.

THE OBITUARISTS

The genealogist is meticulous.
He harries his subject back to Adam
(Forty-two generations – if you can believe that).

Scene 1: the playwright's way in,
Smack in the middle of a river.
Enter a man wearing camel's hair,
Chewing insects.

The novelist deploys more characters
Than Cecil B. DeMille: shepherds, angels,
Emperors, wizards, mother (a mute).
He keeps the hero up his sleeve till later.

Babies, bit players, aren't part
Of the mystic's agenda. He starts with aplomb
And a metaphor.

The subject himself: a man not much given
To writing things down. Once
He scraped a message on the ground with a finger.
No one seems to have noticed.
If they did, it was soon scuffed out.

THE DAGDA

The Celts had a god for it.
Not the handsome sort, with a sportsman's torso,
Manhandling thunder or laurels,

Not arachnoid Indian,
With too many legs for comfort, nor austere
Egyptian, with an ibis's

Profile. A do-it-yourself
God, with artisan's thumbs, and screws, twine, wrenches,
Glue, stuffed in his poacher's pockets.

In sweaty working-clothes, hard
And unbeautiful, shouldering his crude club,
He stands, looking around for work.

Who would employ such a tough?
The gods only know he brews in his homely
Kitchen the recipe of life.

AUTUMN DOUBLE

Celtic Feast

This is the day which is no day,
Belonging neither with what has been
Nor with what is to be.

This is the day which is not,
When the other people come
From the other kingdom,

Missing the boundaries between
Their kingdom and ours, for this is the day
When there are no boundaries.

Tomorrow we shall do many things.
We shall slaughter the cattle, we shall celebrate
The coming together of the goddess and the god.

We shall eat pork, to each
His appropriate portion. The leg for the king,
The haunch for the queen, the head for the charioteer.

For the hero, the whole porker.
We shall drink wine tomorrow, and sacrifice.
There will be races. We shall applaud the bards.

Tomorrow we shall do these things
Which are required of us. Today
Is a day not ours. We do nothing in it

But wait and fear. This is the day
When trees and earth speak in one language,
Being all the colour of fire.

This is the day when the other people
Drift over our boundaries like fog.
We have no power against them

And the doomed cattle are starved, and bawl,
Distressing the children. And the day is short,
Even on high ground. And we are unprotected.

Bonfire Night

We are the other people.
Do our random fires puzzle your night?
Do you seek a word of power to halt
The hornless beasts with golden eyes
That trample our drove-ways?

Our ghost-fires burn
In the wrong places, on low ground,
In gardens. Their reek disturbs
Like a bruised memory. We have lost
The peaceful dialectic of Samain.

We are the other people.
Your seers glimpse our dwarf priests
As on low carts they trundle
The blank-faced god down stone paths.
You are right to be scared of our kingdom.

DRIVING SOUTH

Nothing will happen to us all the way.
Counties drop past, known only to our tyres.
The dog sleeps in the back. The engine purrs.
Sun, trees and cooling towers become a dream,
A world we slip through, never see.

A sudden shriek knifes our tranquillity.
Have we run down a rabbit, killed a bird?
Nothing so harmless. We have passed by Towton.
What's done is quivering here, alive and dying.

The bloody names pursue. York, Selby, Richmond,
Pomfret, where Richard died. History hounds us.
The sign posts stretch like hands, bonefingered, endless,
Pointing us to a sorrow we can't share,
Scorning our ignorance, compelling knowledge.

Here battle was. Here the king bled to death,
The martyr hung in chains. And once we know
The grand, heraldic cruelties, we sense
Enormous suffering behind each hedge.
Here a whole village was wiped out, and here
Hundreds of peasants slowly starved to death.

We break into the present when we stop
For petrol. But the past intrudes here too.
The man who serves us wears the same grim sign.
Has a child died, or is his wife unfaithful?
At least in his case we aren't forced to know.

Suffering riddles England. Rubbish bins
Are not enough for even our modest present;
How can they hold the litter of the past?

THE VULGAR TONGUE

I am old, weatherbeaten, subtle.
Invasion and invention have taught me
Not to be surprised by anything.

One of nature's lifeboats, I survive
Instinctively, out of habit. Sidelong
I am aware of foundering craft,

Sanskrit, Esperanto, Manx. Something
Intransigent in their rig makes them apt
To capsize. I, on the other hand,

Like a prostitute, accommodate
Anything at all. To be alive is
What counts. My mystery persists for

Babies and poets to juggle with
In this dead landscape. And when they touch me,
I go off like a bomb.

CAEDMON'S SONG

Forst ther wes nowt   nowt and neewhere
God felt the empty   space wi his finga
Let's hev sum   light sez God
Ootbye and inbye   so the light happened.

Up ower theer, thowt God,   airy and open
We'll hev a sky   and a shavin' of cloud
Here's a bit watter   we'll caal this whale-road
Dolphin-drive, duck alley   Davey Jones' locka.

Next orth appeared   a canny bit greenstuff
Rhubarb an raspberry   leafcome an leaf-faal.

God saw the heavens wes   handsome but homely
Made sun and moon   an the sharp stars their marrers.
Gannen to be good, sez God,   else Ah'm a gowk.

Friday he thowt on   flatfish an flounders
Halibut, hake   an haddock an herrin
Likewise the cushat   chunterin an clockin
Seagull an skylark   an the shrewd spuggy.

Last cam the fowk, so   canny an careful
Hey, bonny lads, sez God,   how will this suit yez?

'The version of Caedmon's Hymn we are all familiar with is from
Bede's Latin, usually rendered in a Whitby voice. There is also a rather
longer and more detailed MS in Northumbrian OE, here presented
as the modern Tyneside idiom.' (J. G. Collingwood, *The Harp Refused:
Caedmon and his Hymn*)

JONSON AT HAWTHORNDEN

(Drummond speaks)

He must have left a lick of himself behind,
After that famous twenty-stone trudge from London.

Endless infallible views of the man who knows
All about everything (most of it damaging):

Shakespeare lacked art; Sidney was plain; Petrarch
A blackguard for over-production of sonnets.

I wasn't exactly unnerved. But he kept on.
He's killed his two men, twice done time in the Clink –

There's a clutch of eminent mortal enemies after him.
He'll write, he says, about his visit here.

He calls himself The Poet. I'm
Too good and simple, it seems. Would

Be wise to give up on poetry. Won't excel.
And yet this bin of flesh, this brawling bully

Writes O such sweet and O such tender verse.
He is the nonpareil he says he is.

But God be praised, he's gone. I'll write my comment
(*A great lover and praiser of himself*)

Then pace my paths, and listen to my rooks.
Rude swaggerers, they have a touch of him.

(Jonson came to Hawthornden in the summer of 1618, and seems to
have left early in January 1619. See the enormously entertaining
Conversations, noted down by Drummond, who says nothing at all
himself. All this is in *Ben Jonson,* ed. Ian Donaldson, OUP, 1985.)

THE MAN WHO LOVED GARDENS

Being a gentleman
Of parts, he knew the parts
He played included Adam,
Eve, serpent and fiery angel.

He was Adam the mower
With a democratic passion
For grass, and an unhandy
Knack of nicking his own ankle.

Eve, he fancied, had been
Maligned. Sagely he loved
Plain, noble, pre-pubescent
Little girls, grew his hair, never married
But mastered the definition of love.

As for the serpent, being
Beautiful and equivocal, not
To mention belonging in a garden,
He couldn't resist it.

Cagey reporting of parliamentary
Business to the watery borough
That drowned his father
Barred him from other men's Edens,

So he presided with irony
Over sublunary confusions,
Reconciling the irreconcilable
Nature of things with a pun.

HARDY COUNTRY

(*for Nancy Williams*)

Being himself deciduous, he knew
The sadness of the fall of the leaf,
Was moved by the staring heads
Of trucked cattle on their way
To slaughter, suffered all his life

From the fieldfare his father killed
By mistake one bad winter.
A name changed on a Dorchester
Shopfront subdued him. In old age
He avoided his parents' senile
Bockhampton house,
Being himself deciduous.

Being mortal ourselves, we wince
As his leaves go down. We mark
The Americans at the bottom
Of his parents' garden drinking wine
From plastic cups. We estimate
The impossibility of a party
In the shrunken livingroom. We observe
The unimportant letters framed,
And a headscarfed Caucasian Tess
With moody translated eyes
Somehow inching away from Marlott,
Being mortal ourselves.

What was never true is always
Truer than truth. *The Forestry Commission
Has made quite a difference to Egdon,*
But still the path from Puddletown

Greenly unreels, and the young trim man
Steps down it briskly to found
His Dorset dynasty. Cream teas

And juggernaut lorries preside
In Casterbridge, but still the broody Mayor
Paces its littered pavements. Heartless at Stinsford,
Tucked between Florence Emily and Emma Lavinia,
Be comforted, old man. The tree's still growing.

WORKSHOP'S END

'True happiness consists not in a multitude of friends, but in their worth and choice.' (Dr Johnson)

In the old stories, when the band
At last dissolves, they go their separate ways,
Robin, the Friar, Maid Marian and the rest,
The merry men. I'm desolate.
I want them all to stay together,
Whatever the weather,
For ever.

I know they can't. They've other lives to lead,
Must marry, emigrate, turn respectable,
But in my head they're still walking the greenwood
Together, for ever. The last pages
Are never opened.

Now, our last page. Year by year we've walked
The enchanted workshop ground: the dark magician;
The Yorkshire truth-teller; the humble one
Who thought she couldn't do it; me. We have explored
Bravely, in difficult places. We've laughed a lot.
We've loved, not thinking much about it.
We've stayed together,
We thought, for ever.

Now no more. Well, things do end,
However much I like to think they don't.
But we shall keep this rare and sideways knowledge
Of you, of you, of you and me,
Effect of workshop camaraderie
Together. In these poems,
Whatever the weather,
It lasts for ever.

SECRET GARDEN

There's no such thing. Gardens are never secret.
If a single swan (as here) complacently
Inverts itself on a lake, then at once another
Shows up, thrumming its way through air. One human
(As here) in a garden means another somewhere,
Categorizing umbelliferae,
Transmitting a therapeutic kiss, or in search of a cutting.

Then there's the infiltrators. Artists omit them.
But consider the endlessness of worms, the manic
Engineering of moles. Serpents, of course,
Famously get into gardens. And if the painter
Had more room for sky, there'd surely have been
Some gull drifting over, taking a bird's eye view.

The genuine secret garden is suburban,
A couple of cupfuls of sour clay, wrenched
From railway embankments and ring-roads,
Where every grass-blade's cut by hand. No robin ventures
For fear of leaving a claw-mark.

However high their walls, all gardens
Are open cities. And, as astronauts know,
All the world's a garden, all the men
And women jobbing gardeners, discouraging green.

Leave any tarmacked scrap for a moment, and something
Comes quietly through: ivy, grass, bramble,
The great first-footers. Other feet, too.
A fox may winter out in that potting shed,
And lovers know how to climb over orchard walls.
As, if she's lucky, here.

ROUTE DES GRAPPES

Here come the young ones,
The green boys, the dancers.

In spring each coltish shoot
Makes every way a bright gamble.

In summer, tendril by tendril,
They beat the bounds of their domain.

In autumn, dense with cropping,
Gravely they finish the pace
Of the green men's measure.

In other countries, other years,
Drinkers will taste the skin
Of these dancing feet, and music
From the land of green boys will pierce
Expense-account-lunch-flushed
Ears, gorged eyes will grow tender,
As with their rash vines the green ones lasso
The knives and forks, the salt, the clever dealers.

MARRIAGE LINES

Being silent (even her postcards
Were curter than other people's),
She inclined to the company
Of the more reserved plants.

Gardens are safer than men to love.
They betray naturally and

Helplessly. No one expects
A garden to be faithfuL

So she reverted to grass. The stone
Bowls brimmed, the fruit trees' branches bore
Down on the daisies. Nothing much
Was ever pruned or stopped.

The garden grew into the house. Lawns,
Beds and pools amalgamated.
Only robins obstinately
Stayed territoriaL

And he, feeling no fellowship with
Hedges, strayed like honeysuckle
Over other mens' smart borders,
Sowing seeds of children.

HERONS

Trappists, reciting each his
Solitary office from
A damp station;

Executioners,
Patient and precise as death, axing
The lay gudgeon;

Black-queued mandarins, sloping
Off in a bundle of long
Bones, huffily

Assaulting airways to your
High-rise slums, where you turn
Starling vulgar;

Commuters from the M6,
Family men and harassed
Mothers of five

On a limited budget,
With House of Commons manners;

Remote celibate in the
Grey and white of your order;
Fisher of fish,

Or parent, slave to instinct
And procreation; are you
Such artists at

Living that all your selves can
Co-exist comfortably
Uncompromised?

CARAVAN

(*for Eddie*)

Garden grandees, they mince along the way.
Their trains glisten. Black and gold their flags,
Solemn their pacing.

> *Ah! the men and boys, the torches and the singing,*
> *Camels surefooted in the grey sand of morning.*

The straining feet, the heavy precious bales,
The antlered crowns depressed in holy thought,
Sombre their purpose.

> Ah! the last of the town-walls, as the dusty cloud
> Crawls in the mid-day desert. And the singing.

Ah! the fair green flesh of the predestined
Young helpless dahlias.

THE APPLE WAR

The storm troops have landed,
The red and the green,
Their pips on their shoulders,
Their skin brilliantine.

Uniform, orderly,
Saleable, ambitious –
Gala and Granny
And Golden Delicious.

Quarter them, they're tasteless;
They've cotton-wool juice,
But battalions of thousands
Routinely seduce.

In shy hen-haunted orchards
Twigs faintly drum,
Patient as partisans
Whose time has almost come,

From Worcester and Somerset,
Sussex and Kent,
They'll ramble singing,
A fruity regiment.

Down with Cinderella's kind,
Perfect, toxic, scarlet;
Back comes the old guard
Costard, Crispin, Russet.

James Grieve, Ashmead Kernel,
Coppin, Kingston Black –
Someone has protected them.
They're coming back.

WEST BAY IN WINTER

Landscape of absentees, where nothing
Is in itself, but anticipates
Patiently the next coming.

Landscape of withdrawn teashops, of shut
Pizzerias and doughnutteries,
Lavatories out of order.

Brooding self-absorbed till Easter makes
Sense of immense carparks, hides duckboards
And sandbags for a season.

Showers chase us, and mysterious light
Behind clouds falls on water we can't
Quite see. Gulls alone mark us.

Caravans turn their backs like cattle.
Laked fields lie apathetic. Only
The sea, that old ham, relentlessly
Goes on performing.

WOTTON WALKS

These are old paths, designed
And kept alive by feet
For whom walking was
The only way of going.

These are treads of workers,
Plodding early with their bait
To quarries, mills, farms; haunts
Of fishermen; rides for fine
Ladies, cantering sidesaddle
Through polished woodland; sly poaching alleys;
Game-keepers' beats; loitering ways for children
Towards ball-games and arithmetic; paths
For dutiful daughters to mothers'
Picturesque rheumaticky cottages;
By-ways for primrose-finders; the straight gate
To church for tidy-suited hymn-singers;
Trails for dog-tired shepherds to remote
Huts at lamb-time; muddy channels
For heavy patient cows; close turf
And easy gravel for foxes and badgers
To travel after dark.
                    Enter this web
Spun by dead and living round Wotton.
Remember lovers keeping trysts

At special stiles, remember
Gipsies stealing down green lanes,
And the reflective fellows
Who watched and thought by bridges
Over small streams. Attend also
To the punctually returning
Tree, flower, bird, since what you see
Is as new as it's old.
                        Finally,
Come back satisfied, please, at peace,
To where Wotton pleats herself on her shelves
Above the vale, under the edge.

EXTRAS

Two of them, always.
That is part of the story.

Speech, and Silence. The wit,
Who chats up soldiers, speaks the epitaph,
Who knows the score,

And Iras, golden-mouthed,
Says less than Cordelia, even.

There is a soothsayer, to amuse
The women. But she is the one who knows,

Her words being dragged from the future
Into now. One dies before, one after.

The fig-seller's snake articulates them both,
But Iras goes first, dying of a queen's kiss;

Charmian later, contradicting a Roman.

The usual things are happening to the world:
Battles on land, battles at sea, pacts, violations of pacts,

Empire-building, empire-losing, men jobbing, men getting
On with the job, eagles, pyramids, yarns about wives and
crocodiles.

In the dangerous centre of the court,
Eunuchs, messengers, decisions, jokes,

And the two, always,
One before, one after,
Who do nothing but die,
Being part of the story.

A MINOR ROLE

I'm best observed on stage,
Propping a spear, or making endless
Exits and entrances with my servant's patter,
Yes, sir. O no, sir. If I get
These midget moments wrong, the monstrous fabric
Shrinks to unwanted sniggers.

But my heart's in the unobtrusive,
The waiting-room roles: driving to hospitals,
Parking at hospitals. Holding hands under
Veteran magazines; making sense
Of consultants' monologues; asking pointed
Questions politely; checking dosages,
Dates; getting on terms with receptionists;
Sustaining the background music of civility.

At home in the street you may see me
Walking fast in case anyone stops:
O, getting on, getting better my formula
For well-meant intrusiveness.
                                    At home,
Thinking ahead: *Bed? A good idea!*
(Bed solves a lot); answer the phone,
Be wary what I say to it, but grateful always;
Contrive meals for a hunger-striker; track down
Whimsical soft-centred happy-all-the-way-through novels;
Find the cat (mysteriously reassuring);
Cancel things, tidy things; pretend all's well,
Admit it's not.

Learn to conjugate all the genres of misery:
Tears, torpor, boredom, lassitude, yearnings
For a simpler illness, like a broken leg.

Enduring ceremonial delays. Being referred
Somewhere else. Consultant's holiday. Saying *Thank you*
For anything to everyone.
                                    Not the star part,
And who would want it? I jettison the spear,
The servant's tray, the terrible drone of Chorus:
Yet to my thinking this act was ill-advised
It would have been better to die)*. No, it wouldn't!

I am here to make you believe in life.

*Chorus: from *Oedipus Rex* (trans. E. F. Watling)

WAITING ROOM

I am the room for all seasons,
The waiting room. Here the impatient
Fidget, gossip, yawn and fret and sneeze. I am the room
For summer (sunburn, hay-fever, ear wax,
Children falling out of plum trees, needing patching);

For autumn (arthritis and chesty coughs,
When the old feel time worrying at their bones);

For winter (flu, and festival hangovers,
Flourish of signatures on skiers' plaster of Paris);

For spring (O the spots of adolescence,
Unwary pregnancies, depression, various kinds of itch):

I am the room that understands waiting,
With my box of elderly toys, my dog-eared *Woman's Owns*,
Permanent as repeat prescriptions, unanswerable as ageing,
Heartening as the people who walk out smiling, weary

As doctors and nurses working on and on

A BRIEF RESUMÉ AT FIFTY

'Now, let's have a brief resumé.
Ah that's better.' (The Goons)

November. The clocks go back and the lights come on.
In a fall of paper flowers we remember the dead.

Born after Remembrance, in start-again November,
When brooks run high, and Wales is clear over Severn,

When raindrops juggle on fences in early mornings,
And wild swans are drumming their way back to Slimbridge,

Born in the pinched post-war, when, cold and discouraged,
We had too much to remember, too many uncounted deaths,
You came, a wordless message, bringing the future with you,
Into a past-haunted world.

Babies are famous for doing this. But royal babies
Trail our history along with theirs.
At your grandfather's great-grandmother's jubilee, my grandfather
Held up my baby father to see. His first memory

Of anything. Sir, you are past and future, Cerdic of Wessex
And CD Rom. It all comes together in you,

The focus, the pioneer, the first to be born
With a zoom lens in your face. For you the usual
Confusions of childhood were public; for you
Adolescent pratfalls were headlines; for you marriage

A monstrously slow-motion fuss, viewed raptly worldwide,
Which every citizen could recite by heart, errata included.
And then the fairytale death
Of the sad and lovely; and the tongue-tied people,
The angry eloquence of flowers all over the island,
The dogged unweeping slow march behind the coffin.

These things happen to us all, or most of them do,
Only no one bothers to look. (*Zoom*, says the lens.)
Now, for your fiftieth birthday, we wish you
A happier landfall,
A *Now* when the worst things are over, or at least
One knows how to handle them. Not the start of life,
But the start of freedom, of *looking*

(As Shakespeare grandly says) *with such large discourse,*
Before and after.

When you came we were looking backwards. Now
There's the future to see to.
Where you're standing means a lot of going:
Kalahari, Canada, the Caribbean, meeting
Generals, philosophers, artists, people,
Always people, in the rainy streets,
With their handshakes, their flags, their flowers.

And the quiet places, where protocol is different,
Where a kilt is possible and children are safe;
The modest undistinguished bit of Gloucestershire,
Old Shallow's country; all of it,
This fragile special island, mauled by the sea,
Frittered away by speculators, eaten
By money-grubbers. Yours, Sir, by inheritance
To care for.
           With that well-known polite
Diffidence to all comers.

                  It's your birthday.
May the enterprises thrive; may buildings
Be humane and gracious; may broadcasters and writers
Deal fairly with English; may the unemployed
Get work worth doing; may the Duchy
And all its doings flourish; may

Your Gloucestershire garden grow.

Lying on paths and grass the dead flat leaves;
Jutting already on branches, next year's buds.

IN MEMORY

The florist is sympathetic. She chooses
Chrysanthemums of a subfusc tone,
Contributes a card: *with deepest sympathy.*

The undertaker is sympathetic. He
Bares respectful teeth, folding our sad
Flowers close to his expensive black bosom.

The city is not sympathetic. It is
Abstracted. In grassed-over graveyards
Pigeons and children gobble potato crisps.

From vicarages and surgeries, wherever
Sensitive celibate men resort,
Come sensitive celibate sighs of relief.

For you are dead, who pursued them with tiepins,
Cufflinks, tasteful Medici postcards,
And quietly intense conversation. You are

Dead, passed away in your sleep in your chaste bed-
Sitter with the charming rural views.
Tomorrow you will be incinerated,

Like the October leaves. Only leaves return
In a secure succession, and you
Leave just a few embarrassing ashes.

You have much to forgive us. Will you try? We
Are the acquaintances you wanted
As friends, friends who avoided proper passion,

Lovers who preferred the cordiality
Of friendship. Your embers reproach us.
Forgive us our fear, who need professionals

To love and mourn for us, who spread our futile
Euphemisms over suicide,
And ask for pardon from the careless dead.

WHAT ABOUT JERUSALEM?

'Would to God that all the Lord's people were prophets.'
Numbers 11, v. 29

Wallflowers in your garden are stubbornly rooted,
Heeled in by you. Your magnolia sprouts fierce black buds.

In Sheffield and Gloucestershire, babies you drew into light
Flower and grow upright. A knack of giving life.

(*I know 'em all, you'd swagger. At least, their mothers I do.*)
They won't forget you, pain-killer, comforter.

Now you lie here in the chapel in pale wood,
White and yellow mortal flowers, and we sing

Jerusalem tentatively, waiting for you to pop up and exclaim
You've left out the feeling. So we have. I don't want to feel,

Gwen, that you've ended anything. *I will not cease,* we drone.
We haven't even started in the Great-heart way you did,

Who challenged geriatric consultants, hauled your friend
Out of dementia, brought her home to live.

Dear Gwen, who made the worst coffee I've ever tried
Not to drink, who never remembered a name

(*You I mean! Whatnot!*), who told explicit obstetric stories
Loudly, embarrassingly, in public rooms,

Who loved fast cars (*they pull in the birds*)
To my priggish disapproval; whose driving was known to the police.

I argued more with you than with anyone ever,
Though I'd seen you wink as you started to wind me up.

Is this all? Has that relentlessly
Self-educated mind at last run out of steam?

And such a little coffin. There's some trick here.
What about Jerusalem? You haven't ceased, have you?

A WISH FOR WILLIAM MORRIS

(*for Nick Bailey*)

I'd have let him die here
That great lover of things
In the place he loved best.

Not graceless Hammersmith
That he healed in his book
But in the old manor,

Kelmscott by the river,
Where the bed was ready,
That he wrote the verse for,

May curtained, Jane sewed for,
With grass scent, late rose scent,
Invading the window,

Distant shouting of sheep,
A bravura blackbird,
Always his true love Thames.

The last time he came here
In springtime, in springtime,
Cuckoos whooped at seven,

Rooks and appleblossom,
Mediaeval garden,
Friend with a manuscript.

I'd have let him die then,
Saved from the wheelchair,
The hallucinations,

Blood leaping from his mouth,
Not knowing anyone.
He died in Hammersmith.

But they brought him home
In a harvest cart
Vine leaves all over

Past the house he'd found
 To the church he'd saved
By his true love Thames.

O if there were justice they'd have saved him –
Twelve statues at Oxford on Mary Virgin's spire;
Blythburgh church; Peterborough's

Great interior; the north-west tower
At Chichester; the lock-keeper's roof
At Eaton Weir; a little barn
Vandalised at Black Bourton.

Fights of his last three years.

O if there were justice they'd have saved him –
The tower, the Suffolk angels, the non-pareil nave,
The tower, the roof, the barn – they'd have pulled him back
As he did them. And Rouen itself
Rouen itself and little Bourton
Would have come to deliver him.

But things are as they are.
It was raining. Leaves
Still on the lime-trees,
Church ready for harvest.

William Morris died at Hammersmith on 2 October 1896. His funeral
took place on 6 October, at St George's Church, Kelmscott,
Oxfordshire.

THE BENEFACTORS

They come provided with pins,
And buckets of cold water.

They never say *Well done!*
Or *We knew you could!*

They appear in the shape of the widow
Of a Scots GP. Mother has shunted you round

To announce you've won a college place,
First ever in the family.

You'd do better to stay at home, learning
To be the wife of some good man.

Or in the shape of a portly friend of your father's
Whom you overhear saying *Why waste money*

On educating a daughter? It's a poor investment.
You'll get nothing back.

                    O thank you, benefactors,

Who said *Oh no!*

                    You're making a big mistake.

Not at your age.

                    What will the neighbours say?

You'll live to regret it.

                    Not with the pound as it is.

I wouldn't if I were you.

Thank you for believing I couldn't do it.
Without your help, I'd never have brought it off.

CANDIDATES SHOULD PAY SPECIAL ATTENTION . . .

(Examiners' meeting near Christ Church, Bristol)

Papers lie helpless on indifferent baize
By empty coffee cups and frayed cigars.
Here wait the awkward inarticulate
Statements of youth, complete with index number,
Headlong confidings of their shyest thoughts
On music, mothers, loneliness (the lines,
Like the punctuation, wobble with sincerity).

450

Attendant, too, articulated statements
On glossier paper, the poem, the slice of novel,
Exposed to be understood. Superior,
Correctly spelt, with an air of success about them,
Professional. But they are helpless too.
These hearts are pinned to paper, and are judged

By examiners. We sit here, and examine
Each others' accents and taste, and the wallpaper
(Emphatic for this room) and submissive scripts
For our prescribed two hours, while the wedding-party
In the next-door suite brawls on, and the quarter-boys
Of the neighbouring church divide our time between them.

We are examined too. Our standards vary,
We are moved by eloquence to ignore a faulty
Line of reasoning, or a misplaced comma,
Our marking will be marked, like the hotel walls,
The trusting candidates and the candid writers.
Only the flower-marked wedding guests are free
Of critical voices, though the well-fed speeches
Must be taxing somebody's patience this long afternoon,
And the boys on the clock have their measuring eyes on us all.

DEGREE DAY

Autumn brings them out of their
Pupation. They stand in the precincts, gowns
Fluttering in the approving air,
Still sticky from the chrysalis, unused
To wings and freedom. Their parents
Group round them, pleased but dubious,
Knowing they never got beyond
Caterpillars themselves, and wondering

If butterflies are better. Salad days.
Sunshine attached to the hoods
And gowns, inanely askew
In the modern wind. Has our breed always
Sported such fur, such brassy
Mediaeval colours? How will they cope
When it comes to finding a cabbage leaf
And settling down?

NOW WHAT?

I hearby release you from time;
From the tyranny of small comfortless rooms;
From crammed distressful lunch-breaks;
From coffee in paper cups. I divorce you
From the *you* that other people
Have decided you are; I restore to you
Sunday evenings. I have said
There shall be no more agendas;
No more reading of uncongenial papers
About quality control, accreditation, audit;
No more explaining the worth of unparalleled texts
To unimpressed note-takers. No more endless
Phone calls after midnight about
Abstracts, references, funding. No more
Paranoid colleagues, no more
Torpid secretaries. Finally
I invest you with the month of September,
Which you were last able to attend to
At the age of four. Hereby I give you
All this, said the magician. Freedom, it's called.

I thought you'd be pleased?

POTTERY CLASS

They have all lived long enough to know better
Than hope, than children, or the doggedly
Recurring seasons.

Scuffed and weathered like old walls, grey-topped and quiet,
Sore from the banked-up troubles of a lifetime,
They are the clay, near clay, that shapes the clay.

At the end of illusion, you come to clay,
That yields and sulks and moves and thinks for itself
And is almost human,

That goes through fire, like us, and comes out better,
Handy about the house, the unassuming
Art of the scullery and the kitchen-garden.

The sorrowful man sees shapes in his dreams,
And waking shouts to the night *I could make that!*

THE LITTLE CHILDREN AND THEIR WISE PARENTS

(*for Maisie Sanderson-Thwaite*)

Sometimes grown-ups don't listen.
They hear what they think they hear.
Our parents are chuckling, and missing
The sadness of Mr Lear.

>He is very funny, our parents say,
>With his cat and his runcible spoons;
>Just the writer for you young shavers,
>With his drawings and words in festoons.

But can't you hear, O grown-ups wise,
That under the clowning he's crying?
That all his Jumblies have sailed away,
And Uncle Arly's dying?

> *Far and few, and they never came back,*
> *And we probably never shall see them more;*
> *They have sailed away, away, away,*
> *To the Land of the Chankley Bore.*

Lionel worries about the Pobble,
Guy is sad about the Dong,
Violet weeps for the Yonghy-Bonghy-Bo.
Killing the rhinoceros was wrong.

> But he's really awf'ly funny, the grown-ups say,
> It's so pleasant to know Mr Lear,
> With Old Foss the cat, and his runcible hat–

> Violet's crying again. O *dear!*

GRANDFATHER'S WATCH

Grandfather, with his Kaiser Bill moustache,
Who knows only the past and the present,
Trots in his ponytrap from patient to patient,
Charging the poor the least he can.

Tucked in his arm, by the waistcoat tick of his watch,
The child's too young to know who he is,
Nor does she know his enemies: TB, measles,
Pneumonia, the poor man's friend.

He'll never know the future, the National Health,
Antibiotics, sulphonamides, the transplant/bypass world
That she'll grow into. Heathrow, AIDS, computers.
His serious past her sepia history.

The great gold watch stays with her all the time.
Its florid initials. Its waistcoat tick,
Faithful and strong as it always was when he held it
In his helpless hands at the bedsides of the dying.

ROAD RAGE ON THE M6

A killer, officer? Me? I know what I'm doing.
State of the art man, me. Look, I know this road
Like Eddie Stobart's lads, and Norbert Whatsit,
In fog, rain, cross-winds, junction to junction,
Honest-to-God professionals. It's the others –
Mobile phoners, lane-swoppers, old men in hats –
Shouldn't be allowed. So when this cretin
Creeps in at Cannock, cuts me up at Stoke,
I slammed him on the shoulder. Came at him.
He knew what I meant. Somebody had to tell him.
Somebody could've been killed, the way he was driving.

PARTY NIGHT

Busiest night of the year
Six-course corporate dinner,
Everything's gotta be OK –
Coffee, mints, walnuts, wine –
Wassail, as you might say.

Saw at once they had to go –
Not the party spirit.
Him, living on handouts, no doubt,
Her, in the family way. *No,* I said to the wife,
Not this night, of all nights.

Wife's obstinate. Typical.
Bedded 'em down in the shed, in the straw.
Quite envied 'em, rushed off me feet as I was,
Slaving over the wine and the women.

Missed what the wife says she saw –
Fireworks, singing, comets, royals.
Well, she may have. What I say is:
Who made the genuine profit that night?

AGNUS DEI: 2001

When the days grow longer, they come,
White as newness. Life and soul
Of the flock, unlike their dingy elders.

In a good year, grow stockier,
Turn into sheep. In a bad year
Leave the world in summer, behind screens,

Smoke, silence, smell of disinfectant.

This one comes with the very early lambs
Always. Doing the things lambs do,
Lord of the dance in the meadow.

He knows where he's going.

WINTERSPORTS

Winter is rook. He blunders stiffly
Down four hard months, darkness being
His mute barrage. Sometimes he over-reaches
Into powercuts, snow, fog. Then humanity,
Staging survival, the child's romp, swapping
Paraffin, antifreeze, anecdotes, becomes
Humane. Endless gentle erosion,
If only he knew, is his most mortal finesse.

The wretched are king; powerless,
And so beautiful. We revere them,
Comfort them with drugs, parlour games,
Short walks on sunny days, and are
At last checked by their endless
Vulnerability.

I endure winter, and the punctual
Attendance of the distressed
With the pawn's continuous midget acts
Of gallantry. But your absence is
Knight's move, the jagged cut
Clean across expectation.
I have no defence against it.

FOR LEO ON 14.02.2000

Some whim of the calendar. For who
Could imagine the birds would woo
In mid-Feb, when we know quite well
That it's solstice-onwards that they do?

Some whim of the calendar. For who
But a martyr bishop that nobody knew
Would be linked with the business of kiss and tell
When a saucy young saintlet would do?

Ignoring the calendar, as I do,
Year in, year out, and leap-year too,
I may not love you especially well –
But I love you more deeply, I do.

All the same, I deplore the national neurosis
Which believes the best way to celebrate two hearts that beat
     as one is
A dozen long-stemmed martyred crimson roses.

ARTHUR'S WAR

(*for Maisie Hudson*)

Always when it rains I think of Arthur,
Says Maisie, as the tourists huddle
Away from the brusque Venetian downpour
In expensive glittering arcades.
The rain saved his life in Italy,
Says Maisie, as the tourists finger
Curios, wondering who they'd do for.

Animal lover, a gentle man, our Arthur,
Says Maisie. Too imaginative for bayonet practice.
But there he was, in the army, fighting
His way up to Monte Cassino,
The big monastery. That's where he was shelled.
No, not dead. He was lucky. The Germans
Were bayonetting the injured on the ground.

So Arthur played dead. Lay on his face in the mud,
Says Maisie. Rain through his hair, down his legs all night
Till morning. Knew he mustn't move. And always
When it rains I think of Arthur, how the rain
Saved his life, and how he loathed it. Here
I am in Venice, and it's raining again. No,
Says Maisie, no more coffee, thanks.

Only four of them left at the end, only four,
Says Maisie. Arthur got a cushy number, after,
Guarding Italian POWs in Africa. *Bad soldiers,*
He'd say. *Just not good at fighting.* But clever
With their fingers, like the folk are here,
Says Maisie, glancing at the lustrous boutiques.

They were never idle, they'd make something from nothing,
Wood, cardboard, stones even. Whatever they made
Was fine. Arthur bought what he could. We have
Two boxes still, precious things, like in these shops.
He left them to me. That's why all this
Touches me. Reminds me of Arthur.

The filigree spoons. The elbowing crowds. The rain.

ON THE NORTH FACE

1975   Mr Wang (Chinese) meets Mr Hasegawa.
       Mr Wang has seen *a deceased person, an old body.*
       English, English, he says. Next day
       An avalanche kills him. Mr Hasegawa
       Rue he should ask more detail.

       Everest doesn't lose her dead. They sit upright,
       Refrigerated, or lie as they fall, headlong,

Or choke in a crevasse. Few corpses
Break away from the mountain.

1924   Living, they went up the holy road,
Past the prayer stone beyond which
No life must be taken, to the wild North Face
Of the Goddess Mother, rock, snow, wind; implacable.
In tweeds, greatcoats, cardigans and scarves
They climbed, in home-knitted socks and hobnails.

1999   The Yanks who find him look like astronauts
In their correct kit. They're not prepared for this.
O my Gahd! O *my Gahd!* His matches.
His unpaid Gamages' bill. His letter from home
(The children have flu). He's one of them,

For all his old-world gear, his storm-bleached body.
This is Mallory. *A modern person. A man they know.*
We are disturbing him now.

His arm holds the mountain, won't let go.
They pray for him, sing a rather jaunty psalm.
Their awkward reverence needs other words:

O ye compassionate ones, defend Mallory,
Who is defenceless. Protect him
Who is unprotected. Who was last seen
Going strong for the top.

(*O ye compassionate . . . unprotected*: Buddhist rite, from *The Tibetan Book of the Dead*)

460

NEEDLE WORK

I am the genius at the heart of things,
The answer at the middle of the maze,
Secret cartographer who tugs the strings,
The arrow that goes nowhere, but obeys
Earth's headstrong pull North, south, east, west,
And all their subdivisions heed my mark;
The pioneers, the other-world-obsessed,
Follow from Erebus to Noah's Ark
My scarlet finger in the glassy box,
Directing humans through geography,
Through Roaring Forties to the fish-paved docks,
Through unmapped deserts to the tourists' sea.

But touch me not. Unless I'm free to roam,
You'll never set the course that brings you home.

LIBRARIES AT WAR

The more you destroy them, the louder we call for books.
The war-weary read and read, fed by a *Library*
Service for Air-raid Shelters and Emergency Teams.

We can still come across them, the pinched economy
Utility war-time things, their coarse paper, their frail covers.
Such brightness in the dark: *Finnegans Wake,*

The Grapes of Wrath, The Last Tycoon, Four Quartets,
Put out More Flags. On benches, underground,
In Plymouth, Southampton, Gateshead, Glasgow, in the
        Moscow Metro
They sit, wearing a scatter of clothing, caught off-guard,

461

The readers reading, needing it, while terror
Mobilizes in sound-waves overhead,
Lost in the latest. Something long. Or funny.

Fire, fear, dictators all have it in for books.
The more you destroy them, the louder we call.

When the last book's returned, there is nothing but the dark.

NEW POEMS

1 JANUARY

Day of deceitfulness. Brings nothing new.
New Year sales have been raging for weeks.
Resolutions are the old ones, buffed up a bit.
The solstice was last year. Candle wax
And droppings on the floor. We're sick
Of leftovers. Even supermarkets have
A defeated look, waiting for Easter.
Stray people in the streets, not asked to a party.

Only the calendar's eternal optimism
Reassures us; something new *is* happening.
New jobs will start tomorrow; new dates on cheques.
Someone will find a purpose for the Dome.

12 APRIL 2004

(*for R., born 22 February 2004*)

Forty days since you made your first entry
Under the fish, on the cusp of the waterman.

Late in the evening, but sooner than expected,
Ready with black hair, loud voice, smile,

Welcome to here and now, little waterman.
Too late for your birth, too soon for your birthday,

But after your first forty days in this place
(Which is biblical), to make sure you like

The taste of it. So many talents wait
Concealed in your fists, your toes, your ears.

Will you be a sprinter, oboist, wise man?
All we can do is wait, and wish you well,

Fisherman, waterman,
                    Kanga,
                              Ruairadh.

A GARDEN OF BEARS

Fur is soft, skin isn't.
Paw is safe, hand isn't.
Two stiff forelegs, ready
To comfort, not rangy,
Unpredictable arms.
Bears don't speak. Bears are best.

Dolls are too close to us.
They can be trained to laugh,
To wet themselves, shoot from
The hip, explain about
Erogenous zones, need
Clothes, knives, hairdressers. Break.

Remember this: bears are
Brilliant. There was Sam, the
King of the dictionary,
Shambling, myopic, rude
To earls, tender with cats,
Slaves, women, the poor,
Minding their dignity.

Inside homely teddies,
Lolling in cots, lurks the
Grisly intransigent
Ursus horribilis,
Ten feet tall, solitary,
Surly, reeking of meat.

I know a lot of bears.
Most of them look just like
Other people. But there
Are risks. Abruptly bears
Can turn wiser than us
And braver. There are bears
Who rise to their full height,
Rise to the occasion.

ALWAYS

There was always a beast,
And always a human to take it on:
Someone from Samaria; a lamp-in-hand lady;
A body with a cooking-pot, and a pinch of goodwill.

But in our day the beast is bolder,
Thrusts his tainted head into our snug
Domestic screens, shows us the bones,
The shrouds, the fly-filled eyes.

We aren't Samaritans; we have no lamps;
Even a cooking-pot is hard to find.
Our bag of tricks: the versatile goodwill
Of pay-by-plastic, cheque, fax, giro, Switch.

There is always a beast,
And always a human to take it on,
A generous heart to say
I saved this for my tomorrow,

But you need it for your today.

ADMINISTRATOR

Underling too long, though finally you made it
To top dog, you knew the system too well
To bark authentically.

You, the expert on short cuts, on first-name terms
With the influential – stores, post-room, porters; you
Who knew how to fix it,

Whose good deeds were always shady, like
The fiddled day off for Christmas shopping, which
Was rightfully ours;

You who scrounged, never spent, who shook
With fright before committees, who always forgot
Your own authority;

Who dared not sanction our electric kettles,
Whose kindnesses were home-made, compensation
For your servile failure
To improve anything.

ABERAERON

(*for Jean Porteous*)

Like a great cat, the moon licks up the sea.
Small boats in the harbour clatter and bob,
Like dancers on the night before Waterloo.

The tide goes out, comes in, and lovers
Idle along the edge, old dogs
Lagging behind, young dogs sprinting ahead.

Beyond the bridge, serene squadrons of ducks
Navigate between moorings. A grizzled man
Walks, and stops. Watches the water. And passes on.

The ferryman has retired, but he'll be back.
Like a lighthouse the church stands
On the highest place. *Katy Lou, Seren Las,*

Y Marchog, Bingo perch on mud,
Then take to water, ready for anything.
Bright painted houses. Sea shining out beyond the bar,

Waiting quietly to do something violent.

ALL CHANGE

(*CLC: 150 years*)

A place of change. They enter,
Little scruffs, hair in their eyes,
Homesick for gerbils, for Gran,
Hungry for sweets, for the fierce banter
Of brothers; hungry, homesick.

When they leave, so many years later,
They're tall and lean, borzois and ladyships,
Graceful as if the zoom lens were always attentive,
Kind as experienced teachers, looking
For the one who can't follow. Knowing more.

In between, the strange deep friendships
Of adolescence; joint passions for Beckham,
For Branagh, Prince Harry. Sharing,
Sweaty, tearful, giggling, asleep, innocent maybe,
The undesigning equality of youth.

Now, after so much learning to do other things,
Qualified, they come back, with new names,
Different hairstyles, little hangers-on.
Do you remember me? they ask confidently.
O yes, we say (*who on earth is this?*).

O yes, denying it. But somewhere, deep down,
We do, despite the changed façade. These
Are the friends who helped us through hard places,
Loneliness, unravelling Hopkins, *what-am-I-doing-here?*
Through all their elevation to lovely youth,
To wisdom, these are our oldest friends.

AN OLD STORY

A matter of timing; it usually is.
The gods see to it; only gods and poets know the trick.

The body not decayed at all, despite the days passing,
Despite the ritual trailing round; and the old king
Arriving just when dinner was over, Achilles almost alone.

One moment: the king? the body? Achilles?

Yes. You need to know.
Old Priam, King of Troy;
Hector, eldest and bravest of sons.
These are the Trojans.

The Greeks, the invaders –
Achilles, son of the dangerous goddess,
And Patroclus, his true love.
Also various supernumerary wives,
                gods,
                a rainbow,
                heralds,
                cooks,
                and a daughter (prophetic).

Acts find their consequences. Hector kills Patroclus,
Loved by Achilles. Achilles kills Hector,
Eldest and bravest.

So: two corpses. What happens to them?

Patroclus the lover, entombed in a high barrow,
The brave, the lordly, with his grave goods *etcetera*.

What used to be Hector is dragged round the barrow
Three times a day, for eleven days, Achilles whooping
And flogging the horses. (You have to remember
He was given to rages, was partly barbarian.)
Bright Hector, killed by Achilles. Dead in the dirt.
Unburied.
The timing, clever as gods do it, was just after dinner. Relaxing time.
Priam comes after dark to plead for the body.
Priam amazed, finds himself kissing

The hands that had murdered his son, hugging
His knees, like a beggar.
                    And Achilles?
                                    Speechless.

There was Priam, kneeling and kissing, and the old man's words
Struck home. It didn't take much. 'Your father –
Your father will lose his son, as I have mine. Remember your father.'
And he did. And doomed Achilles wept for him,
And for Patroclus too, and for himself, and everything.

'I have done a thing that no man on earth has done.
I have kissed the hand of the man who killed my son.'

The wine, no doubt; that comfortable after-dinner state –
These things played their part. It could have been different,
The dangerous man, facing the father of dead Hector,
Of bright dead Hector who killed his own true love,
After all he'd sworn to do. Not what he'd planned at all,
Lifting the old king gently, both men weeping now,
Filling the house with grief.

Timing is everything. You can't go on for ever
Savaging corpses, seeking vengeance. No need really
For Priam to push it, in the end. The body not decayed at all
(The gods had seen to that), despite the ritual trailing. The old king
Arriving just when dinner was over,
Achilles determined already to hand Hector back.

So that was that, until the next time?

ANOTHER 'LAST SIGNAL'

(TH to PW: a Tribute)

I am the man who noticed with
A raptor's eye; the man who heard
With Wessex the dog's pitch-perfect ear;
Who felt with a woman's generous heart.
Nothing passed me by.

Yes, I was born far lowlier than some.
But stockyard, coop and byre – they didn't
Breed my brain. I am myself, my wayward thoughts
Learned and innocent at once.
Critics can't read me.

I absolve you, Peter, from the critic's taint.
You read, you think, you search, you sympathise,
And as I did, you see, hear, feel, and guess.
What can these modish blockheads tell of tricks
That come of a lifetime's skill?

You live where I should, had I thought
Of dislodging from Dorset; near
Romish Corinium, your Bulwarks,
Their swoops and tumps much like
My homely Rainbarrows.

You've done the things I should have liked to do:
The Cyder Press – the spelling says it all!
Helping the humble bards, Taylors and Clares,
The needy ones. No cash for poetry,
Or the players in Stinsford Church.

You have the eye for what's neglected:
The books that never made it to the top –
Desperate Remedies, Poor Man and Lady,
Ethelberta – I was proud of them.
Their messages were subtle. Only you could read.

You are my listener. From your rough times
To mine, you tune your ear to me. You know
The difficult texts: what counts is love,
In every form. There's no such thing
As a happy ending. So it is.

I wish the stiff-collared gents, the urban know-alls,
Could see as clear as you. Thrush, grass and clouds
Are truth-tellers. I am the man who hears them.
A wave to you, as me-ward once
From Barnes's coffin – *Down with the critics!*
Speak for the inarticulate!

BUT, DOCTOR . . .

A True Story about Confused Referral Letters

Sit down, my dear. I gather that you're not
Feeling too grand. So first things first. How are
Relations with your husband? Do you have
Orgasmic intercourse with him each night?
                    But Doctor, it's my feet . . .

Just move your chair a little more this way,
So that the telltale sun may show me all
The messages of lips, eyes, hands and skin,
The messages you dare not speak yourself.
                    But Doctor, it's my feet . . .

You are a woman. Do you feel fulfilled?
Do you go out to work, and so betray
Your feminine identity? Do you
Nurture your children? Are you on the Pill?
But Doctor, it's my feet . . .

Perhaps I shall prescribe another child,
Perhaps a fresher husband, or perhaps
(Your secret wish) I might prescribe a lover,
Extra-curricular, an understanding psy –
But Doctor, it's my feet . . .

Your tone, my child, is most significant.
Why so aggressive? And your fetishism
About your feet appears suspiciously
Deep-seated and deluded. Tell me all.
But Doctor, it's my feet . . .

Was masturbation early? And how far
Did your incestuous father push his love?
What makes you hate all men? When did you last
Murder your mother? Please be frank with me.
But Doctor, it's my feet . . .

Only together can we overcome
This dreadful trauma threatening to deprive
Your sovereignty of reason. Come, be brave.
. . . . Yes, Mrs Jones. You've got a nasty bunion.

CROP

Now is when squirrels gorge on hazelnuts,
And dormice settle down for the big sleep.

Now is when redwings and fieldfares
Box the compass, and take their bearings

For this modest island. Now is when trees
Explode in a salvo of red, brown, yellow,

And look their bonniest. Now is when humans,
After the tyrannies of career, love-affairs, children,

Relax into the long perspectives of age, knowing
How rich they are in memories, how time is on their side.

DICTATOR

He bestrides the wall-to-wall carpeting
Like a colossus. Imperiously
He surges from comma to semi-colon.

Swaying in the throes of his passionate
Dictation, he creates little draughts,
Which stir my piles of flimsy paper.

If my phone rings, he answers
In an assumed accent

Flexing the muscles of his mind,
He rides in triumph through the agendas
Of Area and District Management Committees

Aborting all opposition with the flick
Of a fullstop. Laurelled and glossy
He paces the colonnades of an imperial future,
With all his enemies liquidated.

When his letters are typed, he forgets to sign them.

EITHER / OR

Once in the age of Gold, poems began with O –
O rare, O fine, O sweet! But that was long ago.

Then, in the age of Silver, If was the poet's word.
Be a man was the message. And the people heard.

Now in the age of Lead, poets don't rate any more.
Instead the managers speak. Their theme is Either / Or.

They say You're X or Y. This is our decree.
You're old, or else you're young. Middle, or Working C.

If you're not rich, you're poor; if you're not gay, you're straight;
If you're not North, you're South; you're skinny, or overweight.

If you're not Bartók, you're Blur; if you're not black, you're white;
Don't spoil your voting paper. We've no programme for
    sometimes, or quite.

You're mad, or sane; you drive, or walk; you're F. Or are you M?
Our final crucial question: one of us? or one of them?

These, they say, are your choices. Just tick the relevant box.
But what if it so happens we don't want to be orthodox?

If we wear our rue with a difference, don't fancy this or that,
If we choose to sport a whole hatstand of different kinds of hat,
If we resist your packaging, range free outside your cage,
Retrieve the grit of the Silver, the zest of the Golden age –

If . . . .
          . . . . . *Oh!*

ENTERTAINING POETS

One of them was sulky
And would speak only
Welsh. One of them had just
Left prison (a sexual
Offence), and one was
Resting between nervous
Breakdowns, and must not be
On her own, ever,
Or she would destroy herself.
One ate, with a passionate
Angry absorption, everything
Available, and cast
Covetous eyes at other
People's plates. One seemed
Unremarkable at the time
But bombarded us later
With remaindered slim
Volumes and obese bills.

It seems wrong to comment
On their difference
From us. After all, they

Did their best to seem the same,
Never mentioned bay
Leaves or inspiration,
But concentrated on
Sales and technique like
Any solid citizen
Who knows how it's done, and is
Willing for a small fee to
Demonstrate unimportant trade
Secrets. Kinder on the
Whole to be fooled by their
Camouflage, pretend
These are our equals, not creatures
Helplessly wired to the wrong
End of the Muse's one-way telephone line.

FRIENDSHIP

Not soul-mates, exactly.
Their names say it all.

Chloe. Kylie. Normally
They wouldn't have met.
One poised, gentle, patient.
The other, a mum straight
From Nappy Valley. Both
Washed up on these sad shores,
Where the brain-damaged, the gibberers,
The obsessive, learn a difficult habit
Of living together,
                    but exclude
Scarred Chloe, who fell in the fire in a fit

And lost an eye, parts of her face.
Whose husband couldn't bear to see her.
And shaky Kylie, muttering endlessly
In the local patois, uncertain of everything;
Where was the canteen? When would her father
(Dead, of course) come to visit?
Hazy memories: who did I marry?
Children? All life's lovely things
Wiped clean by encephalitis. Husband, also,
Keeping clear.
                    What did they say,
One damaged thing to the other? Nobody
Wanted to ask, to talk to them.
But, as they drifted along corridors,
They were always chatting. Kylie feverishly,
Chloe listening with her old-fashioned courtesy,
Enlaced, arm-in-arm, like Victorian sisters,
Like friends.

FRINGE TOWN

She nests between Severn and heaven,
Furling herself round the limestone edge.

She is just Wotton; not glamorous Stow,
Posh Swells or Slaughters or Bourton-on-the-Water.

She's modestly special. Has her own climate
(Fogs on the hill, sunshine below).

Her blackbirds sing louder than others do, her people
Smile when they meet. Their conversation

Rings like birdsong through Long Street. Cotswold Way walkers
Pop out like primroses in March, and swifts

Flick along the summer air. This is an old kingdom,
Self-possessed; way out; out of the way.

FWIW: THE LANGUAGE SPEAKS

HWAET!
Was brought to the island
Over bitter waters
By rowers wielding longswords.
Adam-like named a new world –
Oak, grass, hand, foot, house, sheep, sea.
(Rivers, having their old names,
Churlishly refused my choices.)

HARO!
Smote them at Senlac
The Prince and the people.
Taught them our fashions –
Judge, justice, penalty,
Prison and Parliament,
Fine arts of peacetime,
Gentleman, beauty. April.

HEY NONNY!
Found words everywhere. They came at my calling,
Names for the know-it-alls, arbiter, genius;
And for know-nothings, ignoramus, inertia;
Measurers wanted pendulums, axis and nucleus;

Thinkers craved curriculum and its callow offspring;
Doctors found bacillus, lens, equilibrium;
Travellers asked for omnibus. Got terminus as well.

HEY GUYS!
Shall we move the goalposts?
Try a level playing-field? No wow there.
Use a buzz-word, bog-standard wannabe,
Sex it up? Stay shtumm? Oh, the great
Orchestra of English, played in every key,
Gobsmacked! *Good* hair day! Where we're at!
In a right Horlicks! Braggadocious!

                   f w i w (for what it's worth).

GABRIEL

My spectacular looks make it hard
For the uninformed to know
How to negotiate with me. I'm used to giggles,
Panic, cries of *Mu-um*. This time I was careful,
Furled tight as buds each glowing feather
Of my wings, suppressed my halo, knelt
Down to her level, said the appropriate words,
Hail and *Blessed*. She was a well-brought-up girl,
Asked sensible questions, tried to understand,
Said *Thank you* nicely. I thought she'd do.

Mind you, the harder bits I left unsaid.

GROWING OUT

We enter empty-handed, empty-hearted,
Freckled only by chromosomes and genes,
Novice-naked
(*Born on Monday*)

World, busy gossip, bustles up
Furnishing parents, a name.
A place in the sun
(*Christened on Tuesday*)

Parents erratically bombard us
With gifts – a rattle, love,
Uncles, words – tucking us in
To their particular nook.

The first growing out
Is easy. Bones shoot,
Teeth fall, appetites alter.
Parents officiate for us,
Handing down, or retailing
Through the columns of local papers.

Sometimes, if asked properly, they will
Deal with outmoded friends.

Growing out of parents
Is more expensive. Things
Of unquestioned presence –
A bed, a kettle, space –
Are suddenly unreliable;
They cost money.
We may also find we need
Someone to share them with
(*Married on Wednesday*)

These things, outgrown, become
Recriminatory. Best to consult
A specialist in division,
Who will slice accurately
Whatever is divisible:
House, money, children
(*Ill on Thursday*)

Finally we outgrow
Ourselves. Teeth and hair,
Being deciduous, drop;
Bones buckle and break;
Mind turns anarchist, body
Defects. Before long
We have grown out of everything
(*Worse on Friday*)

Free those who love you,
If you can, from posthumous
Distribution. Avoid
A cluttered end. Give
To the proper heirs before you go.
And celebrate your surrender
(*Died on Saturday*)

HARRIED

They can't ignore it. Larkin in libraries,
Wordsworth in Westmorland, up to the eyes
In stamps, Yeats being senatorial,
Burns fixing taxes, Milton rubbing up
Latin shorthand, Chaucer hard at work
Controlling customs, Wools, Skins and Tanned Hides
(Which must have kept him busy), Marvell hoping
His interest in Hull wouldn't dissolve
Before Parliament did, sad crazy Clare,
Whose plough made crazy furrows in the sad
Northampton earth, and Mr Eliot,
Fault-finding in Lloyd's ledgers, most of all
Shakespeare, enduring conferences with Burbage,
Explaining why he couldn't make the part
Of Hamlet longer, all the time unwritten sonnets
Trickling out of his fingers' ends and running
To waste on the sandy floor. I see them all
Turning an honest penny, perpetually
Worrying that their best thoughts coincided
With a perforation problem, or Cromwell
Declaring war on the Scots. How much better
Poets or employees they would have been,
If they had turned their backs on poetry
Or work. Work doesn't mind. But poetry
Wouldn't leave them alone.

LUMB BANK, EARLY

Hodge and Tigger, home from their night-shift,
Leave small parcels of mouse-meat on thresholds.

The morning chorus has hallooed itself hoarse;
But collared doves still call, unstoppable as MPs.

Between the beds Apollo stalks, god-footed,
Not missing anyone out. Breathes into sleeping ears

His secret gift: phrase, image, first line, last line,
Pattern, whatever it is. The sleepers sigh, roll over.

The gift is god-given. It keeps till breakfast.

NUMBER ONE AND THE BUTTERFLY

A garden, a boy, a butterfly.

The garden gets on with growing, as gardens do.
The boy is at a loose end; boys often are.
You have to wait for the butterfly.

Three boys altogether:
Number Two is learning to talk. *What a clever boy!*
Number Three is a baby. It sleeps a lot.

He is Number One, the oldest. He knows more,
He does more. This is not interesting.
No one notices his vocabulary.

No one's excited when he smiles.
Everyone knows he can do these things.
What's new about him?

Enter the butterfly. It is colossal / gigantic / enormous.
It flaps majestically up the garden
With wings as wide as a smile.
Brown? Blue? No, it's black,
With a thick pale frill, like surf at the sea's edge,
Round each great wing's edge. Compound eyes
Inspect the garden. Great antennae
Explore the scents. It heads for the boy
(He puts out a hand), it lands on his finger.
The butterfly has chosen the boy.

His mum whisks for her camera. Dad watches.
Number Three goes on solidly sleeping. Number Two
Hasn't a word to say. The boy is silent,
So is the butterfly. They have made friends.

Now, he has a photo to remind him
It happened. This convinces them at school,
And Two, and Three. But he doesn't need a photo.

You don't forget a friend with wings.

ON A DEAD SOCIAL WORKER

She steered a firm course through equivocal
Currents, and spoke the language of the seas
Though her own dialect was different.
The shipwrecked liked her, hurled their sopping junk
On to her polished planks, and camped on board
Until they swamped the neat craft, and she foundered.

ON THE WING

(*for Anne Stevenson*)

Obedient to some private calendar
She comes, stays, goes. She knows the others,
The ocean-airborne from Siberia to Severn;
Small brown birds nipping down homely hedgerows;
On-the-wing swifts like cut air falling in shrieks . . .

           Right. Yes. Hang on.
           Is she a bird, your poet?

In some ways, yes. She soars from state to state,
Grounding, leaving a private sign of love,
Her signature, a poem of the place,
In Hay-on-Wye, Oxford, Vermont,
Michigan, Cambridge, Durham . . .

           Ah.
           Some sort of migrant?

Mostly you'll find her silent, spellbound. She broods
On everyday things, has time for unorthodox weeds
That farmers damn: Himalayan Balsam,
Ragwort – of course, they're migrants, too . . .

Just a sec.
What about us, the stay-at-homes?

O she watches the small kempt gardens of Cambridge,
Its cold mercenary bathrooms, the educated earth
Of Oxford. Watches them like a lover,
And the lives inside, around. Remembers
Insignificant people doing insignificant things.
Knows the idiom of children, and of cats . . .

Sounds nice.
Where could I find her?

In cities, and counties, in the weather,
Passing through, wherever there's life,
There, watching it, attentive . . .

But I'm still confused.
Is she a bird or a poet?

Ah, that's the interesting thing . . .

N.B. All the best lines and words in this poem have been pilfered
from A.S.

PHALAENOPSIS

(for Elizabeth Bewick)

A grandee arrives, with a retinue
Of baffled postmen: *Never brought nothing before*
Like this. Garnished with warnings: *Live!*
Protect from Extreme Heat or Cold. A princess,
Veiled from us and our common world
In great swaddling bands
Of tissue, cardboard, expanded polystyrene,
Each single petal intertwined,
Capped on its own in webbing.

The tender lady's maid fingers
That have created all this! Complete, each flower,
With her own stake, and a spare, an A4-full
Of instructions. *Phalaenopsis;* the moth.
I can't pronounce her name, let alone water her.
She stands serene in the east window, fit for her degree,
Purple and white flecked, lofty over
Her gross leaves, looming over our humble usuals –
Cyclamen, Christmas cactus.
                                        Eloquent, strange,
Careless of being different.
Not a flower, but a friend, regarding me
Leonine, as an equal.

POET AT THE FESTIVAL

('. . . school parties welcome . . .')

Not just the lunchtime regulars with *Guardians,*
Handbags, scarves and coughs.
The hall's packed, and half of it has bare knees
And PE next.

(In Thrace they knew what to do
With dangerous folk like you:
Tore 'em in two.)

Some of it lolls legless
In wheelchairs, wades in
On angled feet. The palsied,
The maimed young; and the adults, hale.

They think he's *bonkers.*

Only you, Sir,
Knew what to do
With this bunch. *Right!*
Who's eleven? And hands sprout.

He's used to the cross-legged
Who call him *Sir.* He knows they'll come,
The mad treble giggles,
When he says *bra* or *bum.*

He has a word from the holy mountain,
And a word for the titterers.
He will say both words.

(In Thrace they knew what to do.)

He shows us how to laugh at him
Participation time!
For being Gulliver, for being *bonkers*.

He doesn't laugh at us.
He has spoken both words,
And we have understood one of them.
He has been to the holy mountain in Thrace,
And has come back in two pieces.
He has given us his two pieces.
Laughing, we take them.

Bless us, Sir.

PROBABLY UNIQUE IN THIS STATE

(*for Peter Scupham*)

I've been stupid, shape-changer.
You scattered the clues to your selves
So wittily that all the cul-de-sacs
Shimmer like nighttime motorways,
While motorways dwindle into dead ends.

But now I've rumbled you, shape-changer
(Your passion for Shakespeare gives you away),
You are Puck, the pwca, pooke, poakes
(I mention this to please your bookishness).

Puck who knows woodlands, feels for elms,
Visits the Underground, hears the sea-maid's music,
Has a taste for acting, interferes with sadness,
Has a special relish for transformation,

Who magics tired discarded books
Into volumes of delight, rescues
A *cock-eyed* house (no doubt it needed magic)
Just the place for *a play to be toward.*

Above all poet who acknowledges
Old forgotten things, the whimpering dead,
Who tracks them down and gives them voices,
Resurrects them with his words.

Lover of slim folios and stout volumes,
Discoverer of *1300 vivacious pages,*
Mint yourself, though maybe *rather used,*
You who promise us *No Deep Confessions,*
Football, Sustained Philosophical Thought,
Enmities, or Poems About Dogs.

You who hear, before us mortals,
The morning lark, who follow darkness
Like a dream, you with your flair
For the preposterous, you to whom Shakespeare
Gives the last word, the Epilogue,

Mandeville, Mermaid, Peter, Puck,
This comes with love, and brings good luck.

SOMEONE

Someone came before.
We don't know her name
But Someone cocked up the straw
Before the angels came.

Someone was there before,
Scrubbing the mucky mangers,
Waging the usual housewife's war
On cobwebs, stinks, dust in chinks
For the coming of the strangers.

Someone came who knew
How soft are babies' feet,
The span of angels' wings
How they fit so small a retreat.

Someone got it all ready
No one recorded her name,
But she saw who was standing at the door.
This is the place you're looking for,
She said when they came.

STROUD

You can still smell wool in the air
Down Murder Lane today;
The dye-house chimneys tilt above
In their seasoned trustworthy way.

You cross the bridge, and the water's clear
That the dye once turned soldier-red;
Along the highway, traffic replaces
The thud of the fullers' tread.

A thousand years, a hundred mills –
So much to celebrate:
Snug as a star, where five valleys meet,
Stroud has learnt to be great.

Tariffs, blazes, tonnage, taxes
Altered mills and lives:
Rooksmoor, Ebley, Day's and Ruskin
All changed. But Lodgemore thrives.

From Dunkirk to Egypt, in Gloucestershire miles,
Is a ten-minute bike-ride today
On the green and peaceful Dudbridge Donkey's
Grassy permanent way.

Wool and water, teazels, coal,
She's lived through them all. She's proud.
There isn't much that she can't handle,
Queen of the Valleys, Stroud.

THAMES TALKING

You'd think they'd know better,
The celebrities, the poets,
Who make a living out of me.

Bridges are as far as they get –
Ships, towers, domes, theatres, temples –
Not a word of me and my fickle waters.

Plant a poet down on London Bridge
And what does he see? A crowd,
Each man fixing his eyes before his feet.

What about me, the dark river,
Whose floodgates drown the suicides
And the party-goers? My tides deceive.

My friendly slip-slop at Richmond can turn sinister
At Gravesend. Practical Londoners know,
With their barriers and embankments,

They need to keep an eye on me.
Of the poets, only lunatic Blake
Understood how treacherous I am,

For I am Thames, the dark river,
Who was once part of the Rhine.
The moon is my mistress. Men wait

Uneasily for her and me, wondering
What comes next.

THE BEASTS

After the flood, they left the Ark.
(Two by two. Hurrah Hurrah Hurrah)
Noah had saved them. Life was good.
(All together now. Hurrah Hurrah).

Noah had a vision of his sons
(One and two and three. Hurrah Hurrah)
A vision of fur and tusks and skins,
Of rifles, poison, harpoons, gins,
A whiff of battery hens (Hurrah Hurrah),

Draize-tested rabbits, cattle trucks,
(Thousands and thousands. Money for us. Hurrah)
Myxomatosis and abattoirs,
The pheasant shoot, the *corrida*
(Money and death. Hurrah Hurrah Hurrah).

Noah remembered the forty days
(The Arkful of precious lives. Hurrah Hurrah)
Tiger, panda, bittern, cod,
He knew how dear they were to God
(Who made them all. Hurrah Hurrah Hurrah).

He knelt down so the worms could hear
(No one counts worms. Hurrah Hurrah Hurrah)
He said, *You creatures great and small,*
My sons will soon destroy you all.
Scram! But they didn't scram nearly far
Enough.
        (Hurrah

             Hurrah)

THE C WORD

It was a word we knew but didn't say.
I was born under the sign, but understood
People said *Crab* not *Cancer*.

Routinely he grew a beard every winter
For his annual bronchitis. *Dad's cough whiskers*
We called it, being young and excitable,
Thrilled by changes in the parental landscape.
In the spring he'd get better.

In the spring, when I was older,
Free to roam London, I collected his order
From the shop in Piccadilly: *State Express Three Fives*.
They were dear. *Coffin nails*, we called them,
Being young and flighty.

We took the ten-foot dinghy up the dark river.
He was heavy, unmechanical. The temperamental outboard
Stalled at Henley; we grappled with it,
Ran out of money, had a lot of grubby fun.
Everyone called him *Sir*.

He loved water, and words. On his deathbed
He tested me on how to pronounce
Humour and *indissoluble*. Of course he was right.

Near the end, he lost part of a tooth. He'd always
Looked spry before. The broken-ness haunted me.
I hoped he didn't know.

What did he know? Mother told us not to say.
He doesn't know. It's better for him not to.

I thought he knew. A look in his eye.
But being gentle, preferred to spare us knowledge.
We pretended innocence, pretended he'd recover.

He was a judge. He understood *sentencing*.
On his way up the dark river, he chose
Silence as companion, among all those words.
I wish we could have spoken, shared his knowledge.
In the spring he died.

THIS AND THAT: GUIDO MORRIS AT ST IVES

Once every cottage housed its potter or painter
(Sculpture took up more space), and they kept on the move,
Chasing a better north light, more tolerant neighbours.

They used ephemera to chart their lives:
Change of phone-number, price-list, wife.
Small things some need to know, others to hear.

Familiar unexciting scraps of this and that.

Here to these on-off quarters by the sea
Came Guido, Master of the Latin Press
                    which
HAS BEEN ESTABLISHED TO THE GLORY OF GOD
                    AND
          OF THE ARTS OF PEACE
                  offering
      MOTOR and BODY REPAIRS
        J and J COUCH LIMITED
                    or
        Tickets price 4s, 3s 6p,
                2s and 1s
            may be had from the
            Business Manager.

He treasured the things he worked with, the Bembo fount,
Hard-biting old presses, and paper, the heart of the job,
The hand-made paper of England.
You can gauge the love by the work he did:
By the long-tailed capital Rs,
By his feeling for names like Jack B Yeats –
                    Jack
                    B
                    Yeats.

He was impractical. Ran out of full-stops.
Charged too much, or too little. Didn't finish.
Lost touch with helpful friends. And drank; and drank.

The painters and potters lost their singular printer.
The Underground took him. Gill sans-serif ogled him,
From Barking to Bond Street, Richmond to Rotherhithe.
How the trains lunge, hesitate, shake and stall,
And the faces focus and fade, and are never known.
He served for twenty years, having no choice.

Unique Guido, who cherished the twenty-six
Soldiers of lead which can conquer the world,
Who did the right thing but never got it right;

Who chose narrow paper, and narrowed words to fit,
Like CATALO
            GUE; who used your civilised craft
On Wine Lists, Baptist Teas, notes about ration books.

From the long future, greeting. Be well.

                    FLOREANT
                    ARTES   HU
                    MANITATIS

THREE GODDESSES

(i) *Hecate*

('Procul, o procul este, profani.' Virgil, *Aeneid vi*)

You who do not belong
Keep away at the times
When her dogs give tongue;

She who owns midnight,
Walks with the hollow dead,
Monitor of owlflight;

When her dogs give tongue

She of haunted crossways,
The road to the river
Where the ferryman stays
For the passage to Never;

When her dogs give tongue

She who is the moon,
Lady of the horned dance;
When her dogs give tongue

Keep away, away, away,
You who do not belong.

(ii) *The River Goddess*

From Lundy to Lydney
Subverting the tideway
Fickle and dangerous
Here comes the goddess.

From Welshpool to Worcester
Downriver she dances,
The wilful young creature
Making her début.

Descending she blesses
Fishermen, daffodils,
Birdcalls, fields, festivals,
Our Lady of Waters.

From Gloucester to Chepstow
Shipwrecker, bridge-breaker,
Man-snatcher, field-flooder,
Exterminator.

Two-natured river,
Welshpool to Worcester,
Gloucester to Chepstow,
Lydney to Lundy,
Severn, Sabrina,
Her comes the goddess.

(iii) *The Goddess Superhyper*

Hear the gospel of your goddess
O my people,
You shall get your money's worth,
O my people:
meals in minutes
facial tissues
savoury snacks
in multipacks
And an hour and a half's free parking.

I am your lady bountiful
O my people,
Never knowingly undersold,
O my people:
price protected
longer shelflife
extra value cooking foils
extra virgin olive oils
And an hour and a half's free parking.

Hear your goddess Superhyper
O my people,
See my cornucopia
O my people;
hoki, kumquat
lapsang suchong
filled baguettes
and crêpes suzettes
And an hour and a half's free parking.

O my hungry people, come,
Bring your humble offerings,
Visa, Access, Smartcard, Delta –
All you need to pay the piper
Here are avocados riper
At the shrine of Superhyper.
O my people come.

TUESDAY

Of all the days, the most everyday;
Neither Black nor Good, not used for bank holidays
Nor early closing. Yahweh's day
For creating earth and grass, the usual things;
Named after War, most commonplace of gods.

Just an everyday day,
Though babies and the old notice it.
Is it still Tuesday? they ask.
And schoolchildren, their days distorted
By the flintiness of French and free periods,
Retain in their heads the Tuesday angle.

Only the dying and lovers celebrate
That enormous golden tick in the sky
As each new Tuesday announces itself
Another unrepeatable offer,
With its annual whiff of lemon.

TWO MEN AND A DOG

JK

I was young. In fact, I have always been young.
But a young poet deviates. He needs to be understood.
So I gave all the clues I could: the exact
Date; a very cold winter; St Agnes'
Story; stressed chill and old age
At both sides of the poem, the triptych
Of freezing owl, and storm and coffin-worm,
Between both a feast for epicures,

And Madeleine warm, undressed,
Porphyro, ethereal, flushed, like a throbbing star –
You follow, don't you? The furnace
At the heart of the rose. But this numbskull
Misses the elegant candies, the tastes, aromas,
The iridescence (O the lovely senses,
The lovely words). They miss their chances,
These daubers. I knew Haydon and Severn;
I would have shown them how it should be.

HH

Mine is the subtle version. That's why
I left out all the vapid obvious stuff.
See how he flaunts the spices, delicatessen,
Bosoms, trumpets – not my scene at all.
En plein air is my favourite. I am *not*
A camera. The discriminating eye
Rejects the obvious, the flat. See what I made
Of the porter, splayed along the foreground
(Keats merely gives him a capital P),
I made him a welter of perspectives.
As for the lovers: Keats has them vague
I have them dressed and ready for the road.
Note all the *possible* things: the door might creak,
The dog might bark, the revellers wake –
These are the delicacies paint alone contrives,
Not the rude boorishness of poetry.
I'm sad he's dead. He could have learned from me.

Dog

Both got it wrong. You have to feel for dogs
Before you paint or write them. I, the dog,
Recognise the inmates. What does a dog do?
Silently wag his tail, of course. Neither of them
Got that.
        And, incidentally,
How many dogs are there supposed to be?

TWO NURSERY RHYMES FOR TODAY

Little boy Red
Come blow your own trumpet
New Labour is ageing
You've lost your best men.
Kennedy's stirring
Ken Clarke's on the war-path –
You'll not see a socialist landslide again.

Oh where is our leader
Who looks after the sheep?

He's under a gooseberry Bush
        Fast asleep.

———————

Boys and girls come out to play
The pubs are opening night and day
Come on a blinder till break of day
Tessa has told us it's quite OK.

Let's have a booze-up and boil our brains
Let's have a skinful and bung up the drains
We don't give a damn for the cops or the law
We'll smash all the furnishings, break up the bar.

We'll throw up and punch up and get pie-eyed
And terrify everyone else outside.
Boys and girls come and see what you've missed
The government says we can all get pissed.

VILLANELLE TO ORDER

Diana asked us for a villanelle.
Sorry, dear friend, I can't, even for you.
Mostly I try, but this time I rebel.

Intolerable subjects come pell-mell:
Days; water; Yeats. Then, last turn of the screw,
Diana asked us for a villanelle.

And rhyming's not my forte. Hard to tell
The endless petty tinkerings that ensue.
Mostly I try, but this time I rebel.

There's things that I *can* do. Of course, not well,
Just odd schemes I was hoping to pursue.
But you insisted on a villanelle.

If workshops go like this, then, friends, farewell,
For Eddie's next. What will he make us do?
(Mostly I try, but this time I rebel.)

My mind's made up: A W O L.
Now, if my tally's right, I'm nearly through.
Mostly I try, but this time I rebel.
Diana, this is *not* a villanelle.

WILL THERE BE TRUMPETS?

(*for Linda Whalley*)

Will there be trumpets? I asked,
horses, and Romans?
                              Perhaps,
said Mum and Dad. *But maybe.*
That was enough. We set off.
                              And crowns?

A real let-down. All these people –
honestly, embarrassing, messing around
with palm leaves in the dust, making it grand,
they must have thought, poor guys. But it wasn't.
Just messy.

And a clown, straddling a midget donkey
with people's coats across its back, no saddle;
a drop-out, trailing bare feet in the dirt,
and the poor little donkey, only a colt,
never been ridden before, you could tell
from how he slithered and shook his ears,
every now and then forgetting himself . . .

Then worse. These two oldies came skidding along the road,
leaping over ruts like four-year-olds,
yelling *Hannah! Hannah!* Then everyone yelled *Hannah!*
except me. I didn't know who Hannah was,
or where to find her. Mum said the oldies
had been blind, and the Healer
had made them see. *What healer?* I asked.
Dad pointed at the drop-out. *Him,* he said.

I looked, and suddenly I saw. Saw it all,
crowns, donkey, trumpets, oldies, the clown.
I can't explain it, but I saw. Like everyone else,
I shouted *Hosannah!*